DRAWING FASHION

Illustrating Fashion Poses

Illustrated by
Vasanthi Puttigampu

Written and Organized by
Jennifer Lynne Matthews-Fairbanks

Illustrations by Vasanthi Puttigampu

Written by Jennifer Lynne Matthews-Fairbanks

Book Design by Designarchy

Photography by Jason Tidwell

Models: Kassy Macias, Maya Huyana, LaMeshia Jones

Services for our readers:

Universities and wholesale purchasing:
Fairbanks Publishing, LLC offers special rates for universities and wholesale purchasing.

Wholesale purchasing is available through Ingram Distribution or directly through Fairbanks Publishing LLC, at Porcelynne.com.

Contact Us:
Fairbanks Publishing LLC DBA Porcelynne
Jennifer@porcelynne.com

Your feedback is always welcome. Let us know if we can do anything to improve this title.

Copyright © 2020

Publication by Fairbanks Publishing, LLC

All rights reserved. No part of this book may be reproduced electronically or by other means without permission in writing from the author, except by a reviewer who wishes to quote passages in connection with a review written for inclusion in a magazine, newspaper or digital press medium.

Black & White Edition ISBN: 9798642746387

Color Edition ISBN: 9781733274036

PREFACE

Four years ago, I ran a small nonprofit design school in Redlands, California. During that time, we created the material in this book, but only recently have we been able to complete this book. As a designer and educator, I am always striving to create the best educational material available.

I had an amazing teaching staff at my school, and while we were unable to complete this book for our students at the time, we created an amazing curriculum for our young fashion design students to work from. The illustrations within this book were created by one of my talented instructors, Vasanthi Puttigampu.

This book is designed to teach fashion students to develop their skills in mastering fashion illustration. The focus of this book is to illustrate the fashion figure and understand how different body shapes and sizes are interpreted.

We worked with three models in the creation of this book. Each model represents a different market in the fashion industry, juniors, misses and plus size. The industry has changed drastically over the years and while most fashion books focus on the smallest size model, we chose a more inclusive approach to illustrating fashion figures.

Working through the book and take note of the body proportion changes for each model being illustrated. Additional poses are provided at the end of each topic for further practice.

The outline for this book, and the course taught at my school, was created by the amazing Han Vu, an illustrator and fashion designer from Anaheim, California and myself. While Han was unable to see this book through to its completion, I would like to acknowledge that this book would not have been created without her guidance and insight.

The illustrations throughout this book were created by another one of my stellar instructors, Vasanthi Puttigampu. Vasanthi is a fashion designer from India. She joined our team in the last year of our school and it was a pleasure to have her teaching with us. This is Vasanthi's first book and an amazing addition to my educational library.

I have been producing educational content and books for the fashion industry since 2007. While my educational background was in intimate apparel, my teaching career covered all aspects of design, from sewing and pattern making, to business education.

I am pleased to provide this fashion illustration book for your use.

-Jennifer Fairbanks
Designer, Author, Entrepreneur and Mom

Website: Porcelynne.com
Instagram: porcelynnesupplies
Facebook: porcelynnesupplies
Twitter: porcelynne
YouTube: YouTube.com/c/Porcelynne

ABOUT THE ILLUSTRATOR

From an early age, Vasanthi loved sketching and painting. It grew during her youth, when she spent much of her free time in her mother's clothing boutique, surrounded by the colors and fabrics that grew her affection of fashion. These interests grew into a passion which pushed her to seek her first diploma in Garment Technology at Kamala Nehru Polytechnic College for Women in India.

Vasanthi continued her post graduate studies in Fashion Technology at Wigan and Leigh College (WLC) through their program beginning in India and graduating in the United Kingdom. During her time at WLC, her coursework placed her with Indian designer, Vinita Pittie, as a mentor. where she worked on her first collection.

Her first industry job positioned her in the design department of sportwear company, JJB Sportswear, in the UK. In this position, she assisted in the online design department and printed t-shirts, as well as other duties relevant to online order fulfillment.

Upon returning to India, Vasanthi furthered her experience working at Lakme Fashion Week with designer Asmita Marwa. This experienced spearheaded her into the position of assistant designer for this renoun Indian designer. Her reponsibilities placed her in the middle of every aspect of the business, from managing tailors to selecting fabrics and more.

After the thrilling role of dressing India's top movie actors and touring fashion shows, Vasanthi returned to her family roots and helped run her mother's fashion boutique. Running her mother's boutique, while her mother was overseas, inspired Vasanthi to follow her dreams of starting her own business.

Upon her mother's return, Vasanthi opened her own couture custom fashion boutique. With the eye for fashion and the skills of a couturier, Vasanthi created beautiful hand embroidered clothing items using techniques of Aari, Tambour and Luneville. She designed her wares and operated her boutique for 2 years prior to relocating to the United States with her husband.

When she arrived in the United States, she switched her focus to education and started her career at Jennifer Fairbank's nonprofit design school, Porcelynne Design Institute, teaching pattern making, sewing and illustration courses. It was during this time, that she began working on this book with Jennifer.

TABLE OF CONTENTS

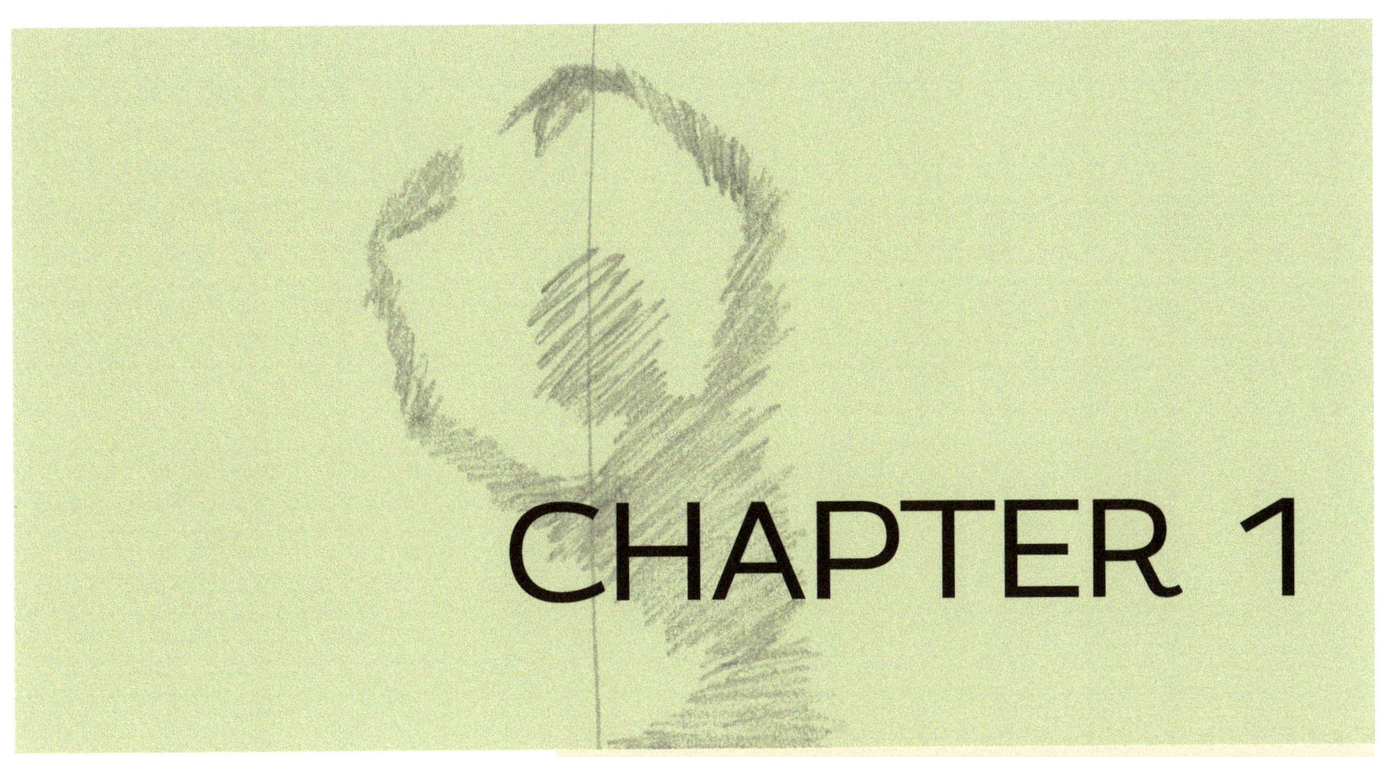

CHAPTER 1

Introduction

GESTURE DRAWINGS

As a beginning illustrator, it helps to warm up both the hand and the mind. This warmup method is called gesture drawing. Gesture drawing helps focus the mind, to the shape and proportion of the human body. The following exercises are quick and easy. Try to create the shape of the body by not removing the pencil from the paper. Warm up exercises can often be messy due to the softness of the pencil lead. You may wish to consider practicing these gestures on a separate piece of paper, rather than directly in this book.

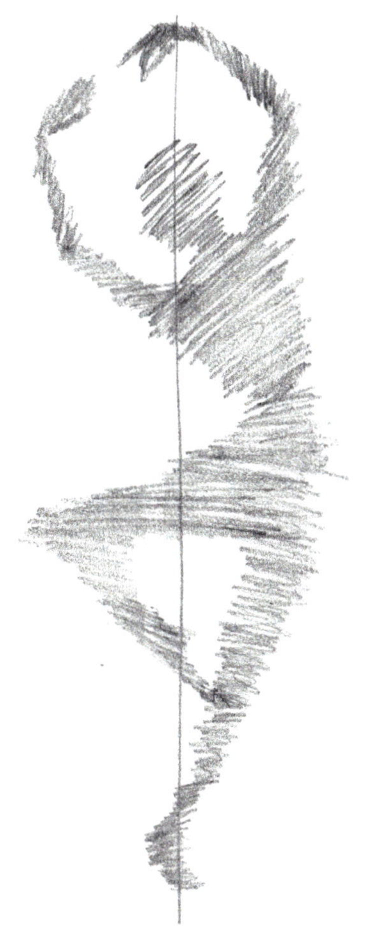

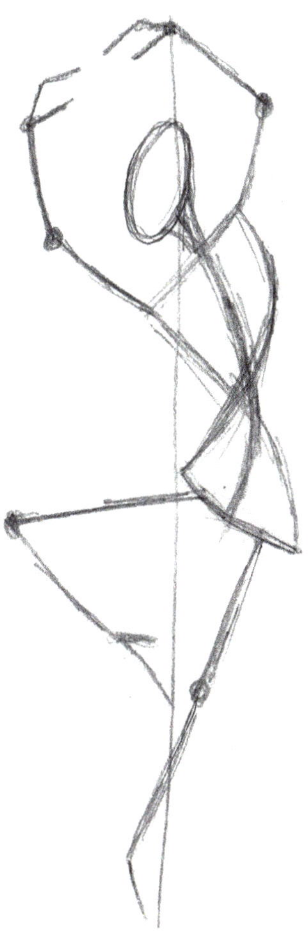

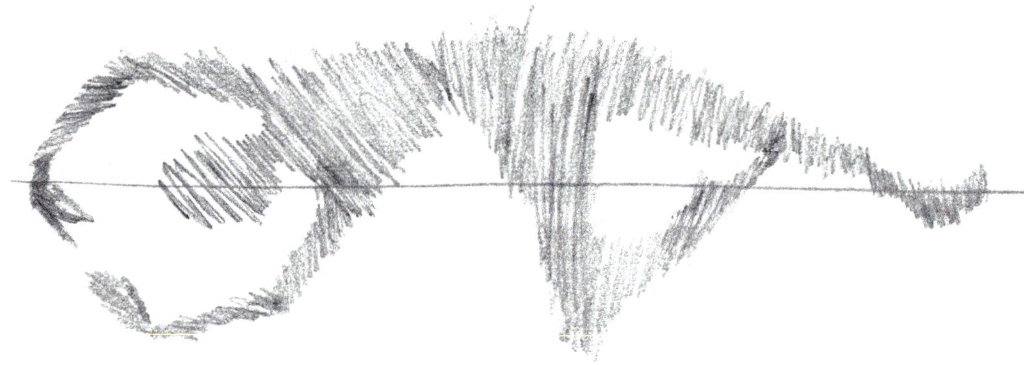

SHADED GESTURE

Sketch the center balance line. Follow the pose of the body to create a quick shaded gesture.

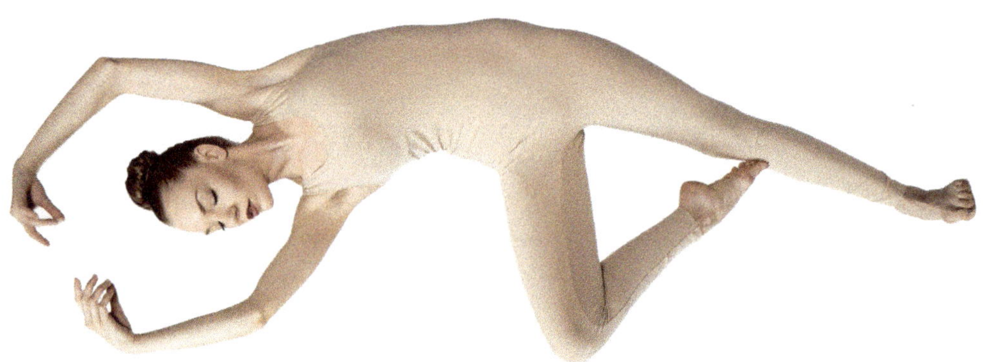

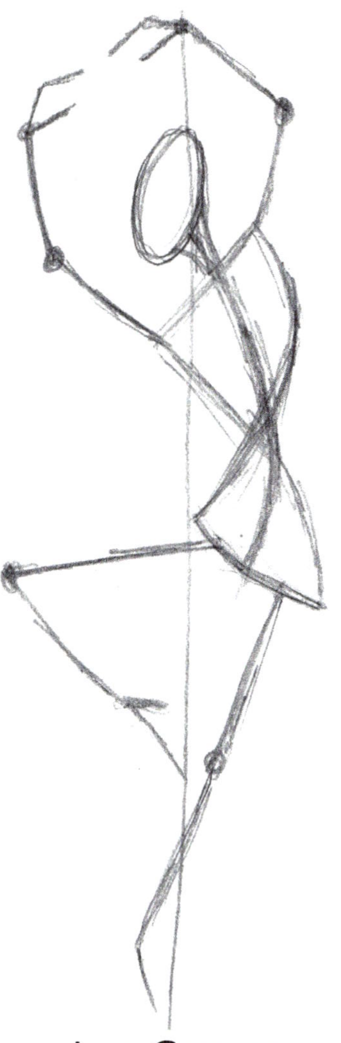

Line Gesture

Sketch the center balance line.
Follow the pose of the body to
create a quick line gesture.

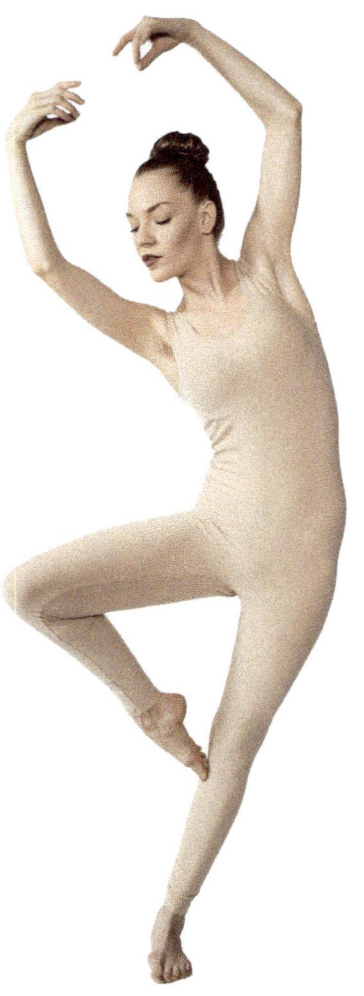

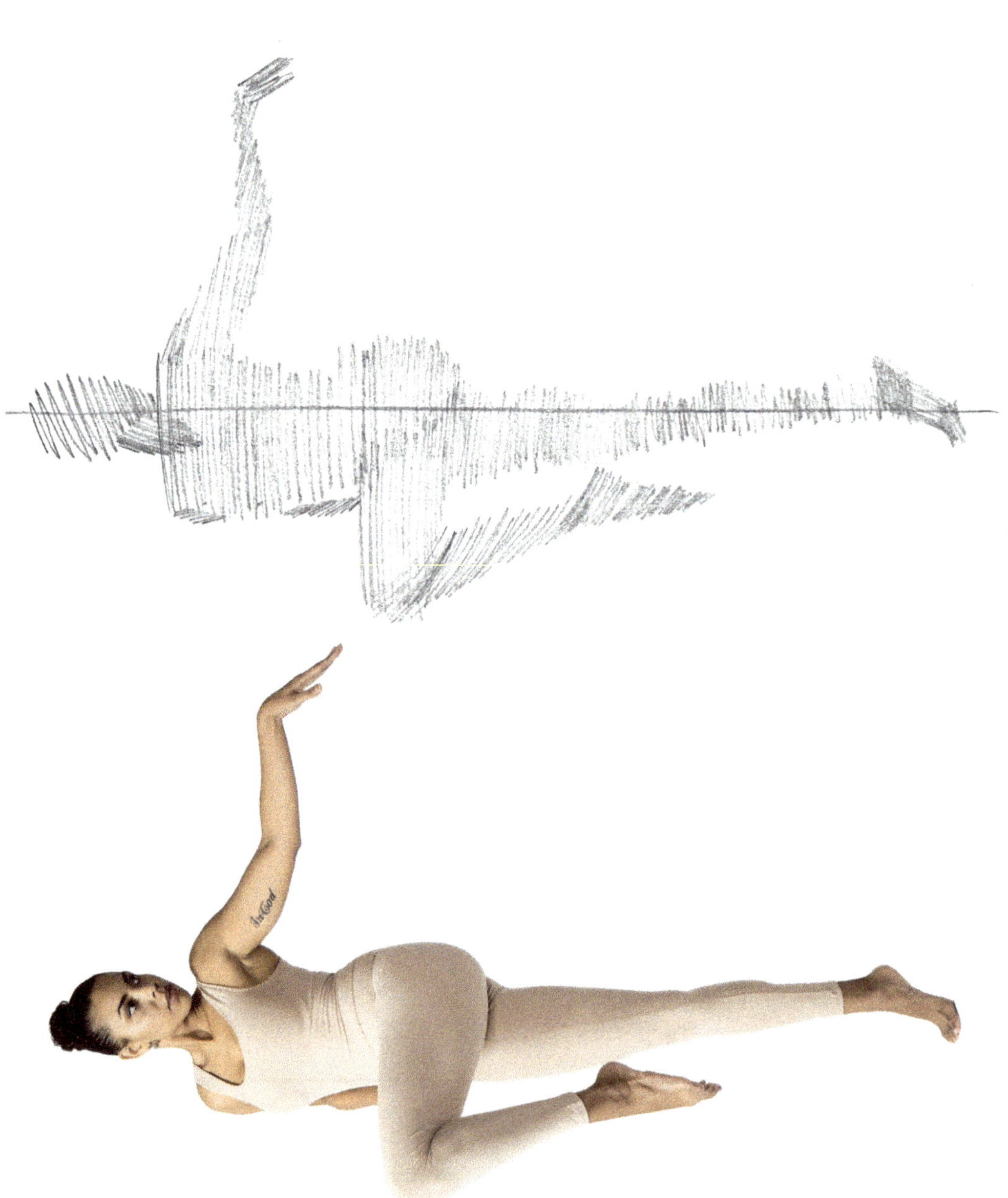

Shaded Gesture

Sketch the center balance line. Follow the pose of the body to create a quick shaded gesture.

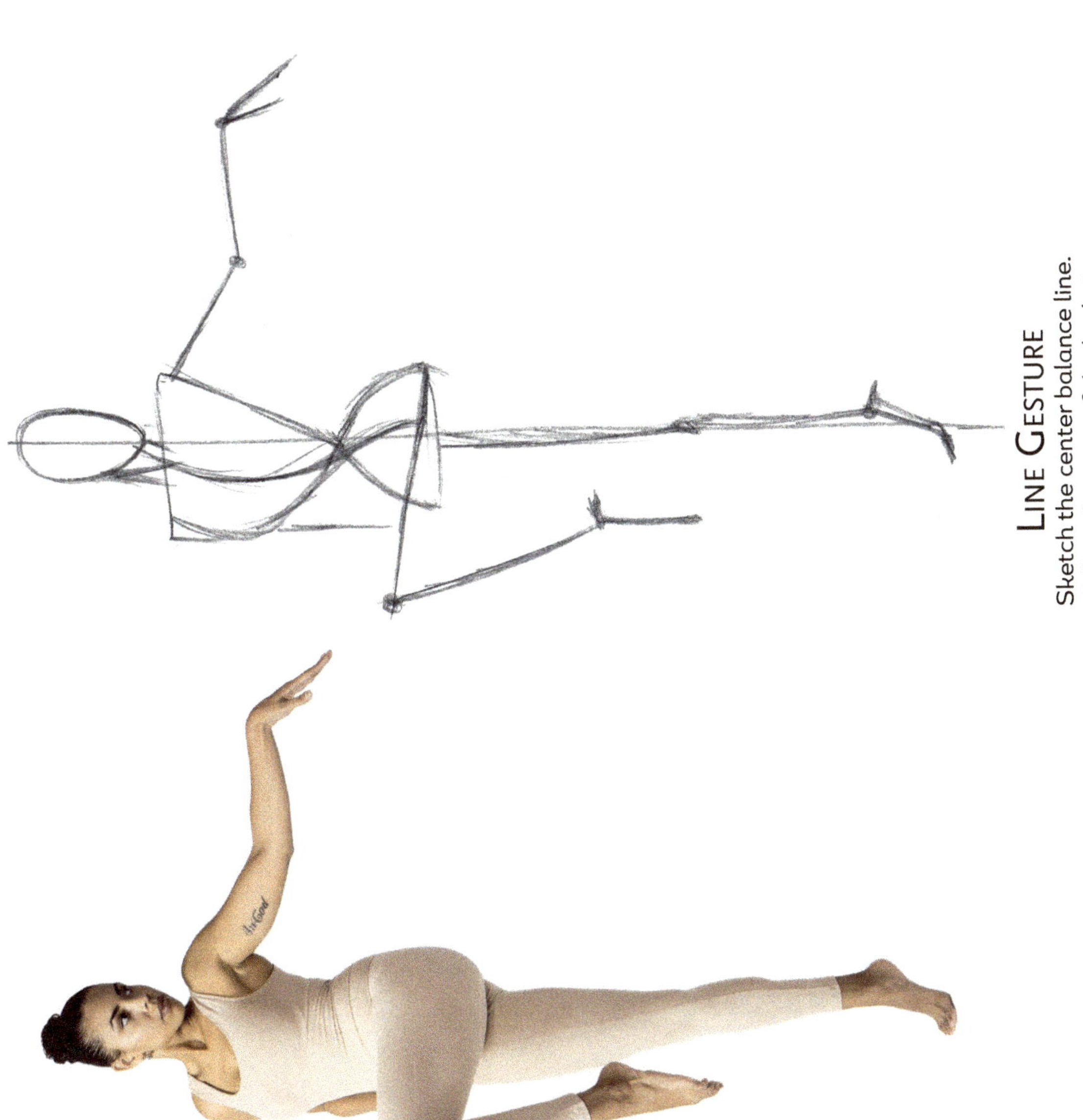

Line Gesture

Sketch the center balance line. Follow the pose of the body to create a quick line gesture.

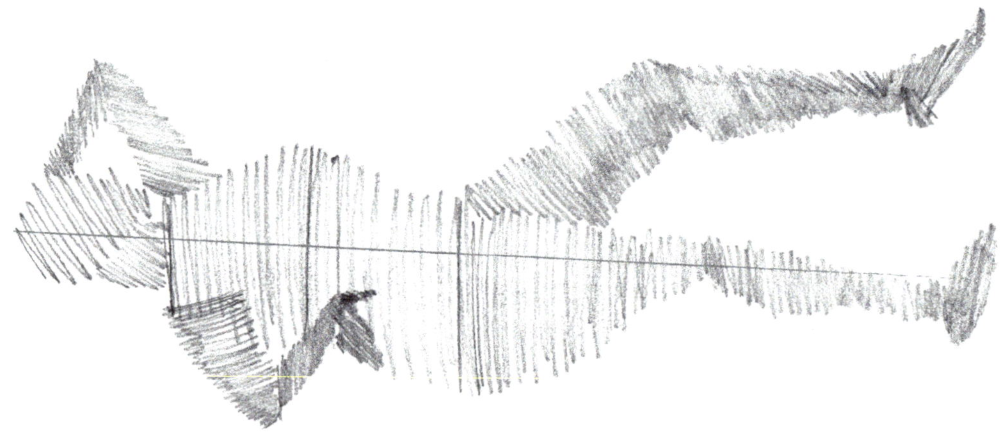

Shaded Gesture

Sketch the center balance line. Follow the pose of the body to create a quick shaded gesture.

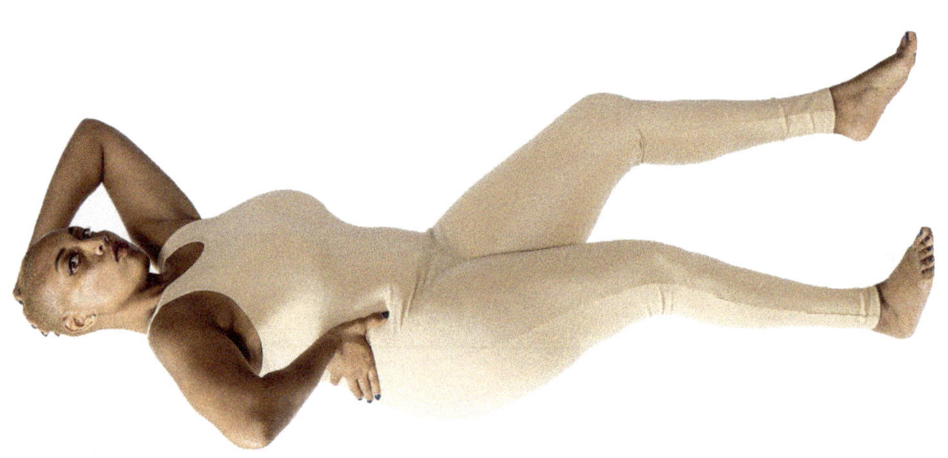

Line Gesture

Sketch the center balance line.
Follow the pose of the body to
create a quick line gesture.

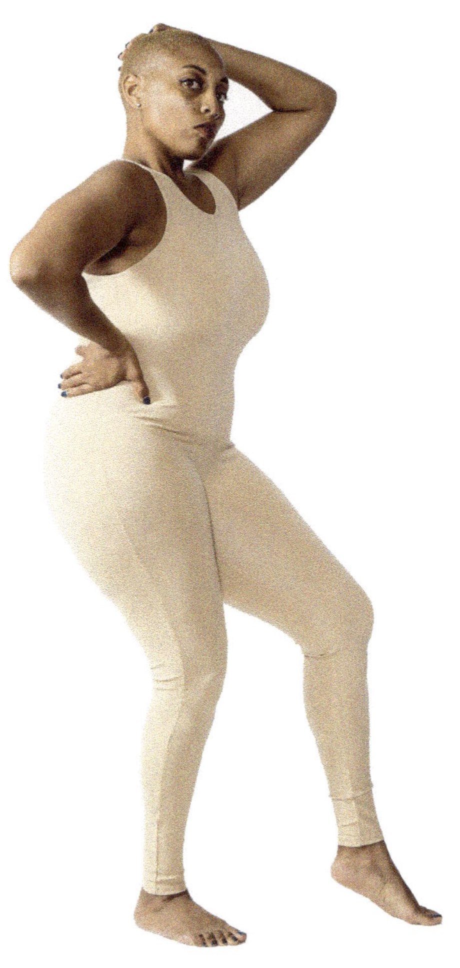

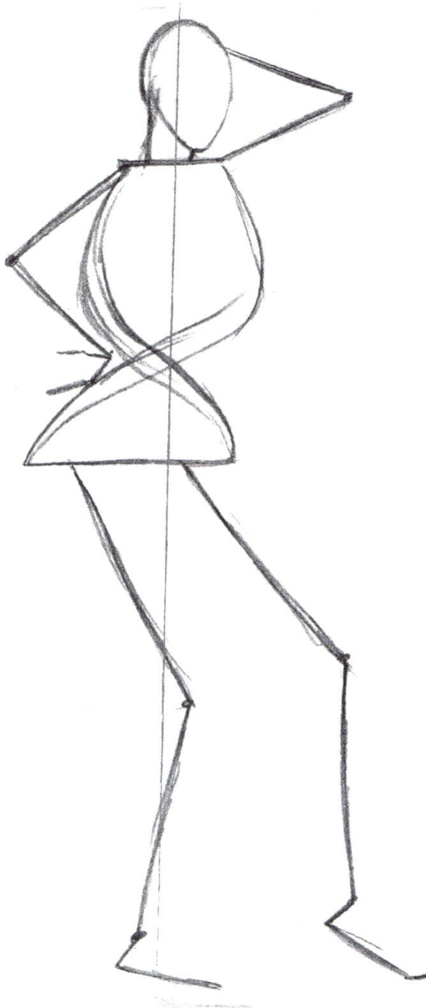

Practice Line Gesture

Sketch the center balance line.
Follow the pose of the body to
create a quick line gesture.

Practice Shaded Gesture

Sketch the center balance line.
Follow the pose of the body to
create a quick shaded gesture.

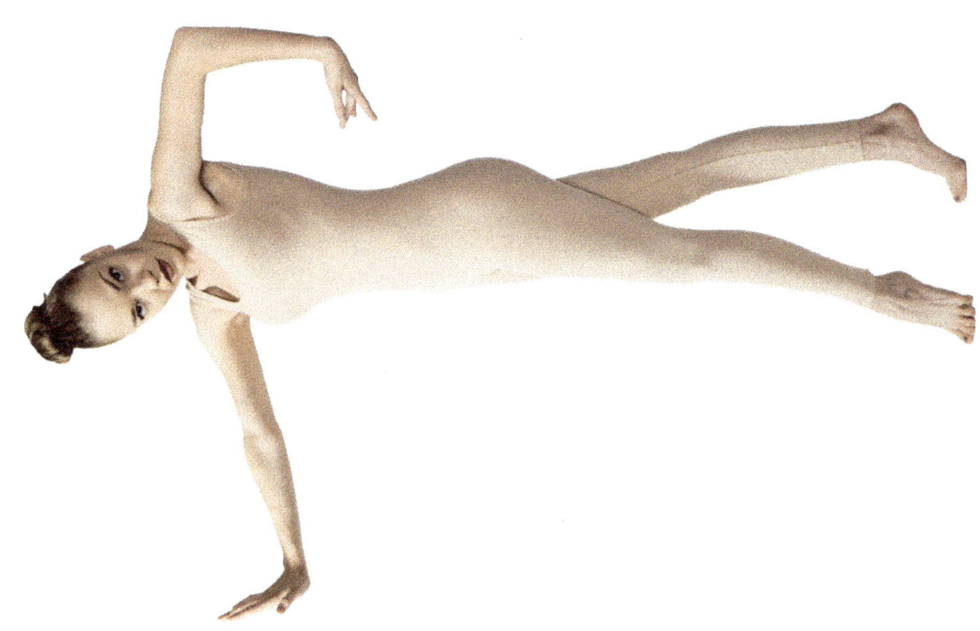

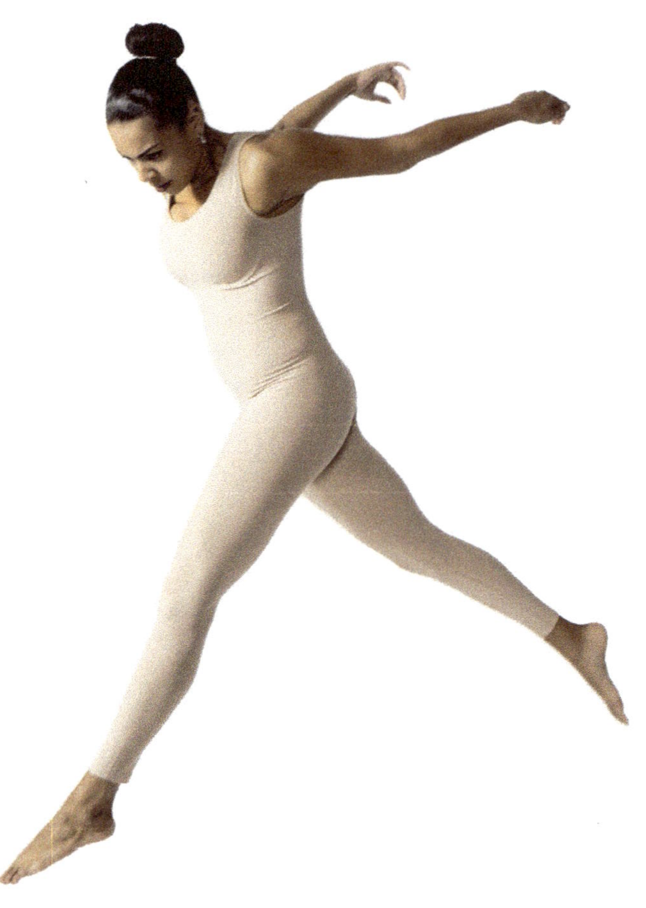

PRACTICE SHADED GESTURE

Sketch the center balance line.
Follow the pose of the body to
create a quick shaded gesture.

PRACTICE LINE GESTURE

Sketch the center balance line.
Follow the pose of the body to
create a quick line gesture.

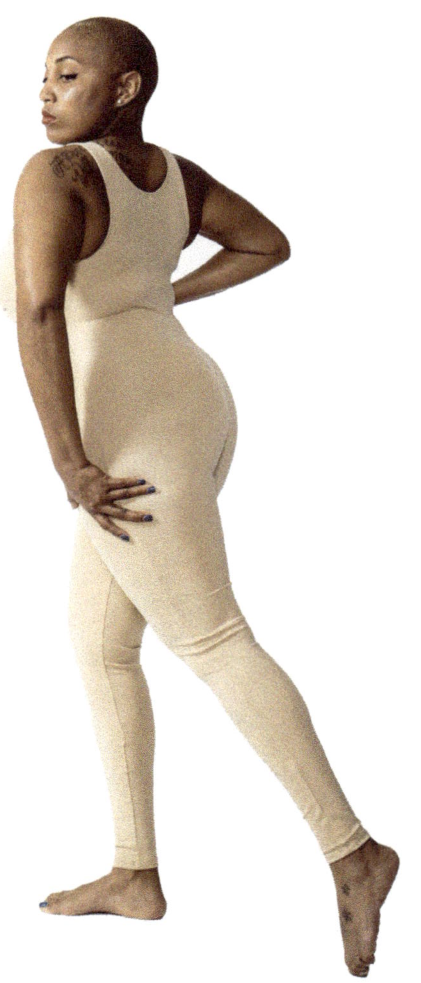

Practice Shaded Gesture

Sketch the center balance line.
Follow the pose of the body to
create a quick shaded gesture.

Practice Line Gesture

Sketch the center balance line.
Follow the pose of the body to
create a quick line gesture.

COMPARISON OF FIGURES

In the fashion industry, the fashion figure is generally based on a 10 head figure. A 10 head figure is an elongated version of the human form. Proportionally, the height of a person is approximately the size of 8 heads. The main difference, between an 8 head figure and a 10 head figure, is an elongation of the torso and the legs.

We instruct the 10 head figure in this book, but for a frame of reference, we first demonstrate how to draw the 8 head figure. This provides insight for understanding proportion of the human body and a knowledge of how to change a figure to a fashion figure. The sketches to the left illustrate the side by side comparison of the 8 head and 10 head figures.

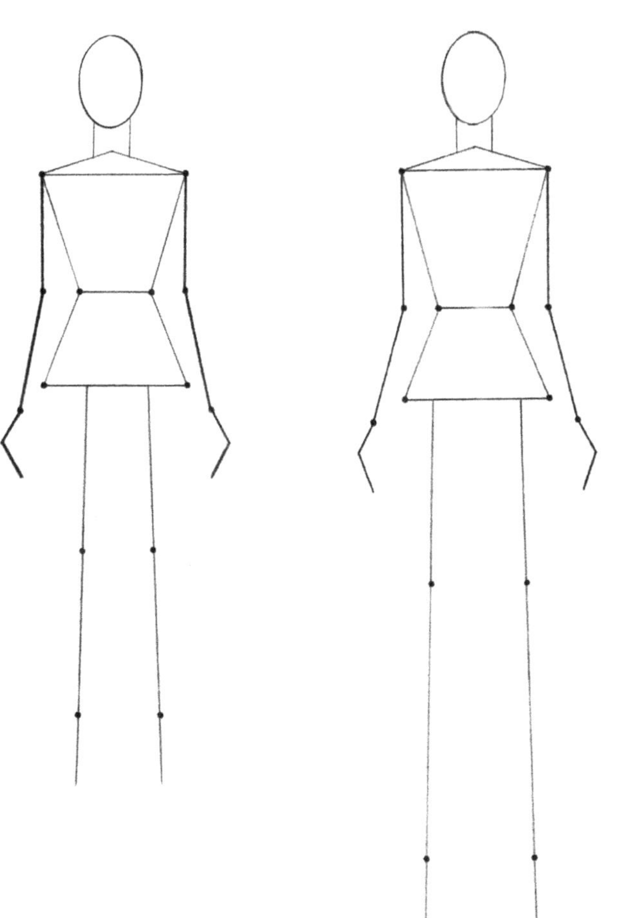

Tip: When drawing your figure, always reference the center balance line of the figure, to the position of knees, ankles, wrists and elbows.

8 HEAD FIGURE

To fully understand the fashion figure, one must understand the proportion of the human body. The 8 head figure is an illustration of the proportional body.

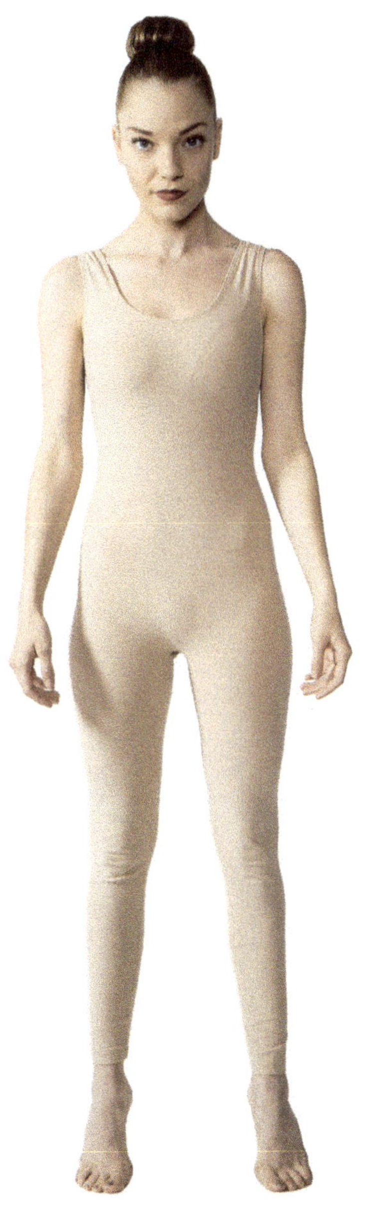

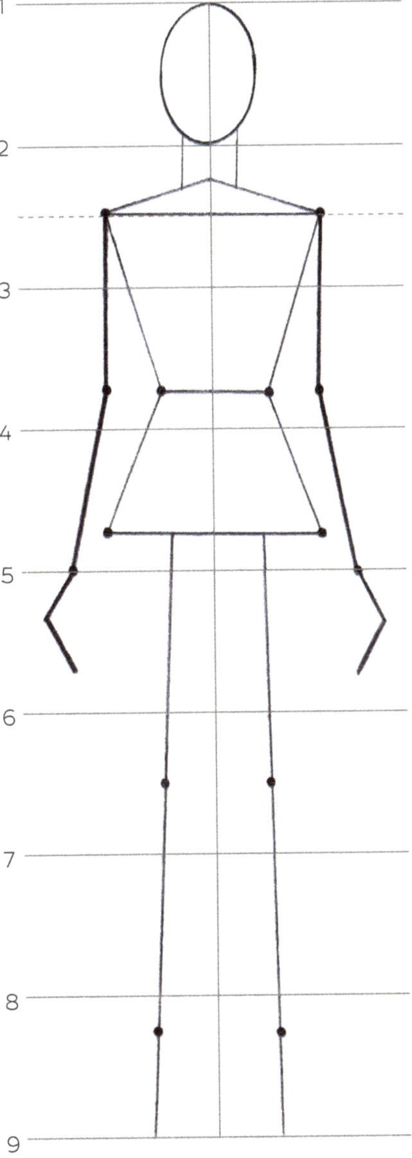

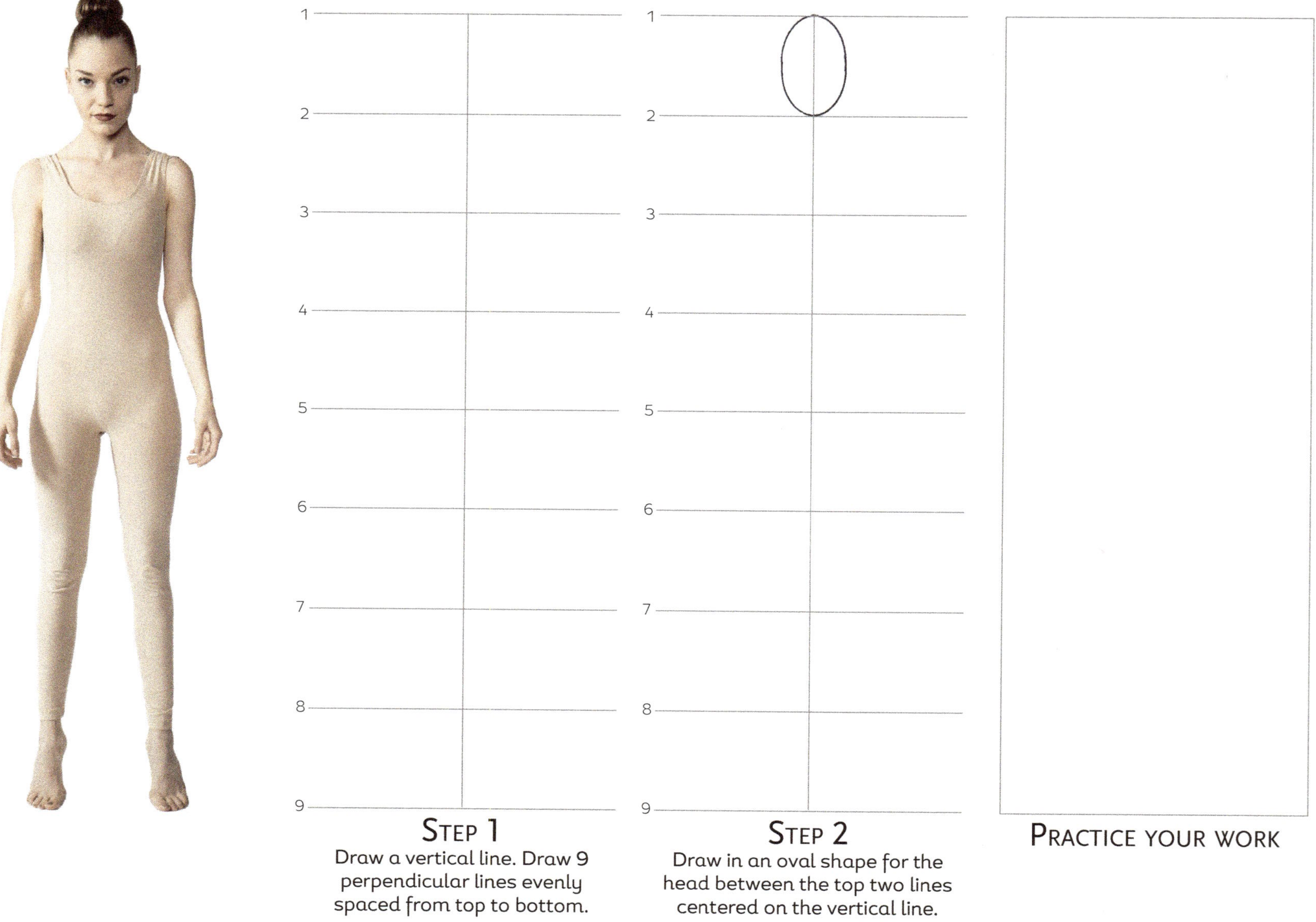

STEP 1

Draw a vertical line. Draw 9 perpendicular lines evenly spaced from top to bottom.

STEP 2

Draw in an oval shape for the head between the top two lines centered on the vertical line.

PRACTICE YOUR WORK

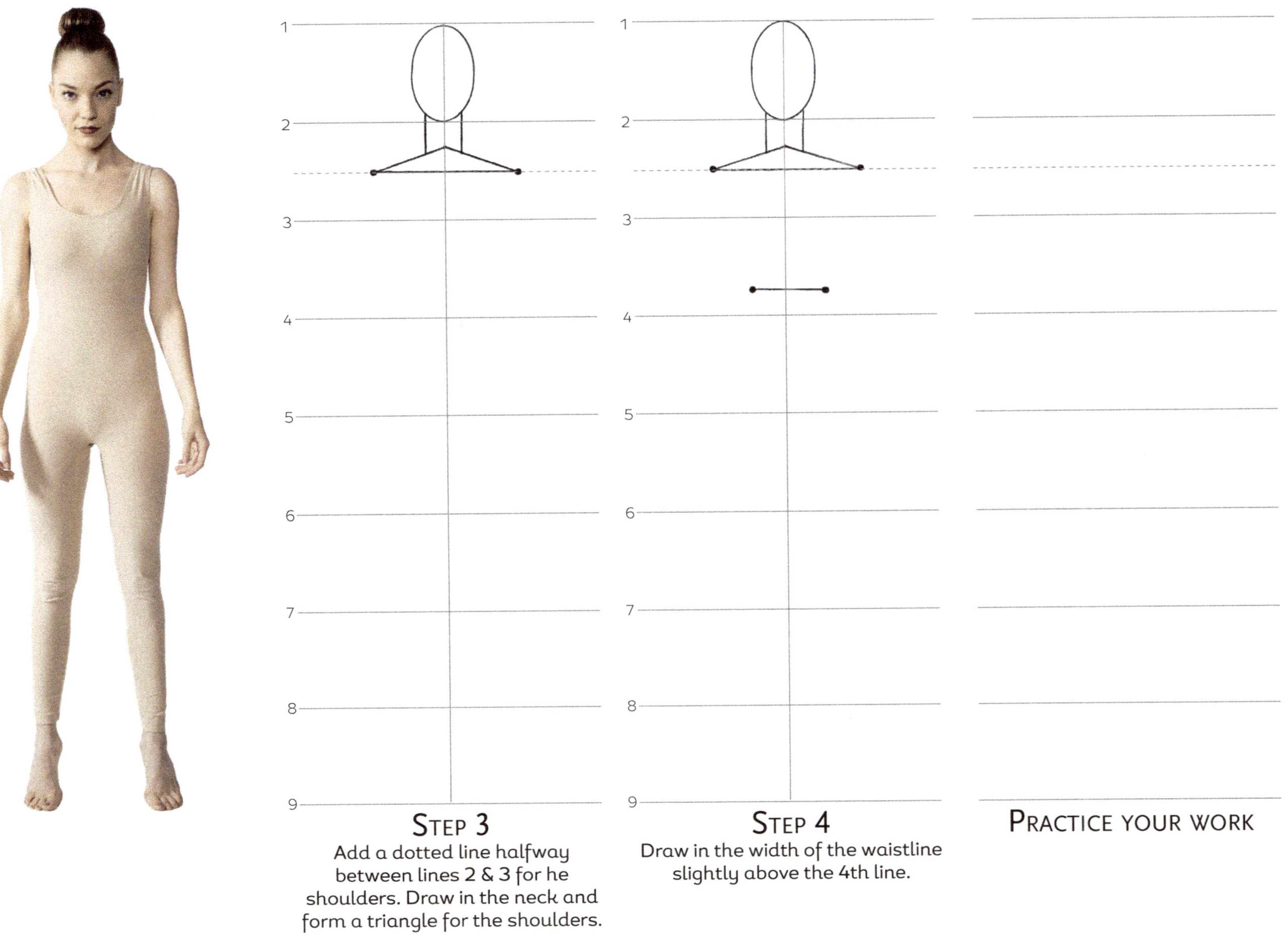

Step 3
Add a dotted line halfway between lines 2 & 3 for he shoulders. Draw in the neck and form a triangle for the shoulders.

Step 4
Draw in the width of the waistline slightly above the 4th line.

Practice your work

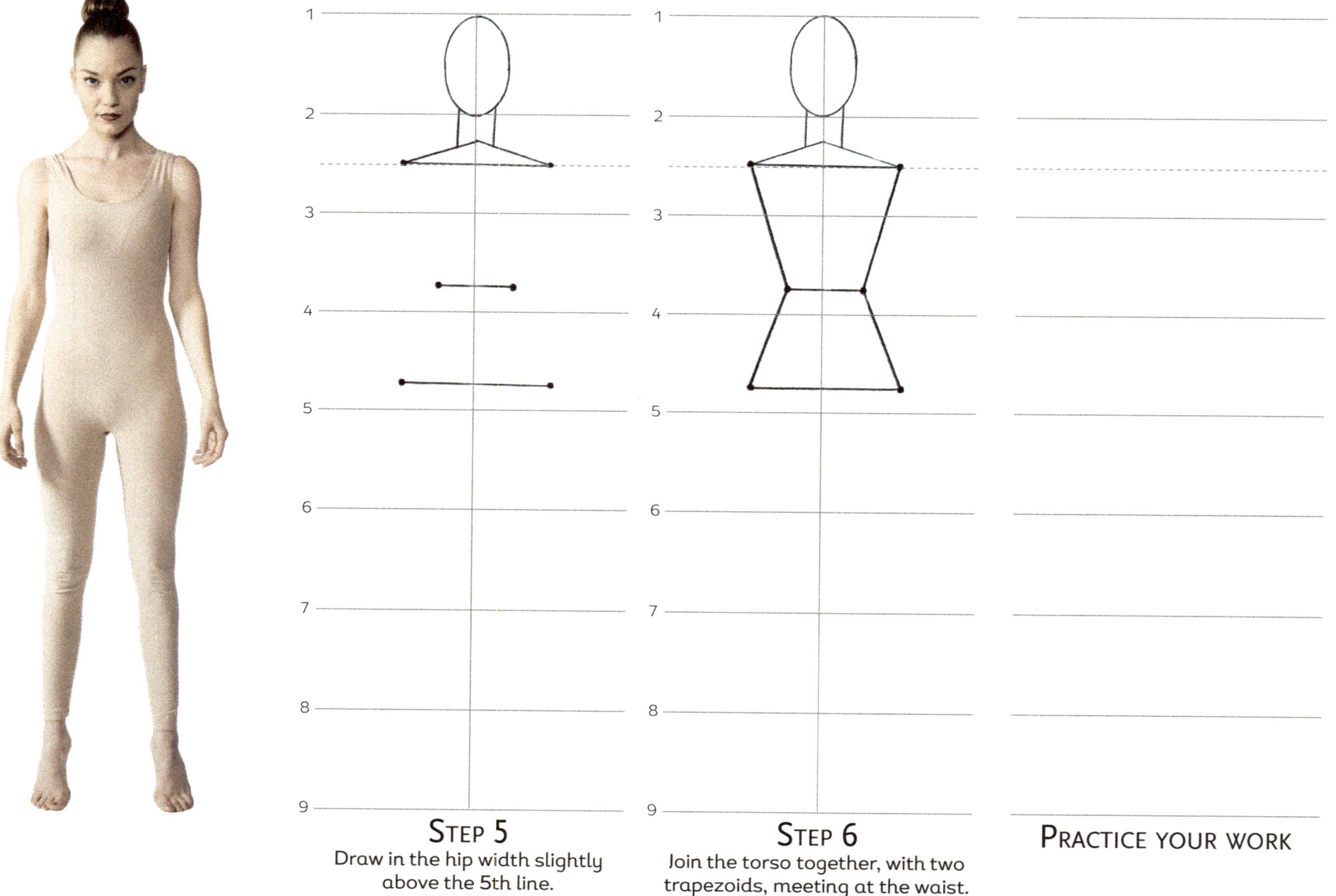

STEP 5
Draw in the hip width slightly above the 5th line.

STEP 6
Join the torso together, with two trapezoids, meeting at the waist.

PRACTICE YOUR WORK

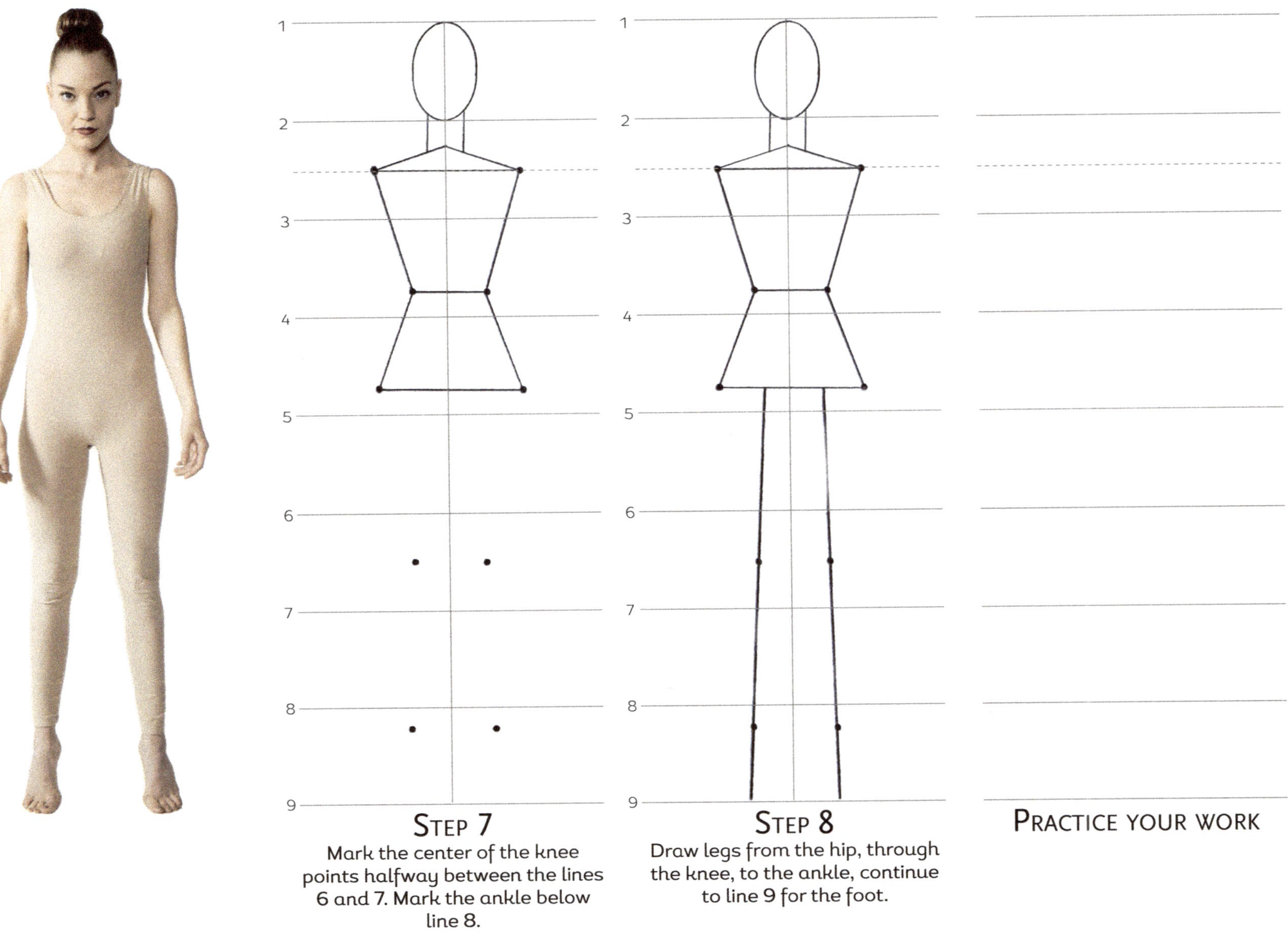

Step 7

Mark the center of the knee points halfway between the lines 6 and 7. Mark the ankle below line 8.

Step 8

Draw legs from the hip, through the knee, to the ankle, continue to line 9 for the foot.

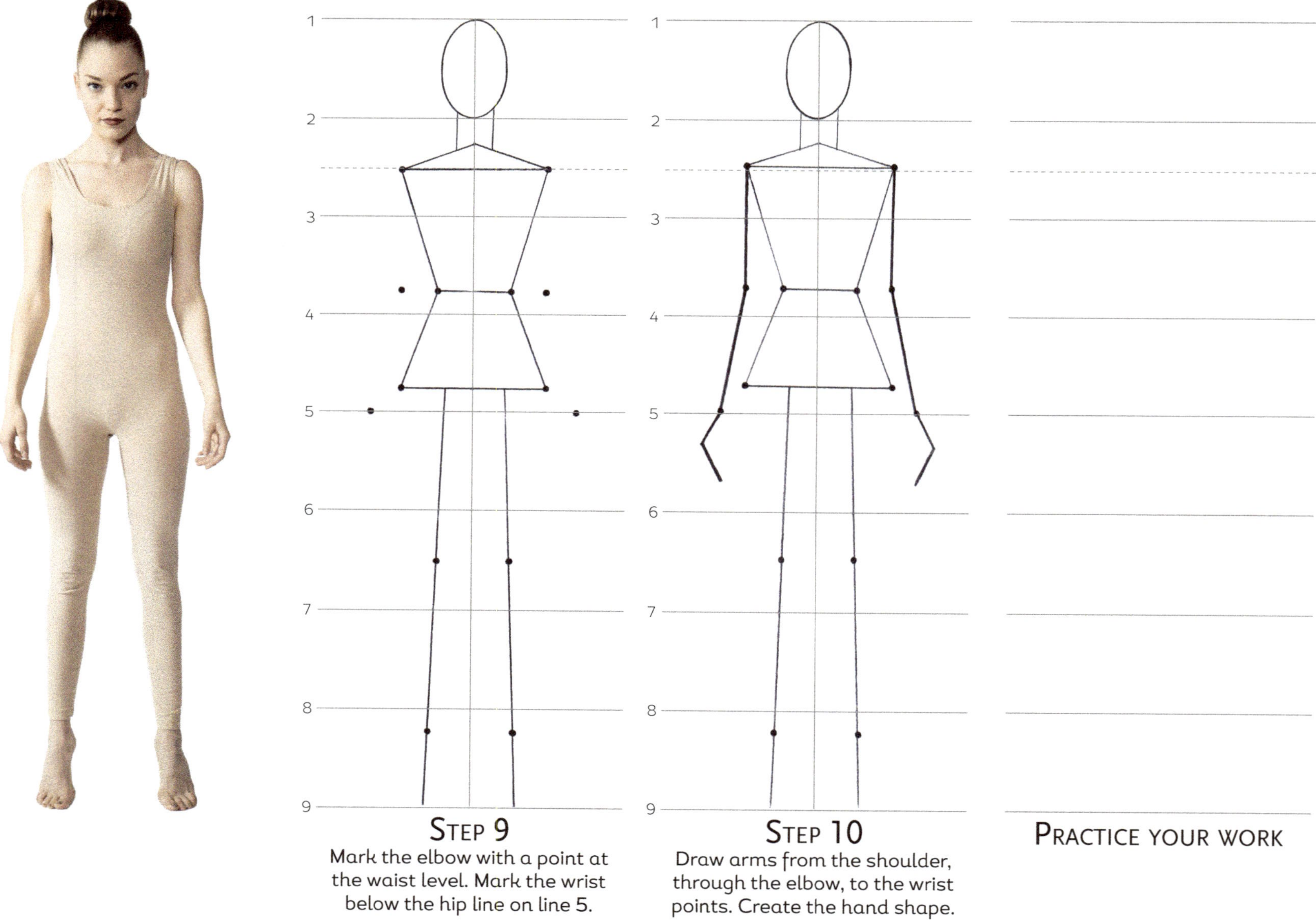

STEP 9

Mark the elbow with a point at the waist level. Mark the wrist below the hip line on line 5.

STEP 10

Draw arms from the shoulder, through the elbow, to the wrist points. Create the hand shape.

PRACTICE YOUR WORK

10 HEAD FIGURE

The fashion figure is 10 heads in height, altering the proportion of a normal body. This creates additional length in the torso and legs, which accentuates style lines when illustrating clothing. For visual proportional reference, the model has been lined up to the 8 head lines for this example and all future examples in the book.

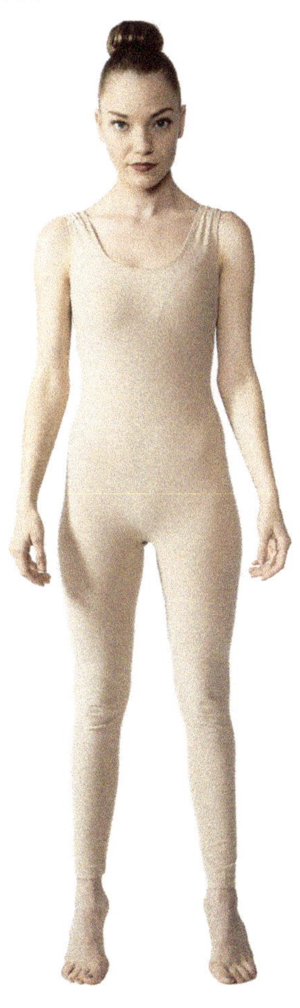

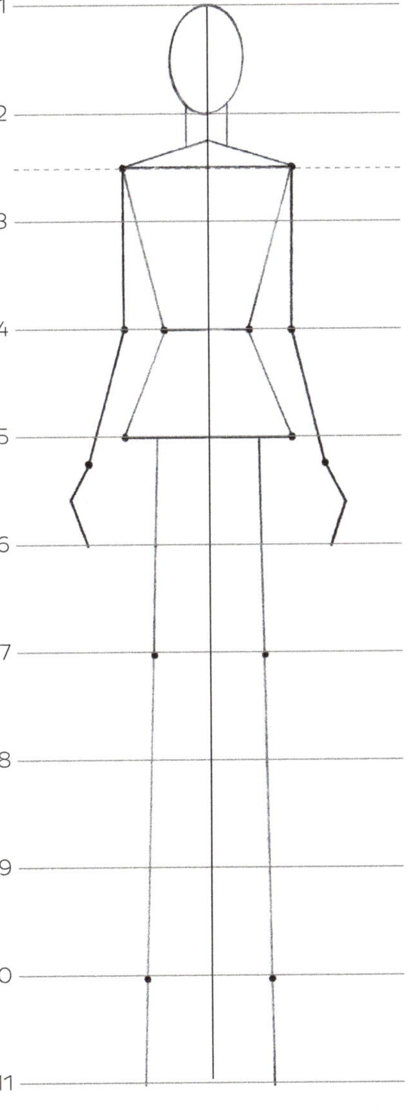

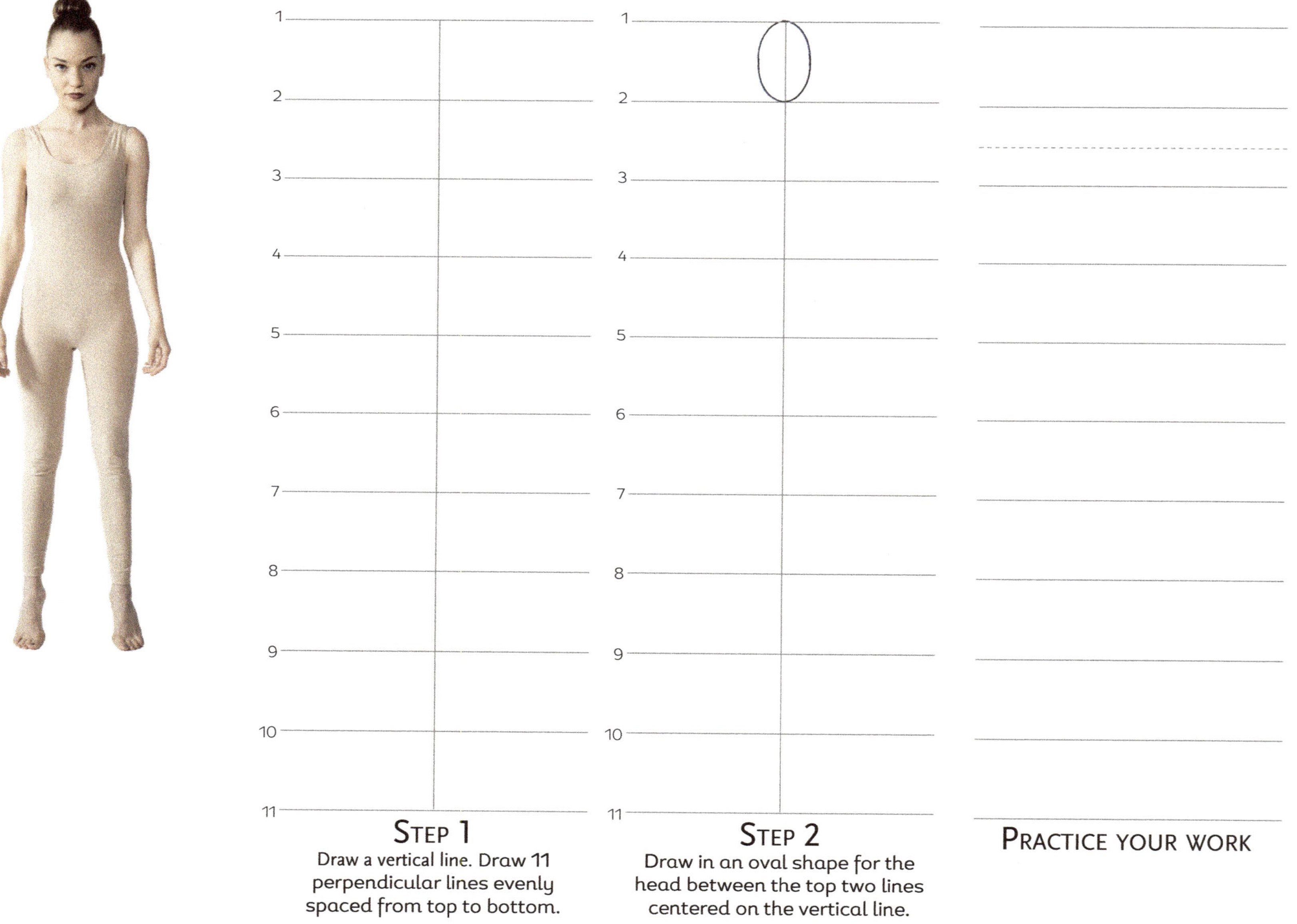

STEP 1

Draw a vertical line. Draw 11 perpendicular lines evenly spaced from top to bottom.

STEP 2

Draw in an oval shape for the head between the top two lines centered on the vertical line.

PRACTICE YOUR WORK

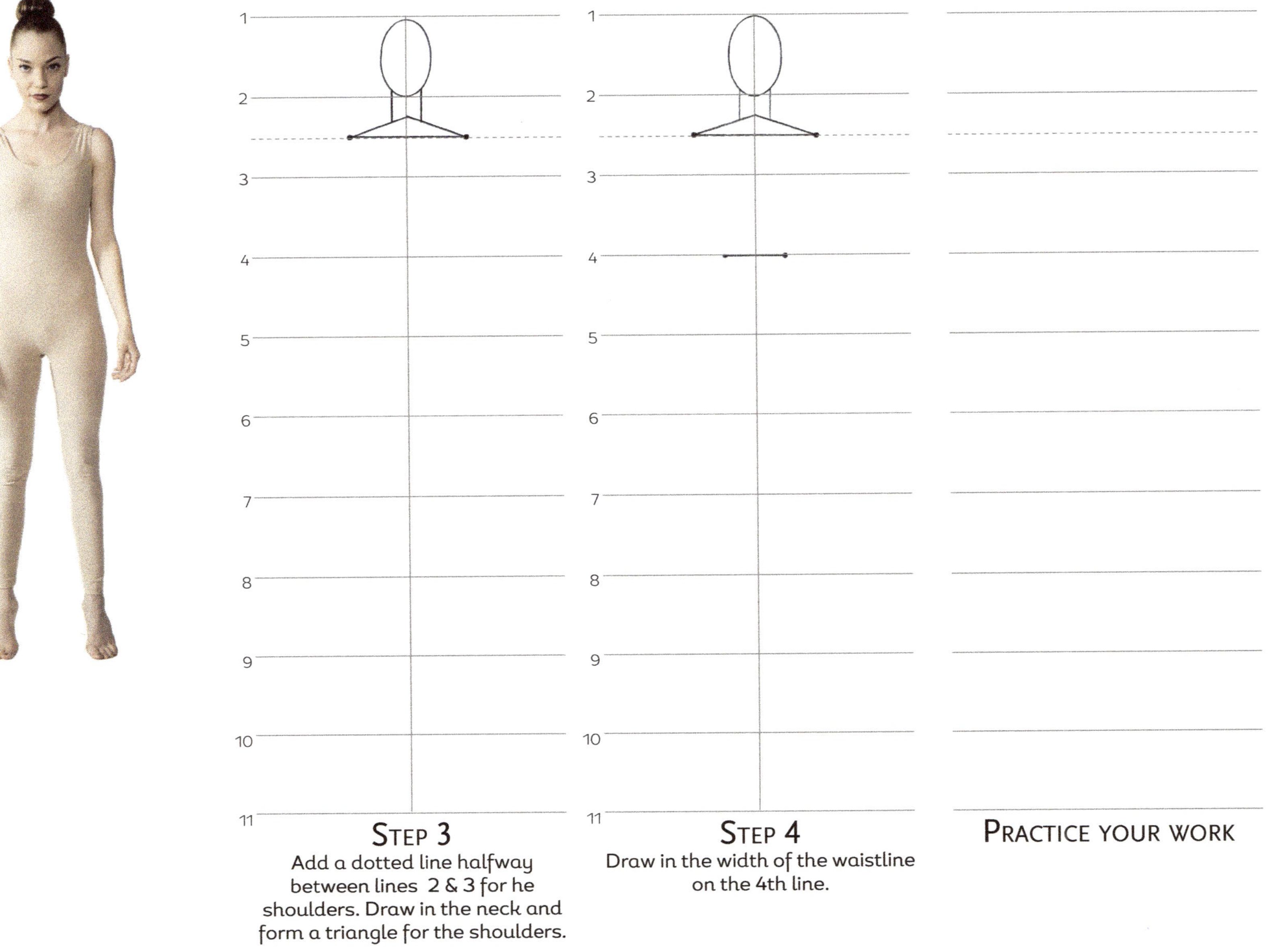

STEP 3

Add a dotted line halfway between lines 2 & 3 for he shoulders. Draw in the neck and form a triangle for the shoulders.

STEP 4

Draw in the width of the waistline on the 4th line.

PRACTICE YOUR WORK

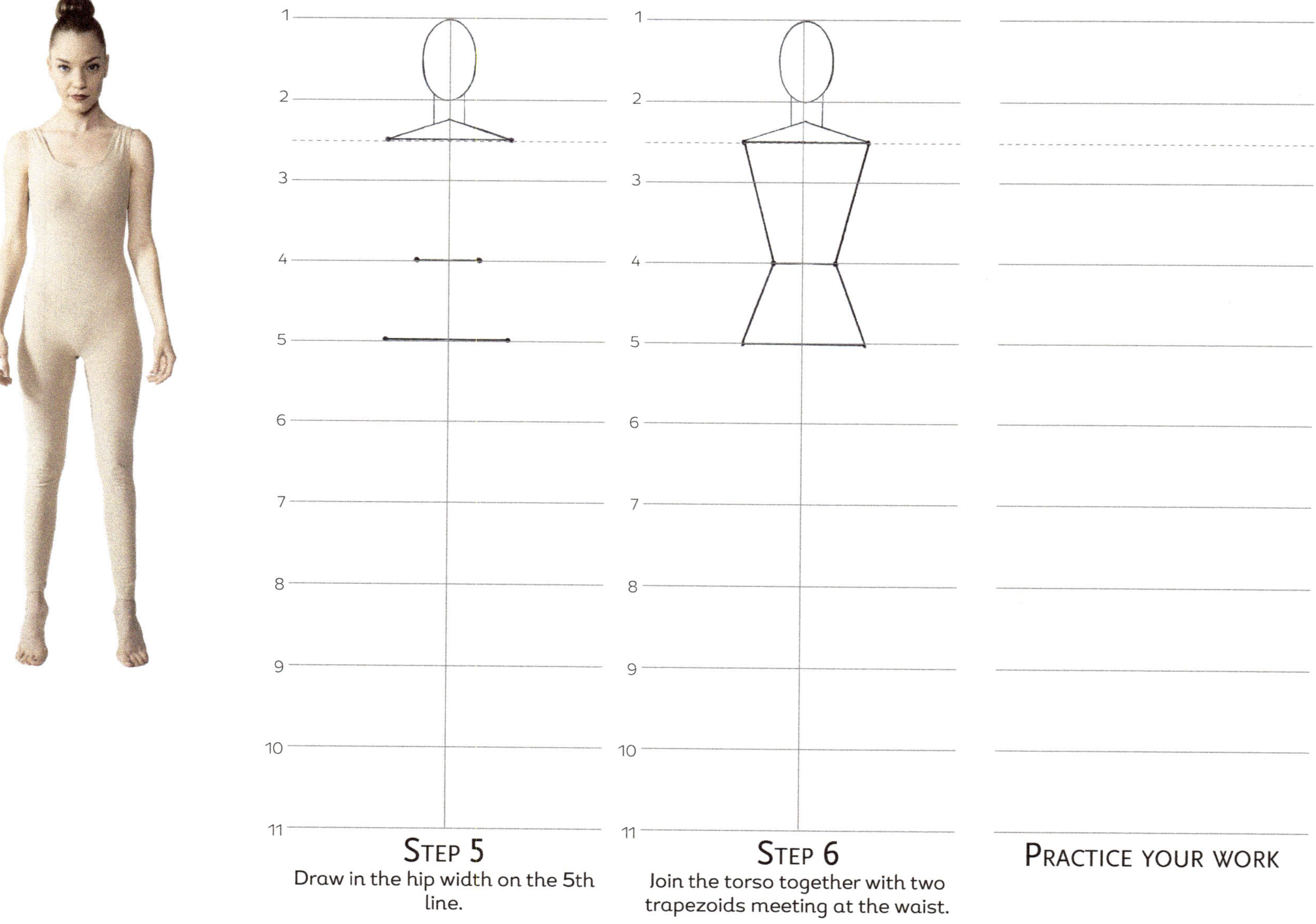

STEP 5

Draw in the hip width on the 5th line.

STEP 6

Join the torso together with two trapezoids meeting at the waist.

PRACTICE YOUR WORK

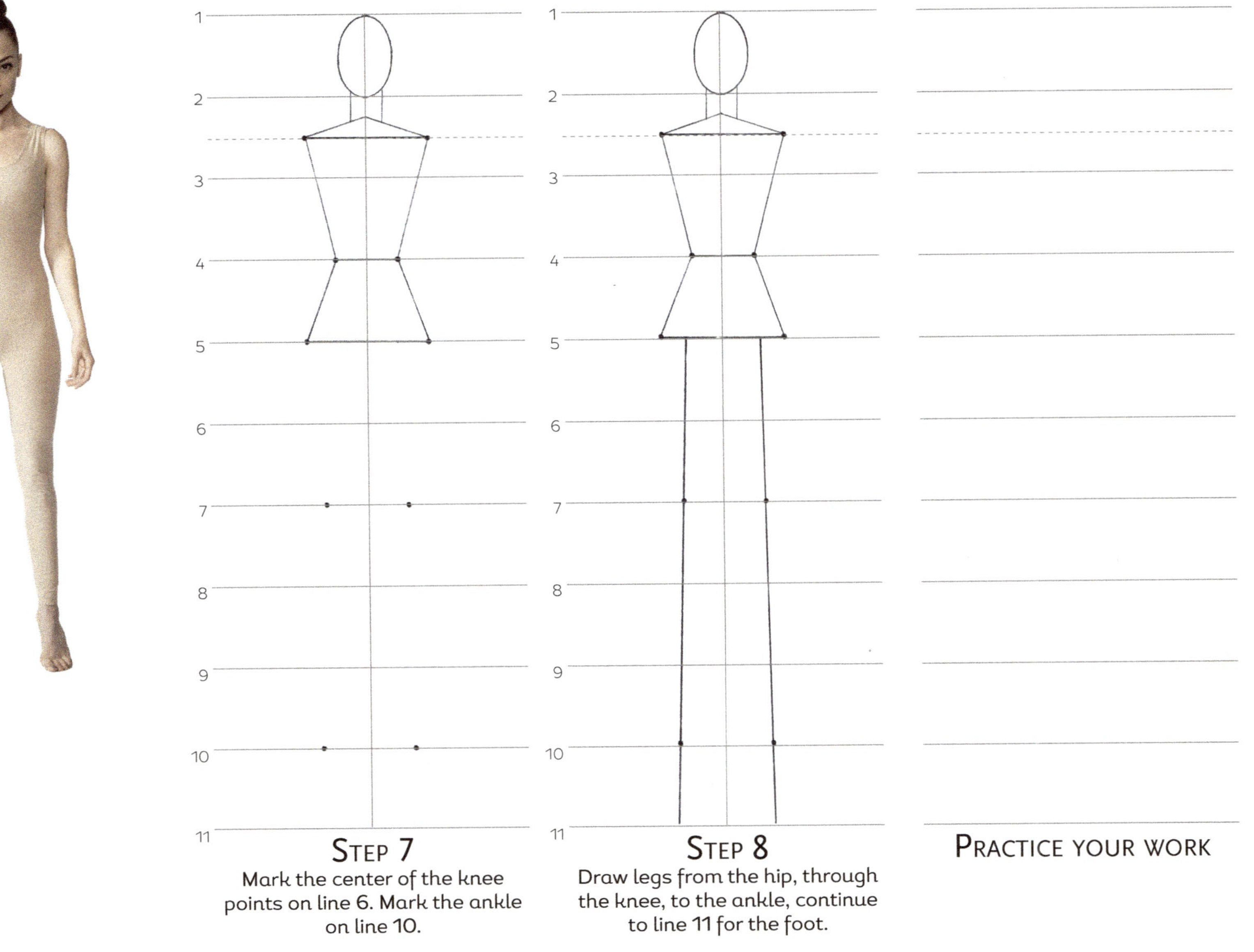

STEP 7

Mark the center of the knee points on line 6. Mark the ankle on line 10.

STEP 8

Draw legs from the hip, through the knee, to the ankle, continue to line 11 for the foot.

PRACTICE YOUR WORK

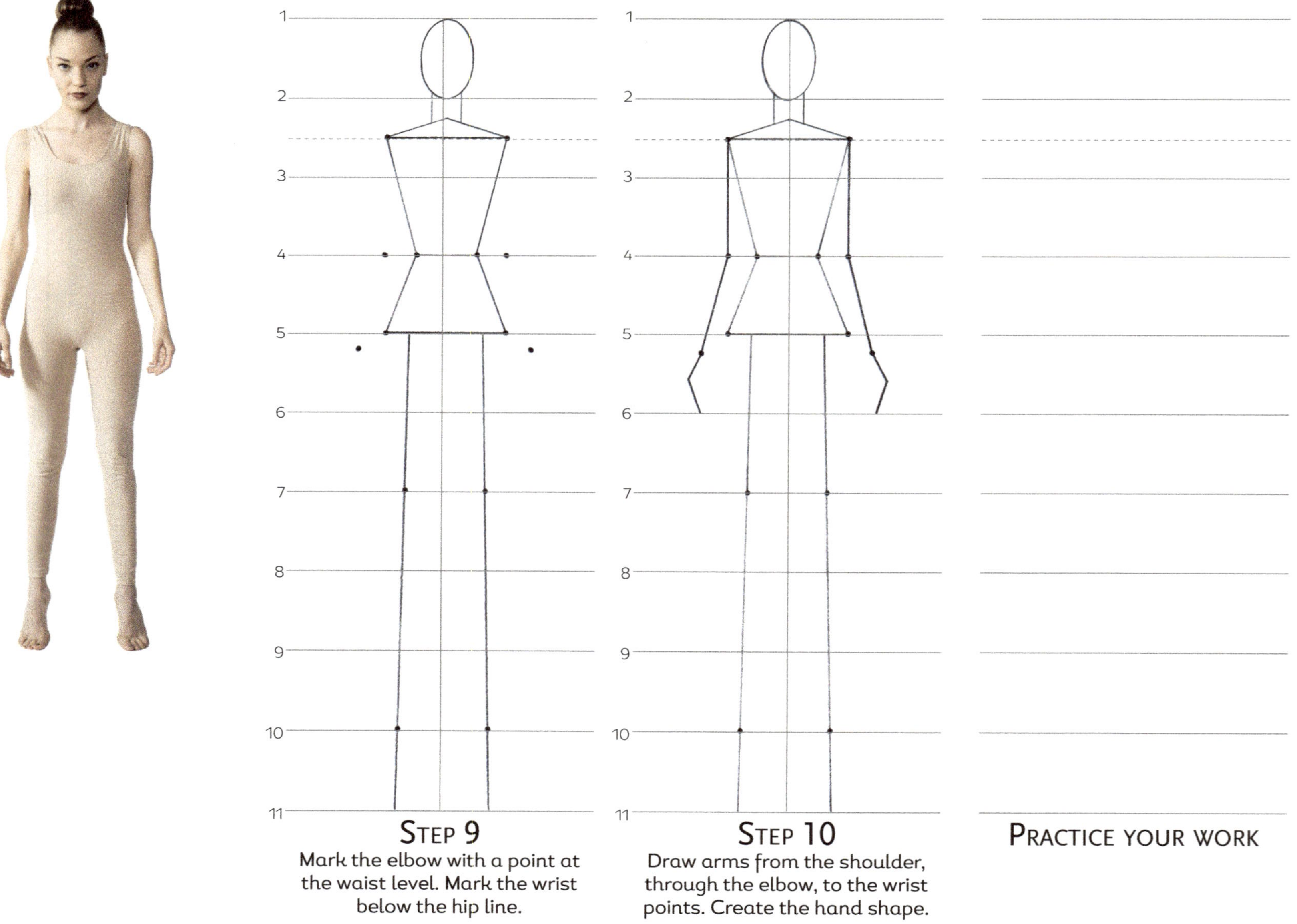

STEP 9

Mark the elbow with a point at the waist level. Mark the wrist below the hip line.

STEP 10

Draw arms from the shoulder, through the elbow, to the wrist points. Create the hand shape.

PRACTICE YOUR WORK

PRACTICE
10 HEAD FIGURE

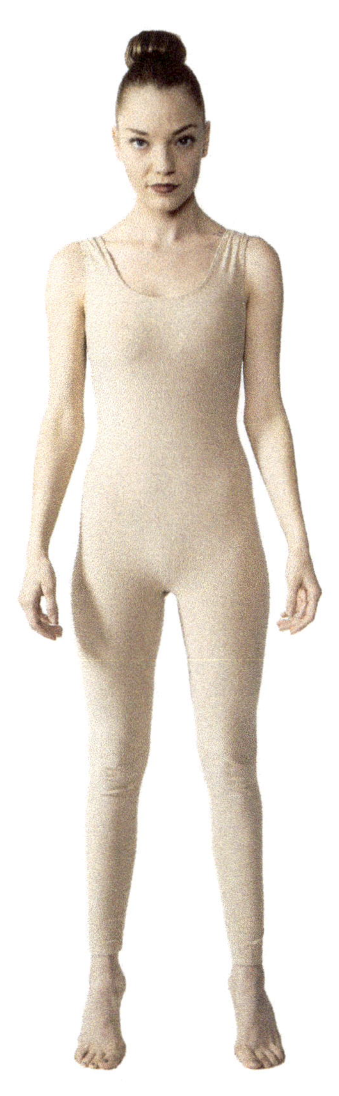

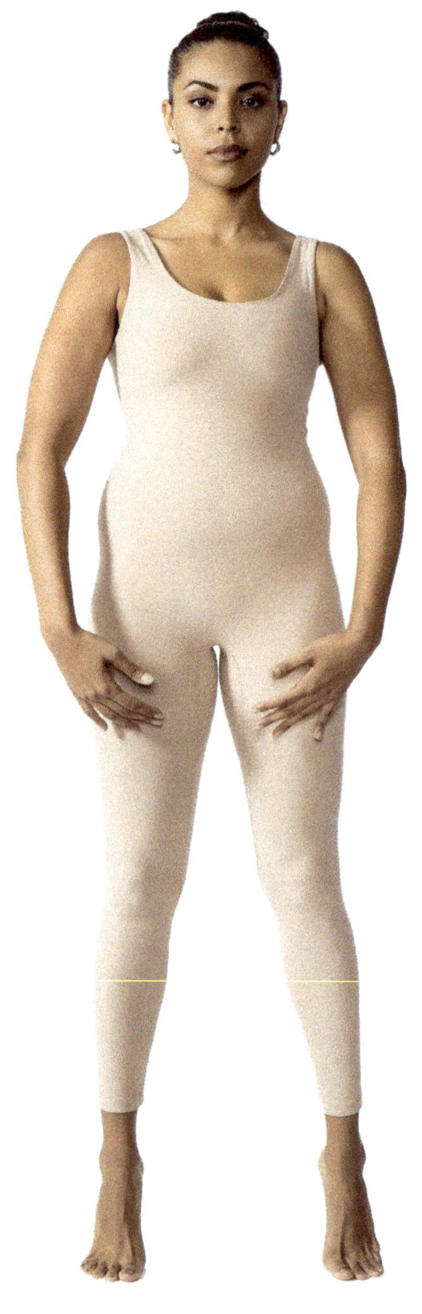

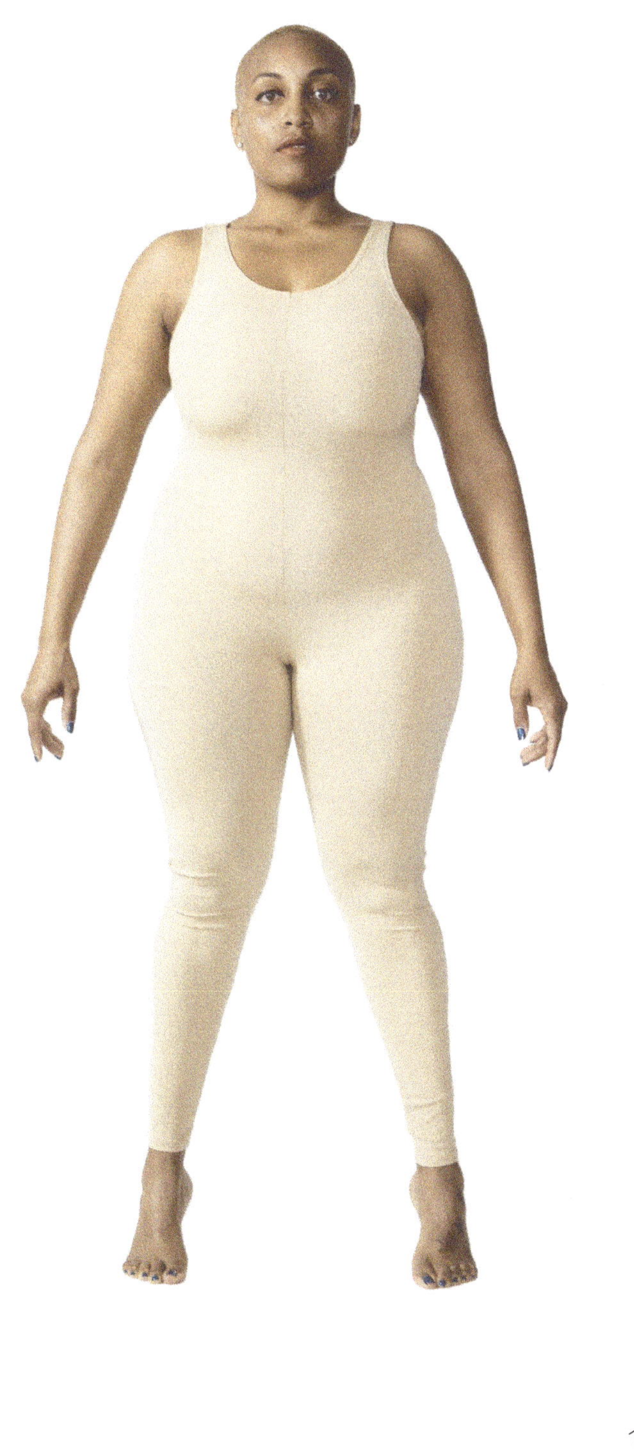

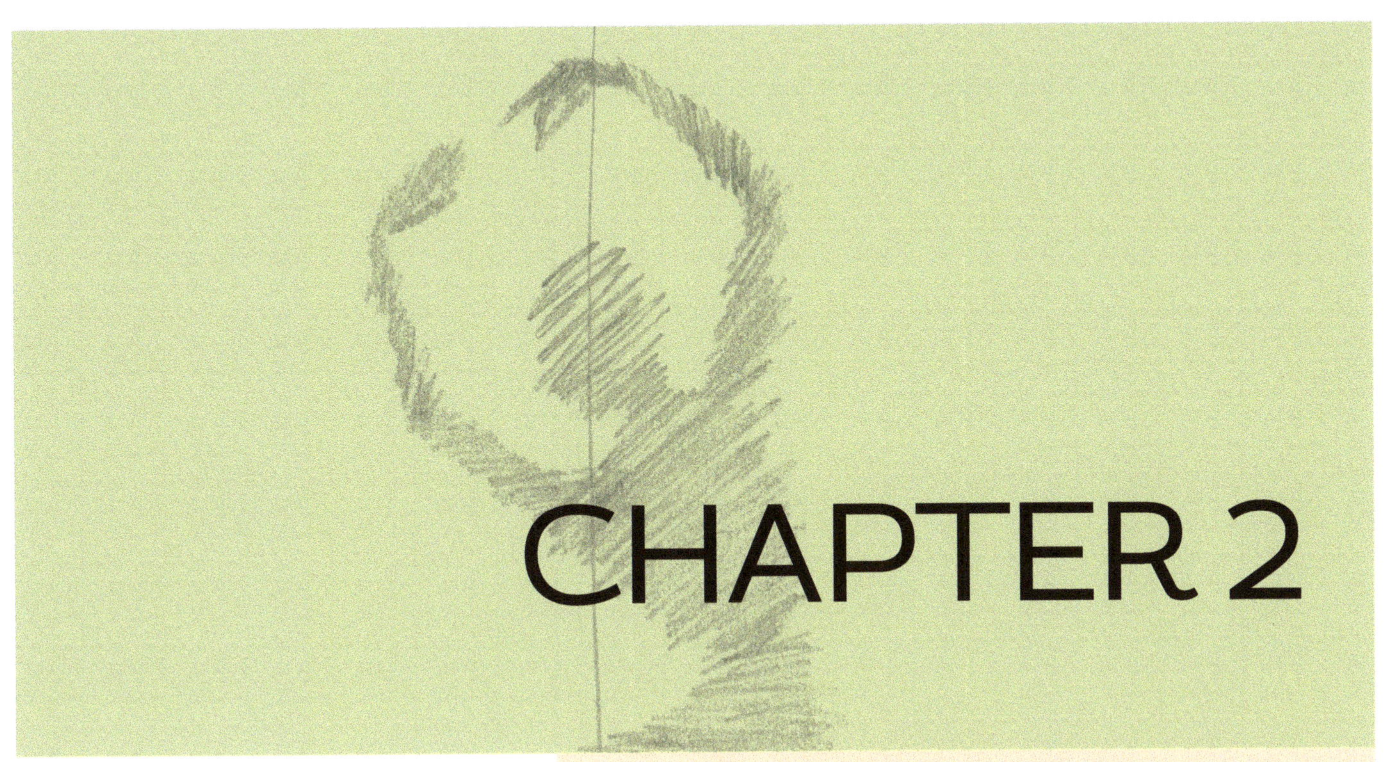

CHAPTER 2

Simple Poses

FRONT VIEW FIGURE

In the first two exercises, the sections of the body were addressed for both the proportional figure and the fashion figure. In the following steps, we approach the fashion figure in terms of shapes, rather than lines, to help you better understand the body shapes.

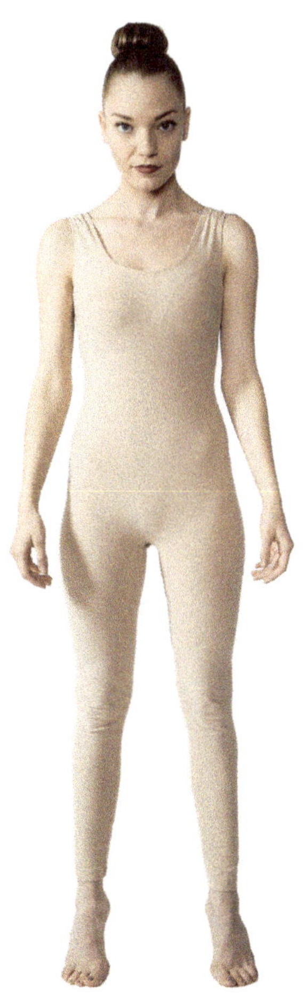 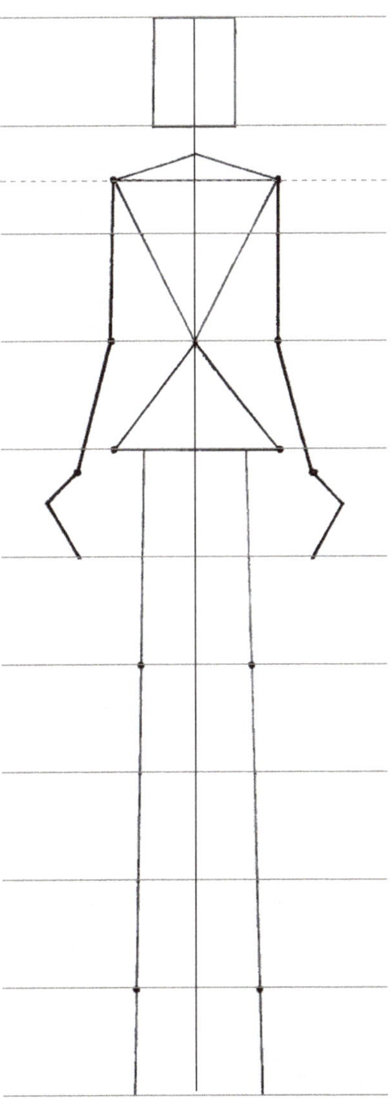

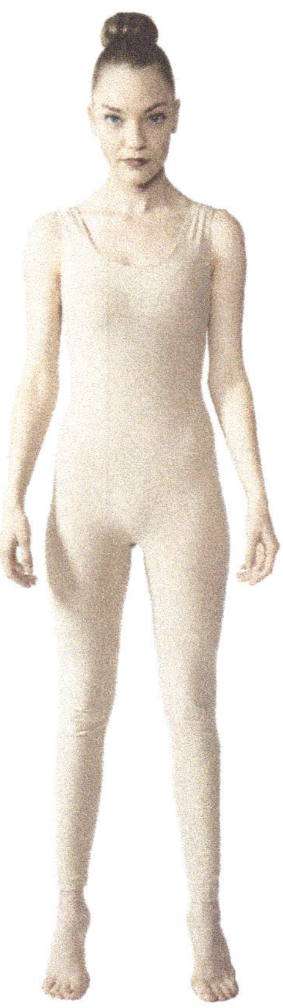

STEP 1
Draw in the head as a rectangle.

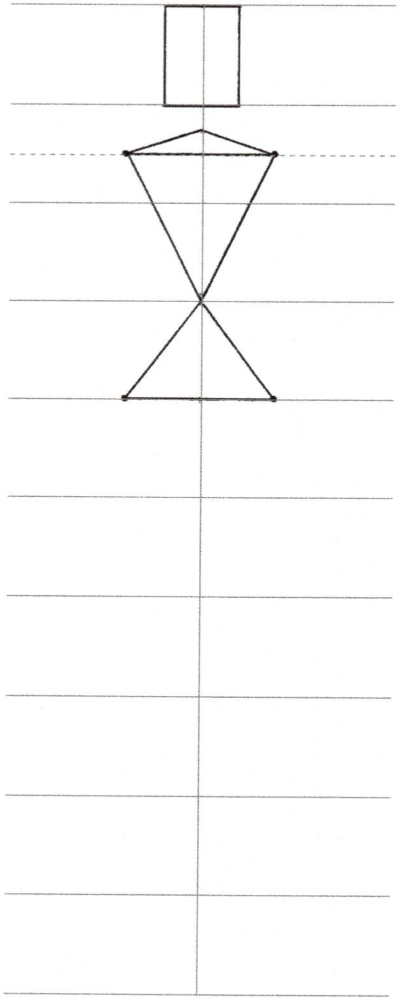

STEP 2
Create the shoulders and torso shapes as triangles.

PRACTICE YOUR WORK

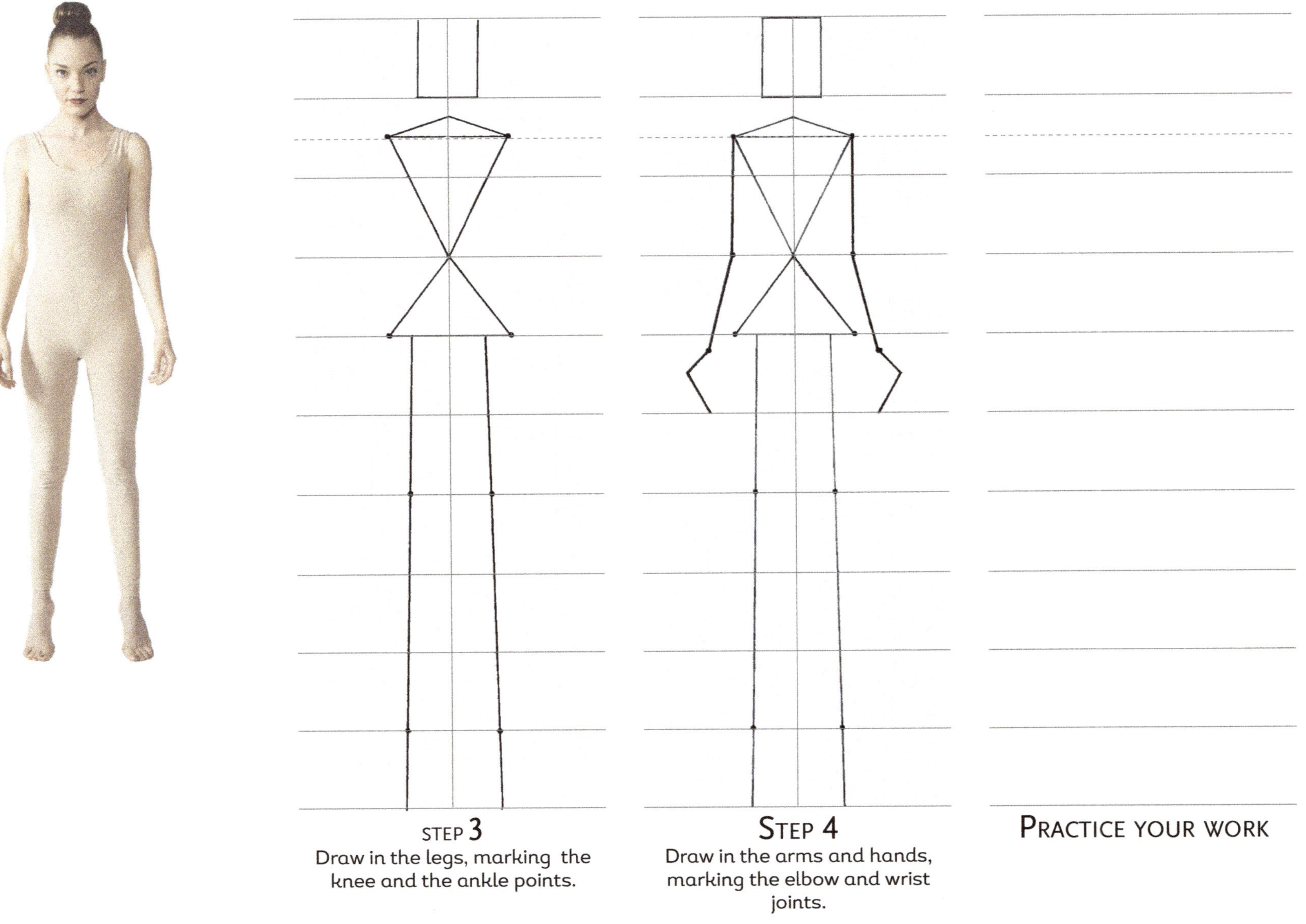

STEP 3

Draw in the legs, marking the knee and the ankle points.

STEP 4

Draw in the arms and hands, marking the elbow and wrist joints.

PRACTICE YOUR WORK

BACK VIEW DETAIL

In this exercise, we introduce the body shape to the figure. The back view is the easiest figure to begin with. Follow the basic figure illustration steps from the previous exercise for this all and all future exercises.

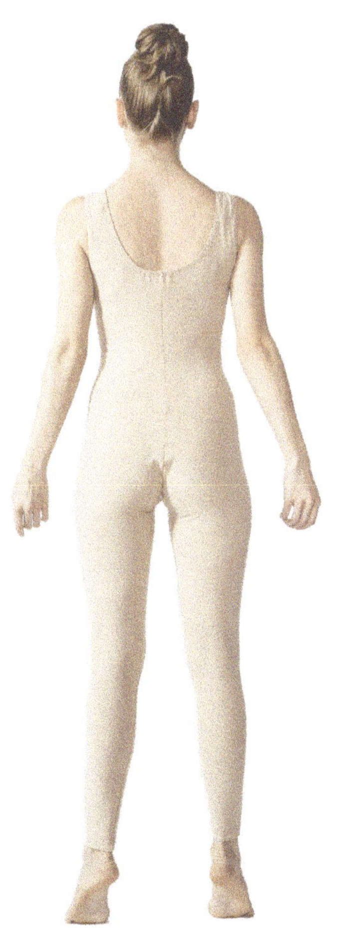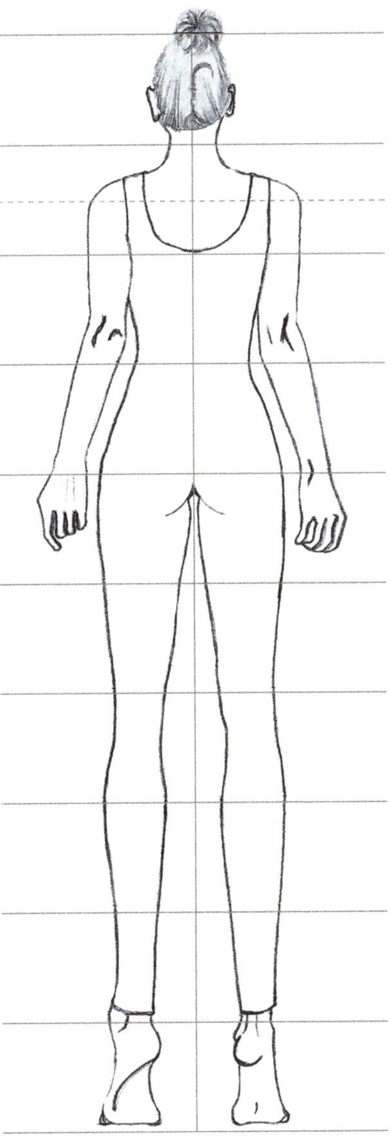

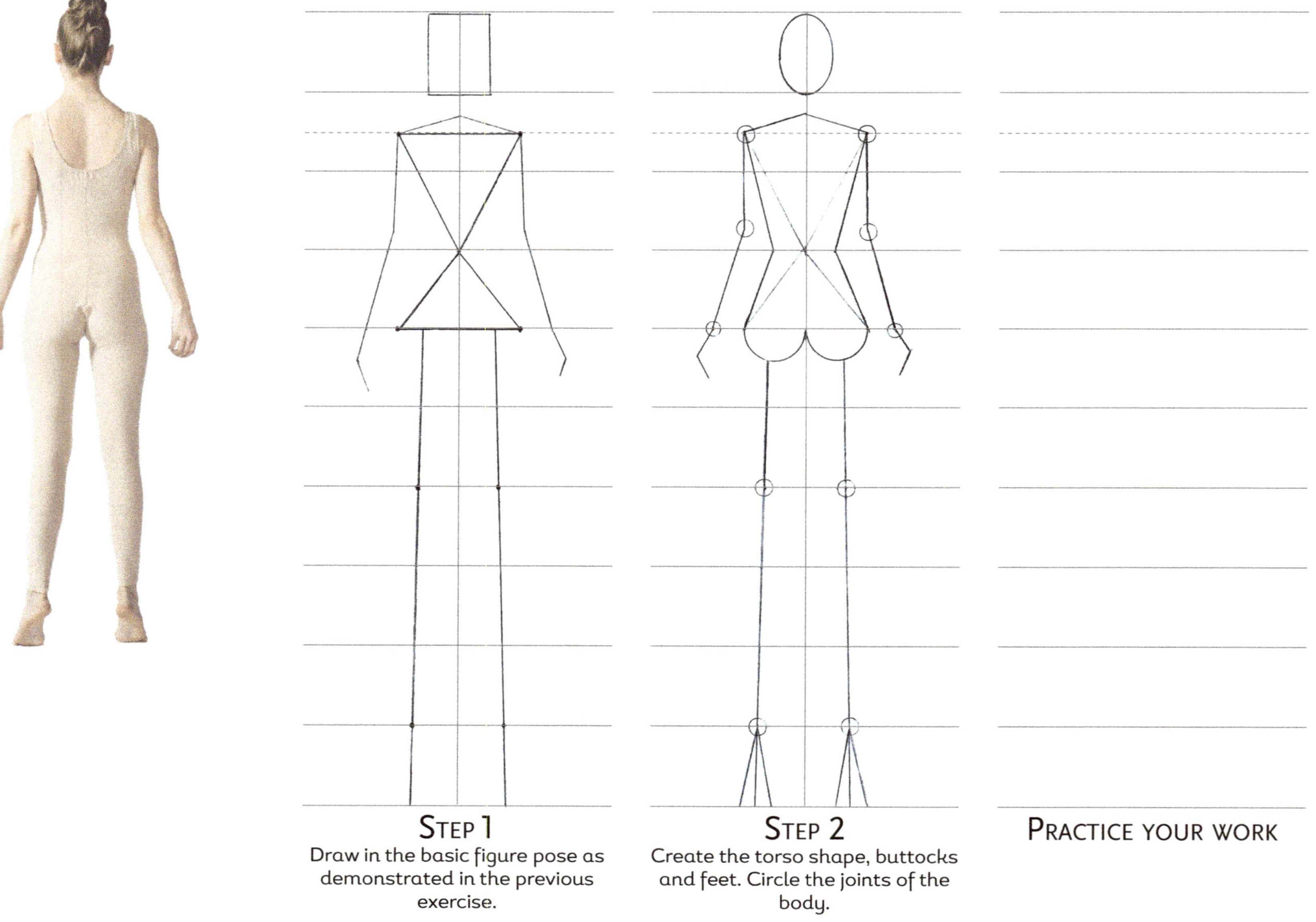

Step 1

Draw in the basic figure pose as demonstrated in the previous exercise.

Step 2

Create the torso shape, buttocks and feet. Circle the joints of the body.

Practice your work

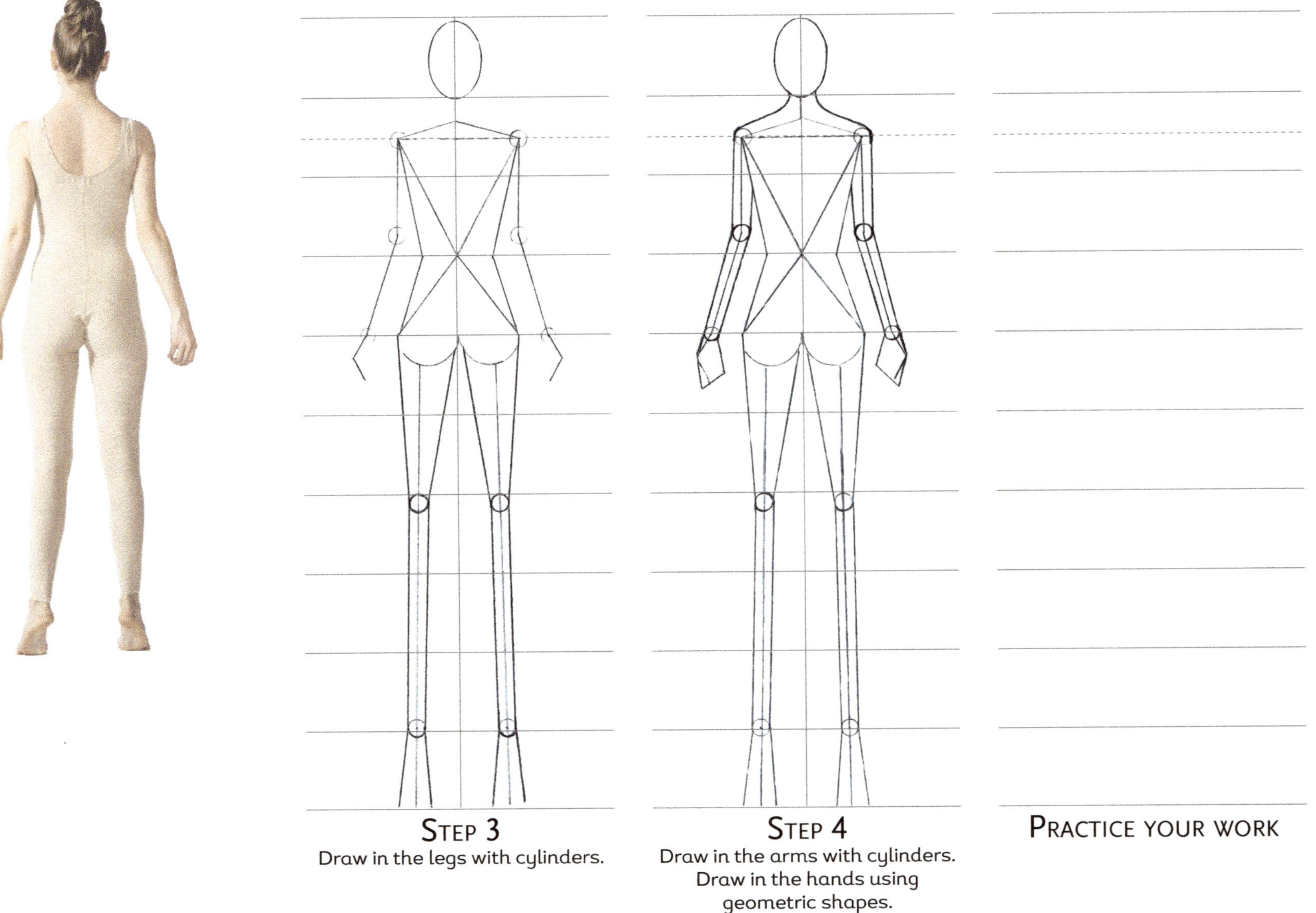

Step 3

Draw in the legs with cylinders.

Step 4

Draw in the arms with cylinders. Draw in the hands using geometric shapes.

Practice your work

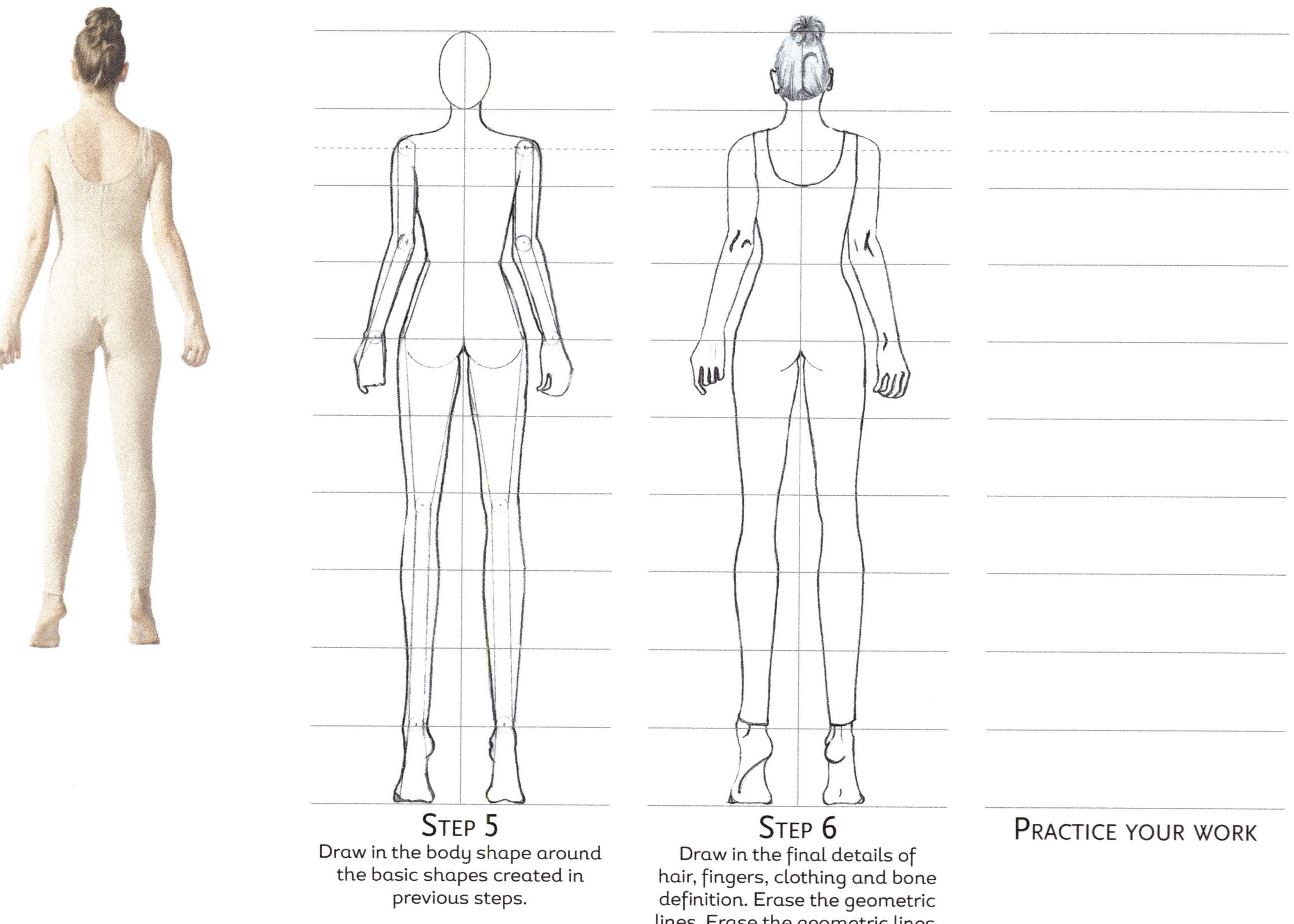

STEP 5
Draw in the body shape around the basic shapes created in previous steps.
STEP 6
Draw in the final details of hair, fingers, clothing and bone definition. Erase the geometric lines. Erase the geometric lines.
PRACTICE YOUR WORK

SIDE VIEW DETAIL

The side view exercise follows the same steps as the previous exercise to include the body shape and details. We follow the same proportion for the 10 head figure as previously demonstrated. The side view is modeled by a different size model, but the steps remain the same.

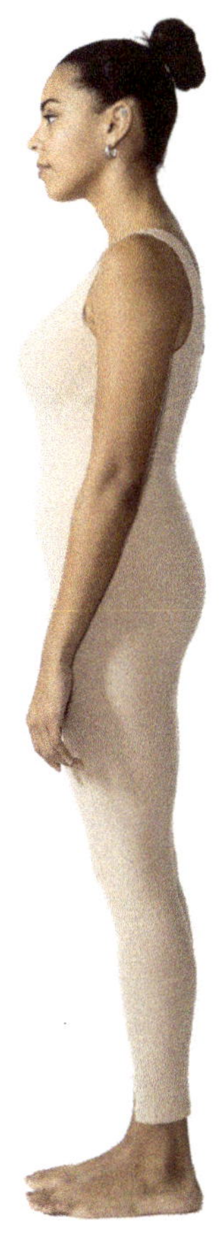
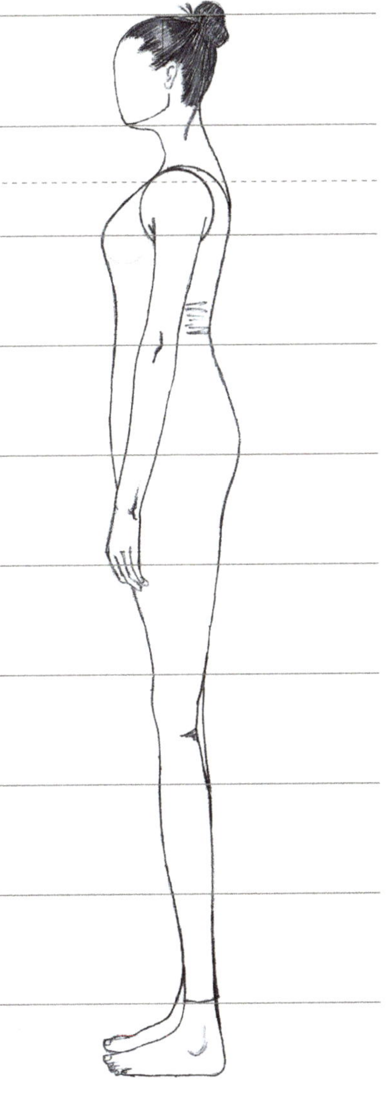

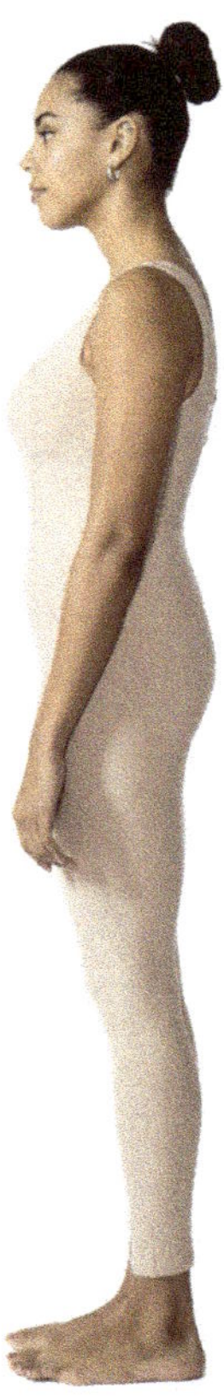

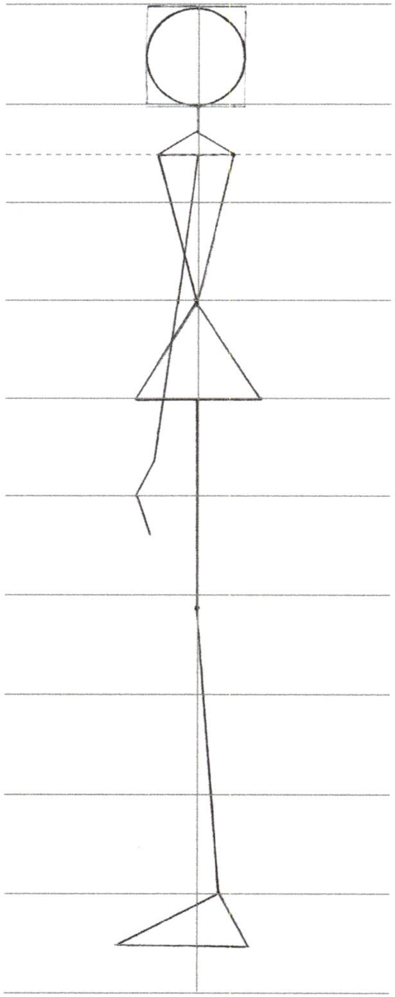

STEP 1

Draw in the basic figure pose as previously demonstrated. Draw in the foot with a triangle.

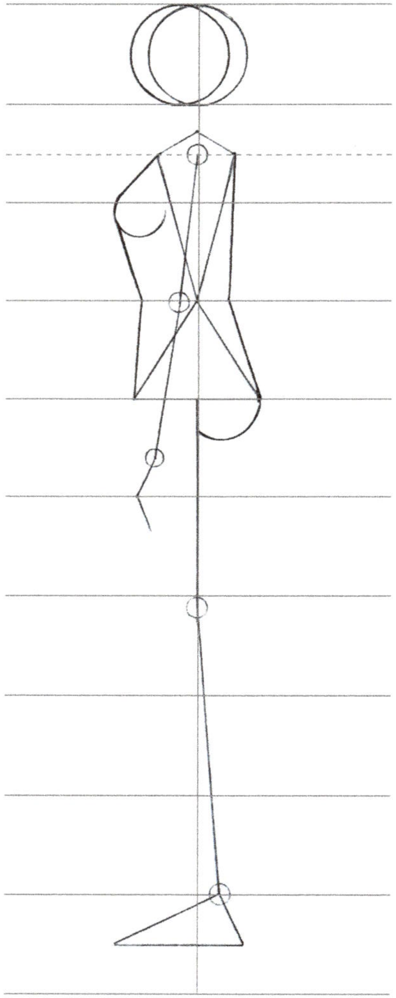

STEP 2

Create the torso shape, buttocks and bust. Circle the joints. Adjust the head positioning.

PRACTICE YOUR WORK

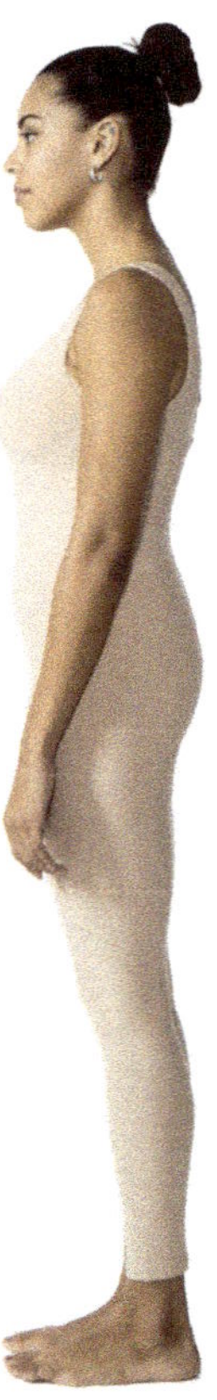

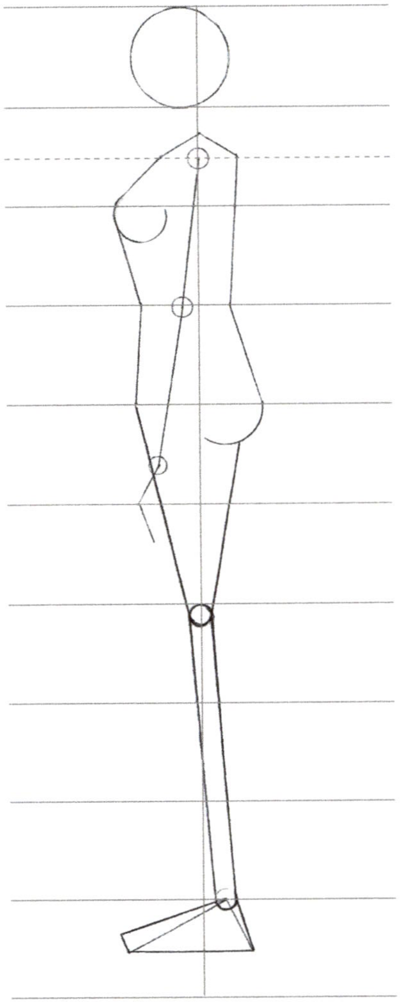

STEP 3

Draw in the legs and feet using cylinders and geometric shapes.

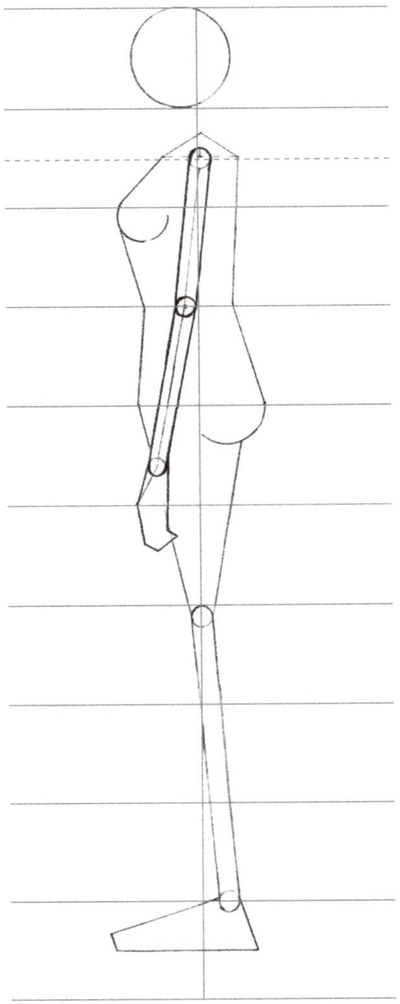

STEP 4

Draw in the arms with cylinders. Draw in the hands using geometric shapes

PRACTICE YOUR WORK

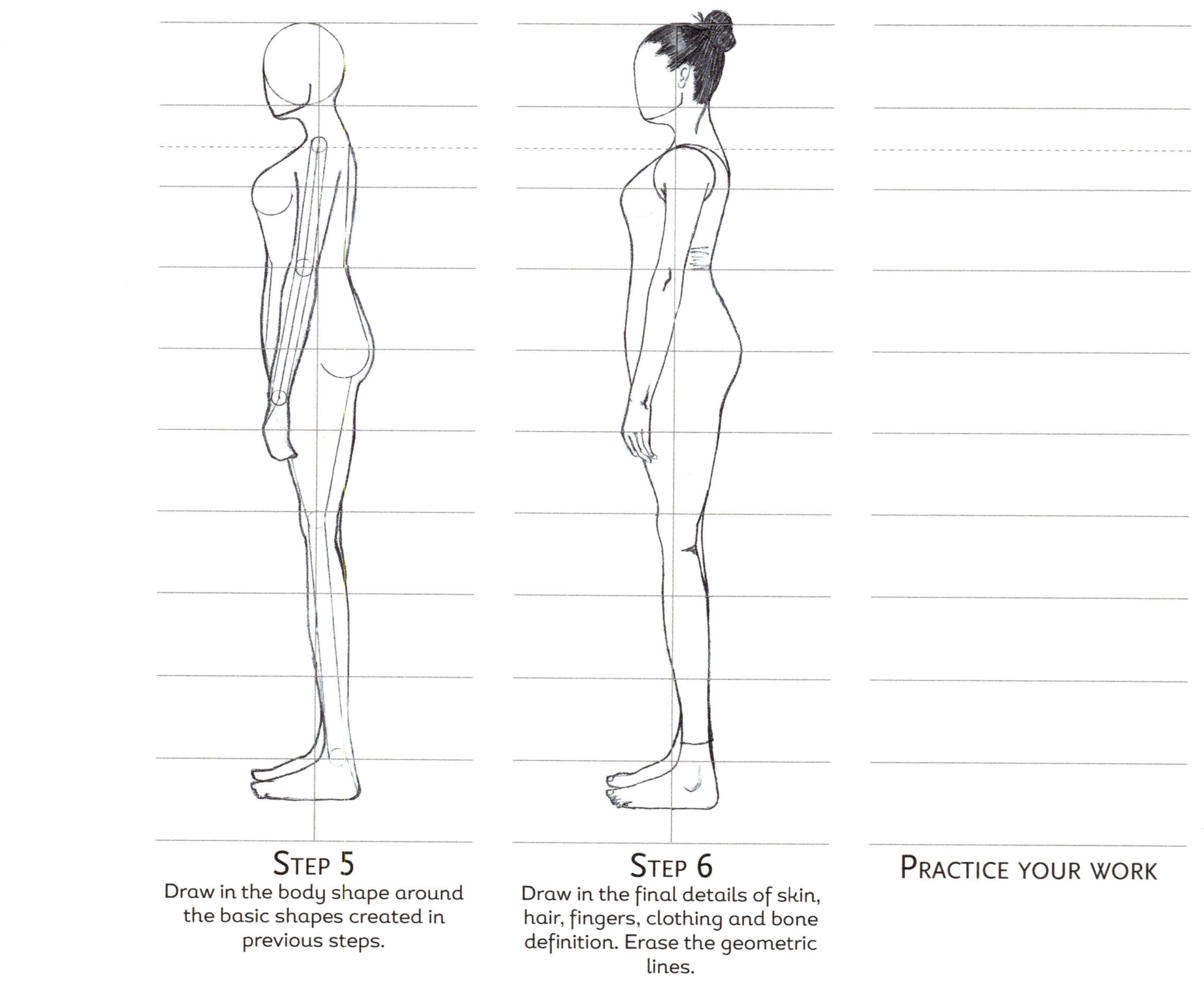

Step 5

Draw in the body shape around the basic shapes created in previous steps.

Step 6

Draw in the final details of skin, hair, fingers, clothing and bone definition. Erase the geometric lines.

Practice your work

FRONT VIEW DETAIL

This exercise details the front view, on a different body shape. The figure is extended to 10 heads. For proportional analysis for this and all future exercises, the model is lined up to the 8 head lines. Follow the basic figure illustration steps as previously demonstrated

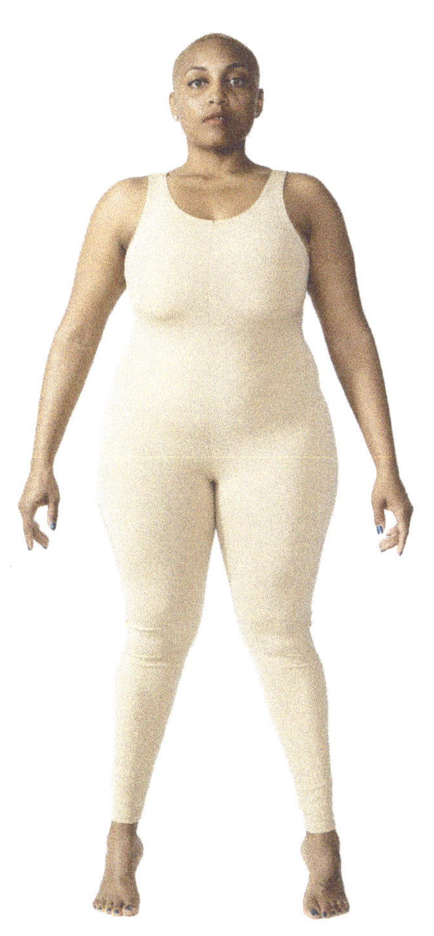
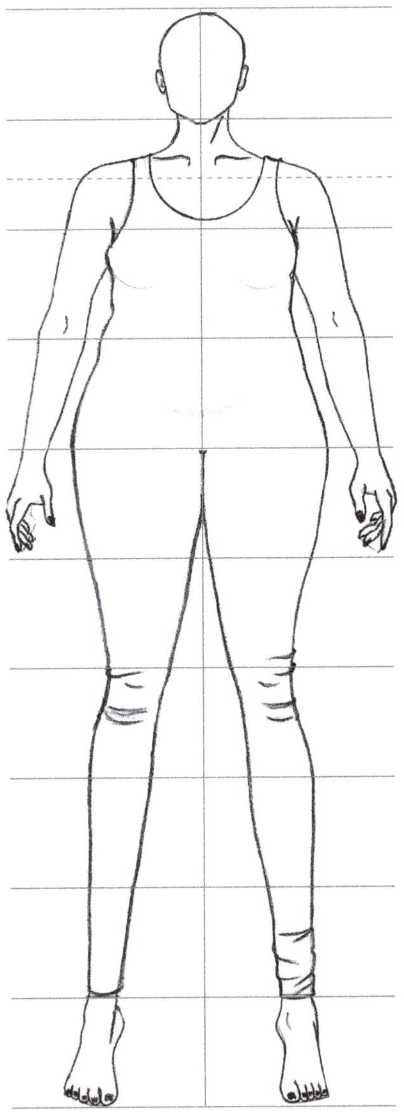

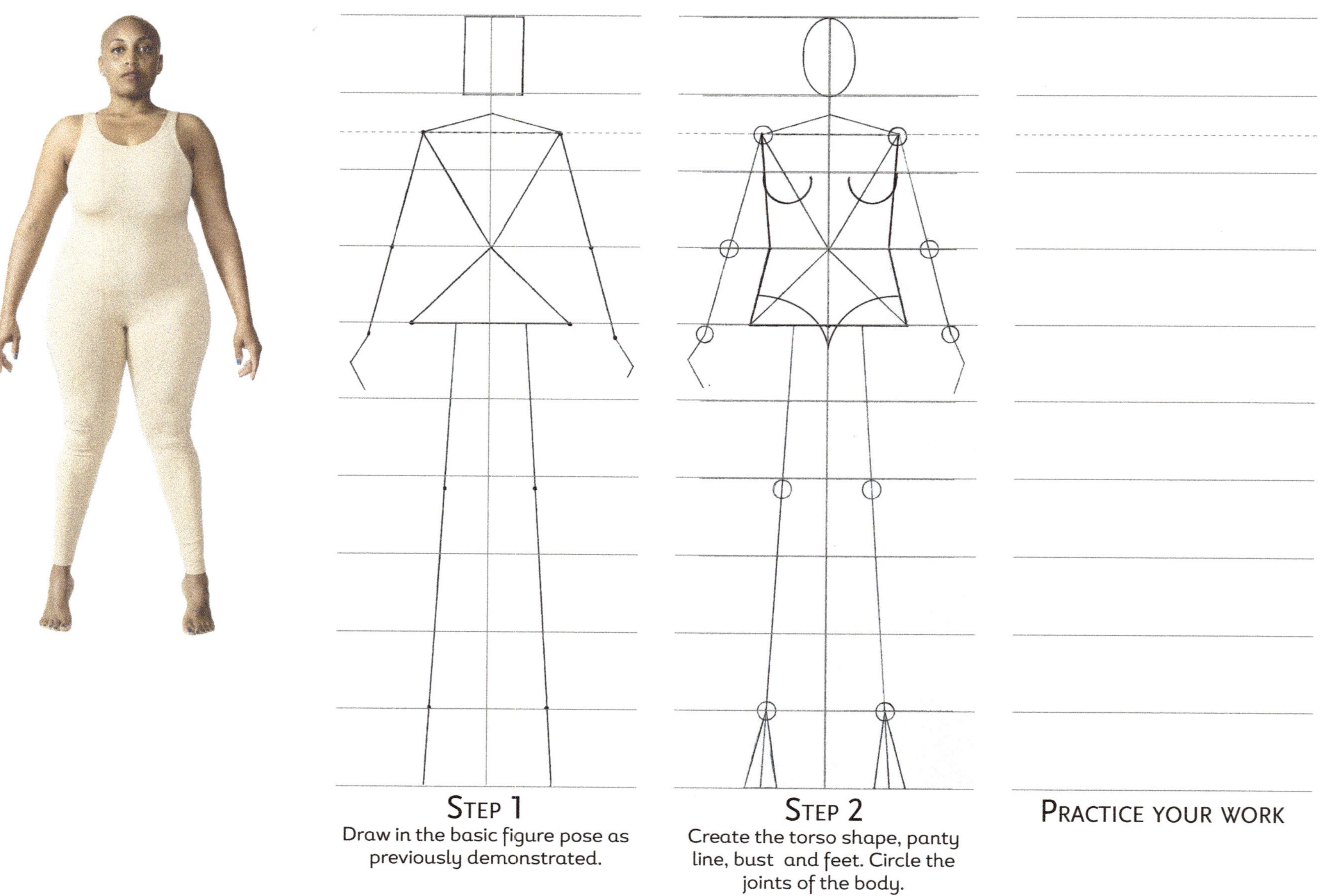

STEP 1

Draw in the basic figure pose as previously demonstrated.

STEP 2

Create the torso shape, panty line, bust and feet. Circle the joints of the body.

PRACTICE YOUR WORK

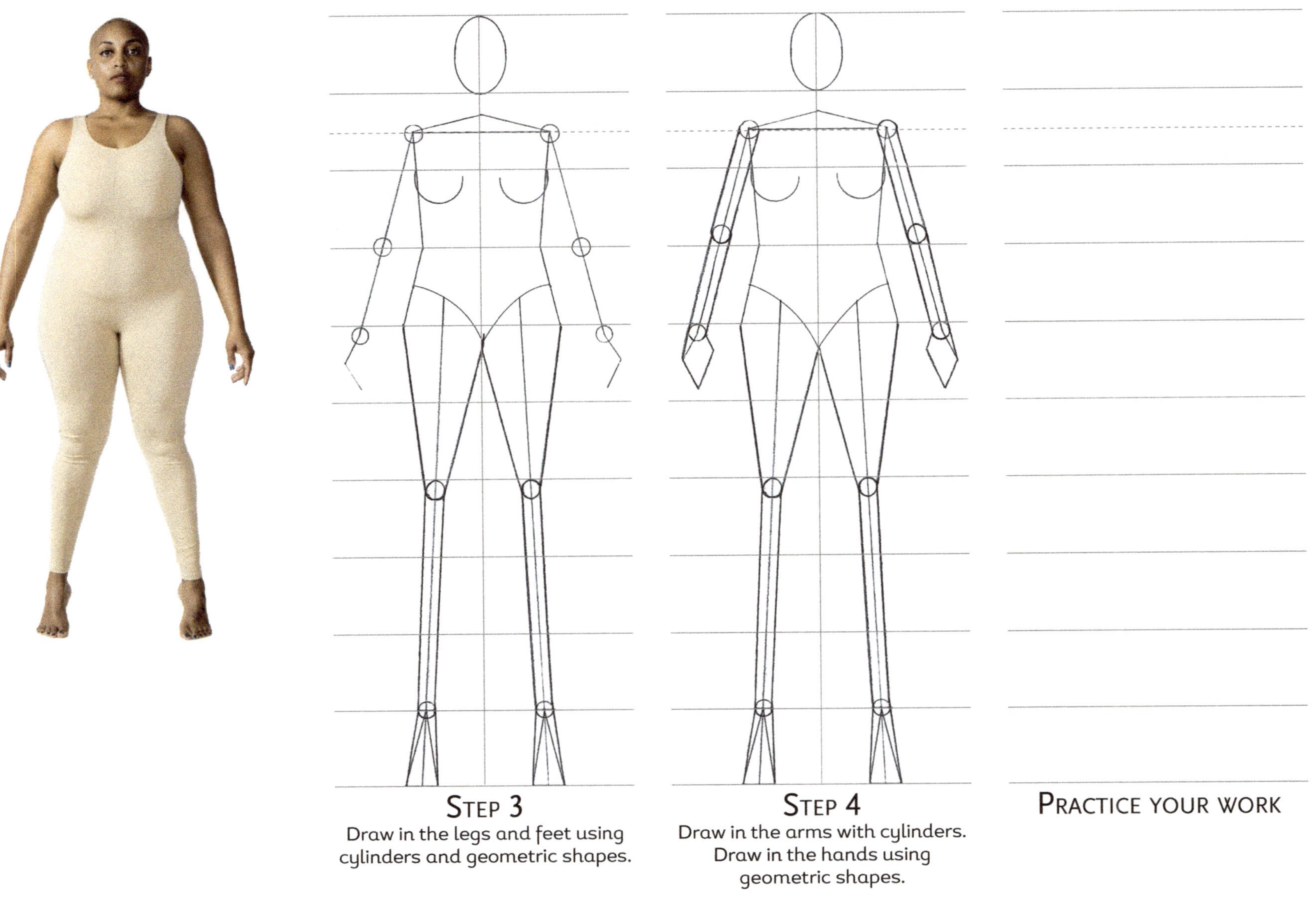

Step 3

Draw in the legs and feet using cylinders and geometric shapes.

Step 4

Draw in the arms with cylinders. Draw in the hands using geometric shapes.

Practice your work

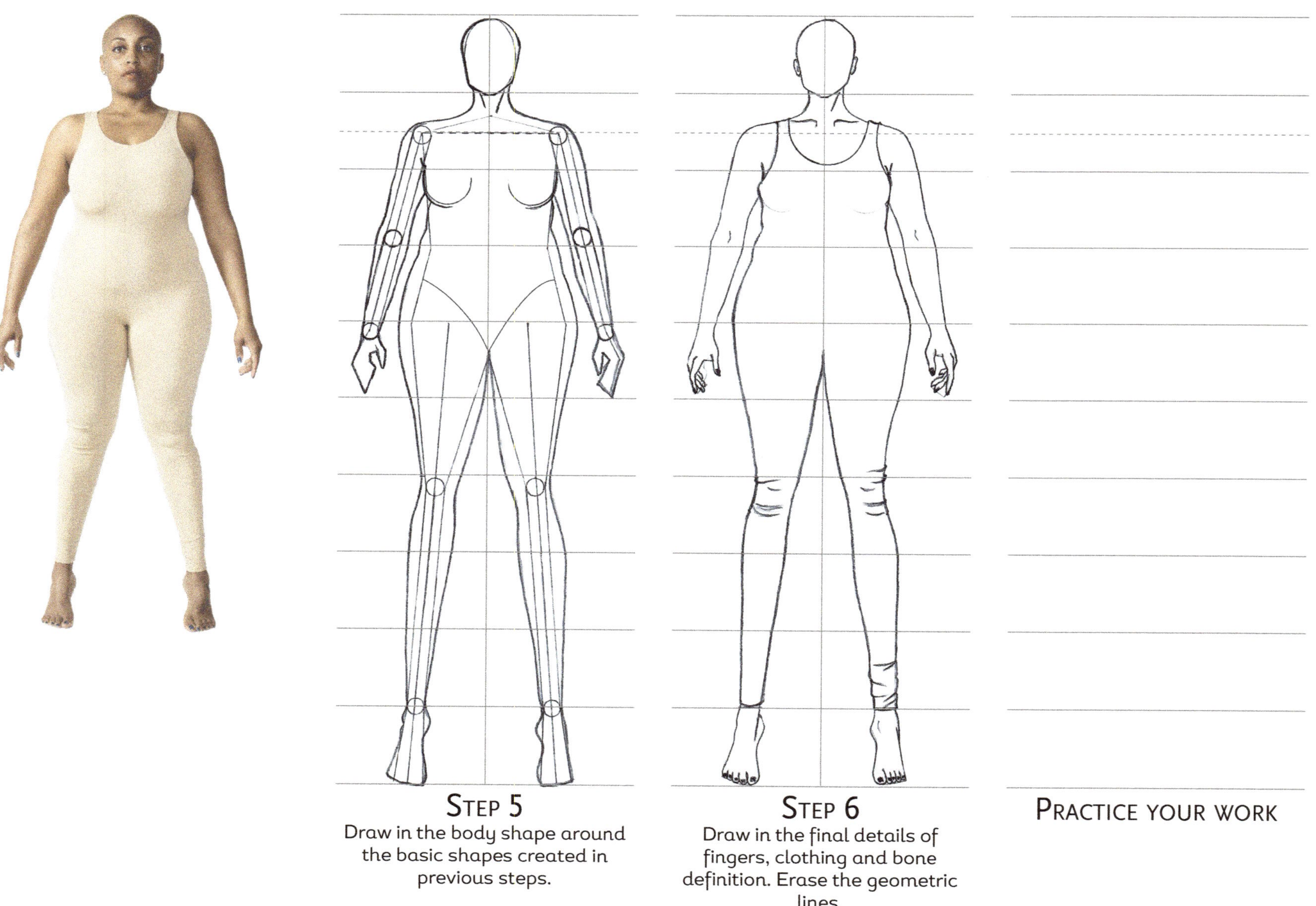

STEP 5

Draw in the body shape around the basic shapes created in previous steps.

STEP 6

Draw in the final details of fingers, clothing and bone definition. Erase the geometric lines.

PRACTICE YOUR WORK

PRACTICE SIMPLE POSES

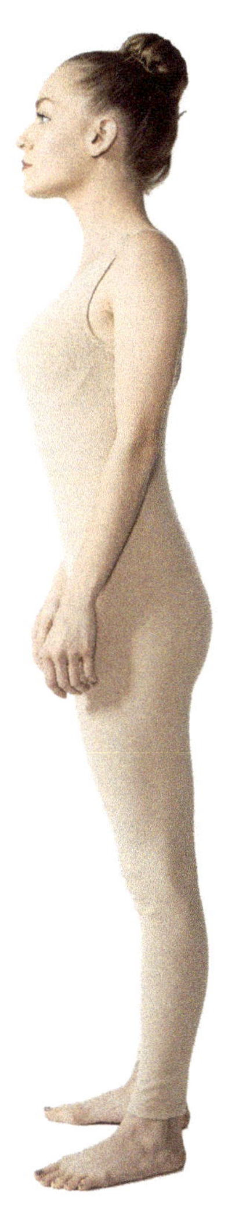

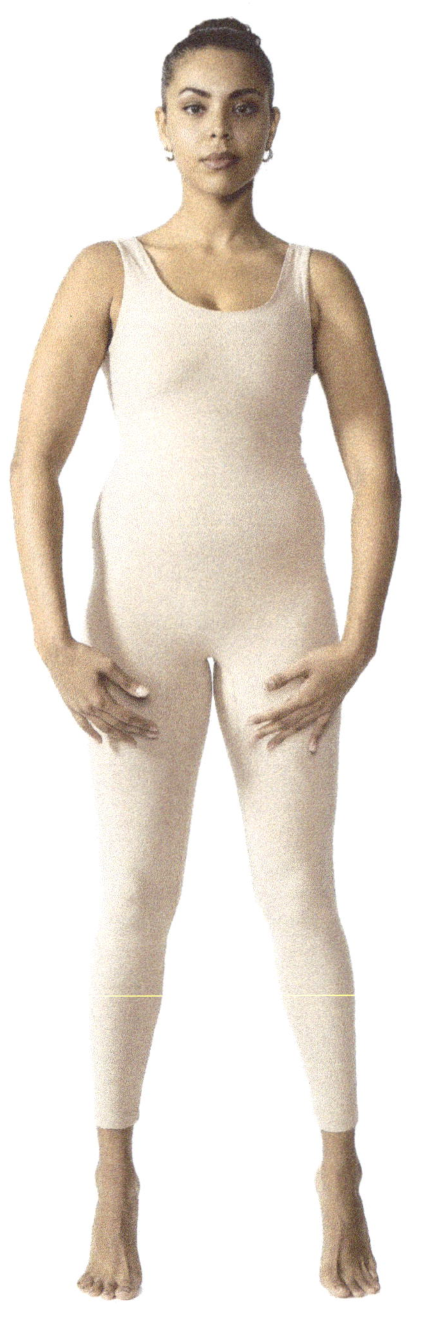

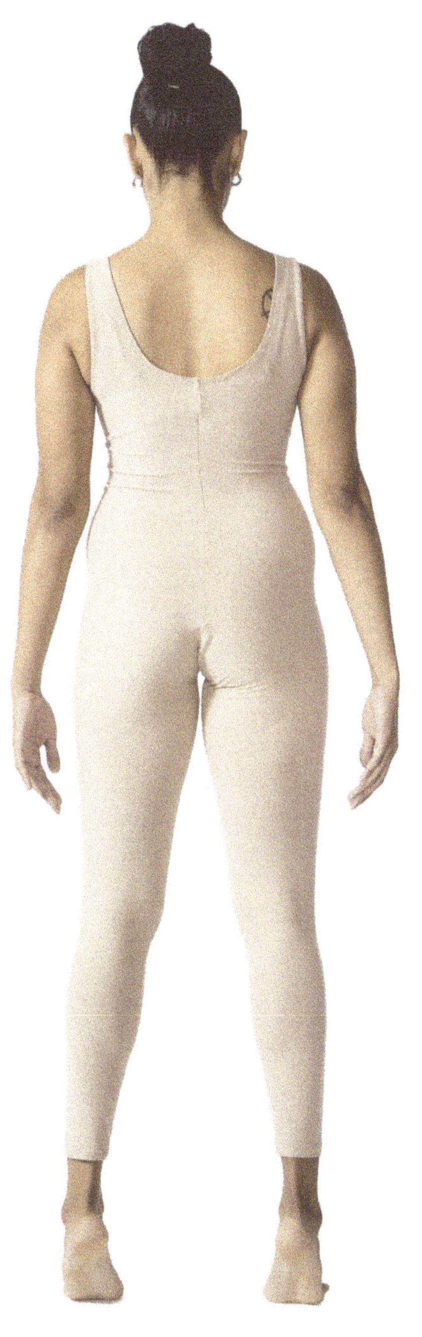

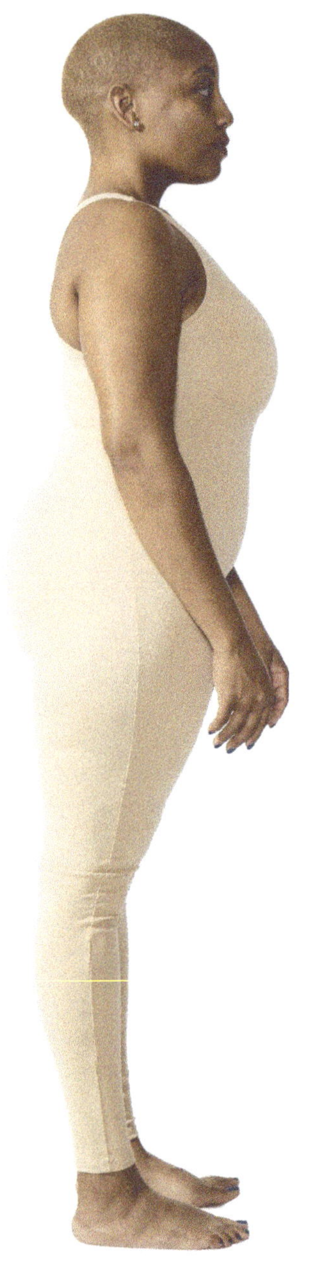

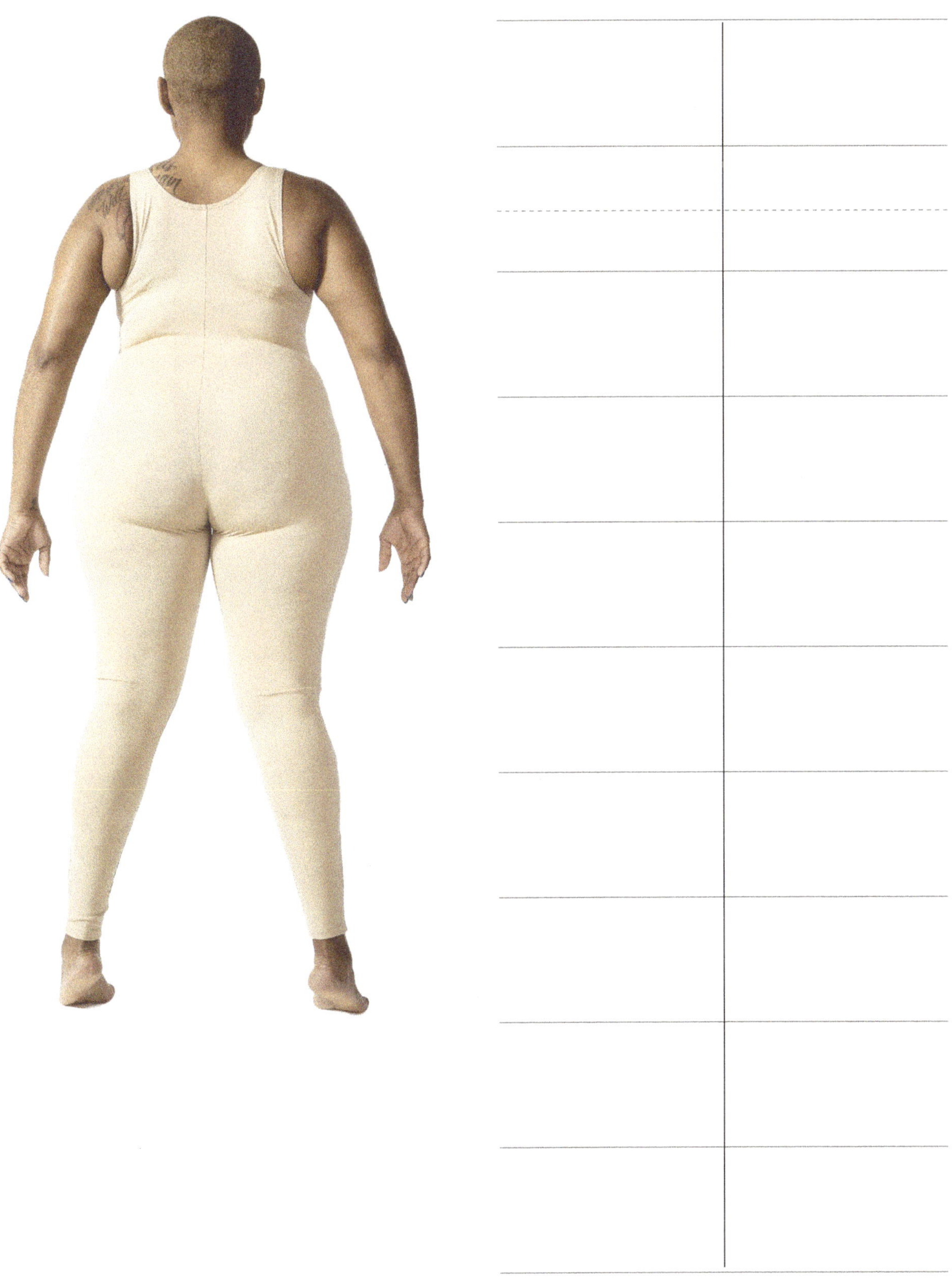

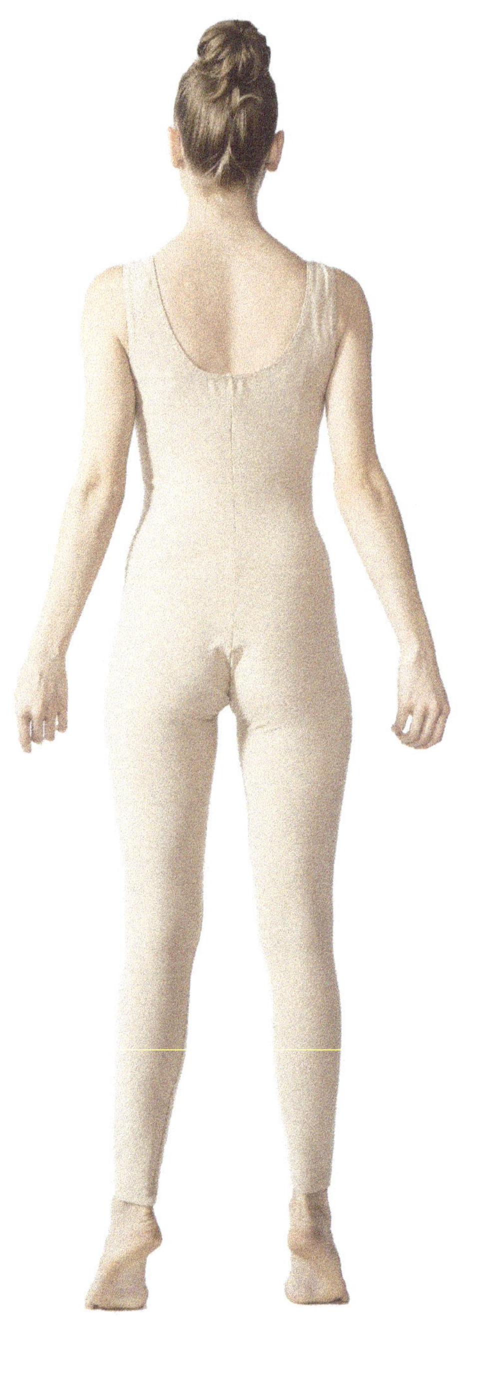

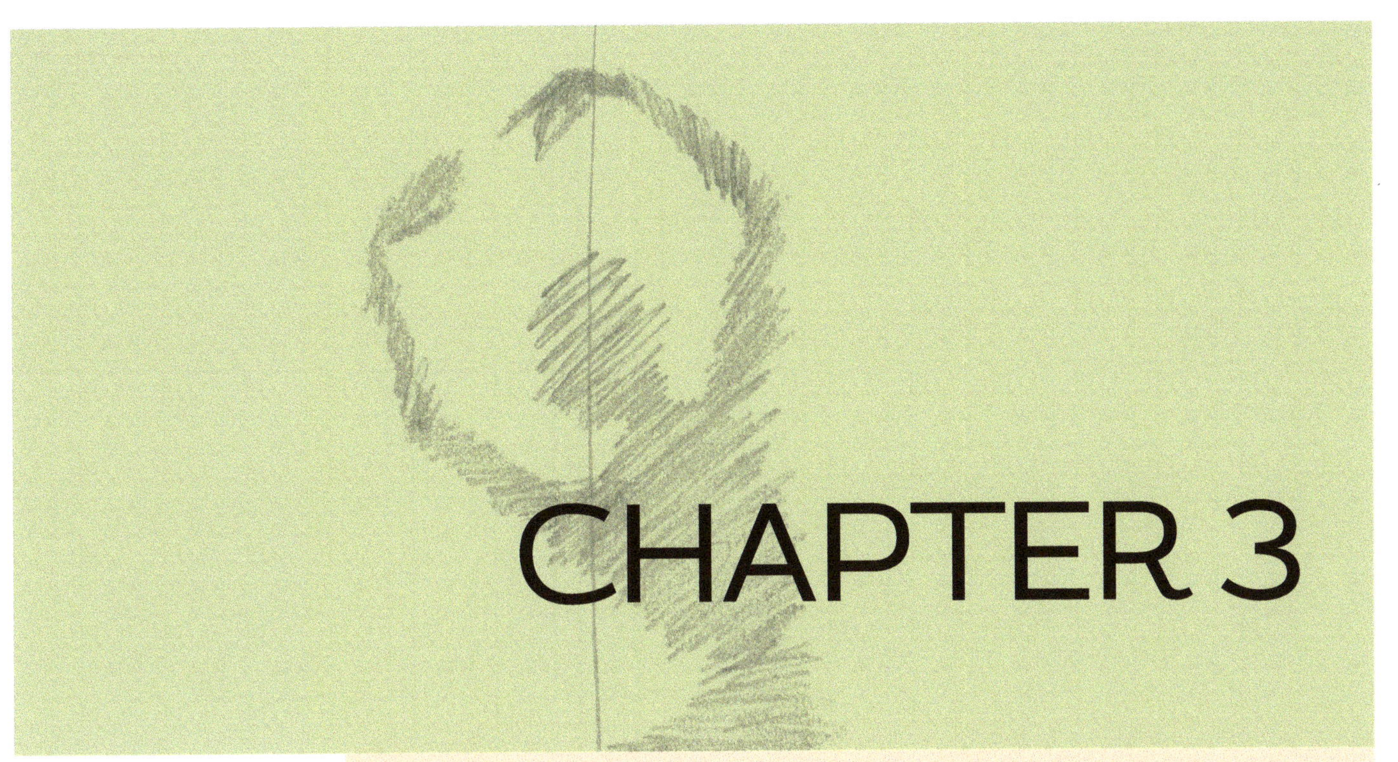

CHAPTER 3

Simple Movements

3/4 TURN - POSE 1

In this chapter, simple movement poses are demonstrated. The following pose is a 3/4 front view. The perspective of the body proportion may differ, but keep in mind the shape of the spine, waist and hip. In this pose, note the tilt of the hip and the positions of both knees and ankles.

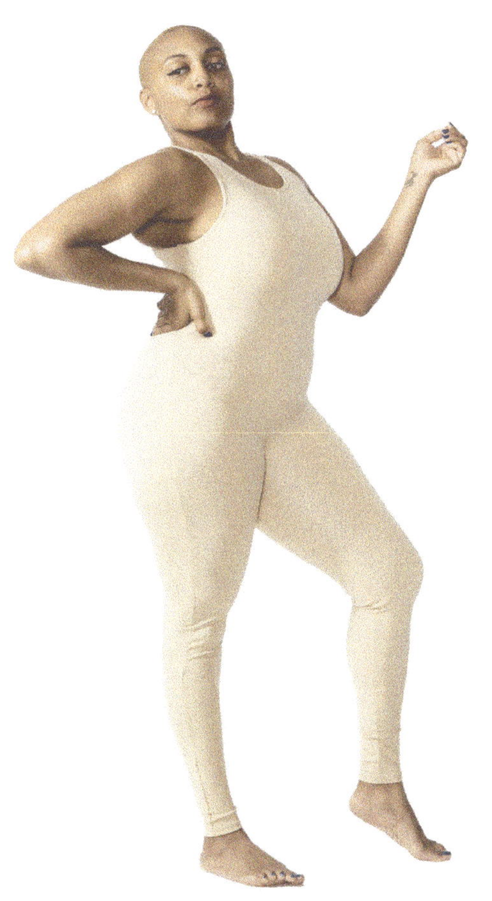

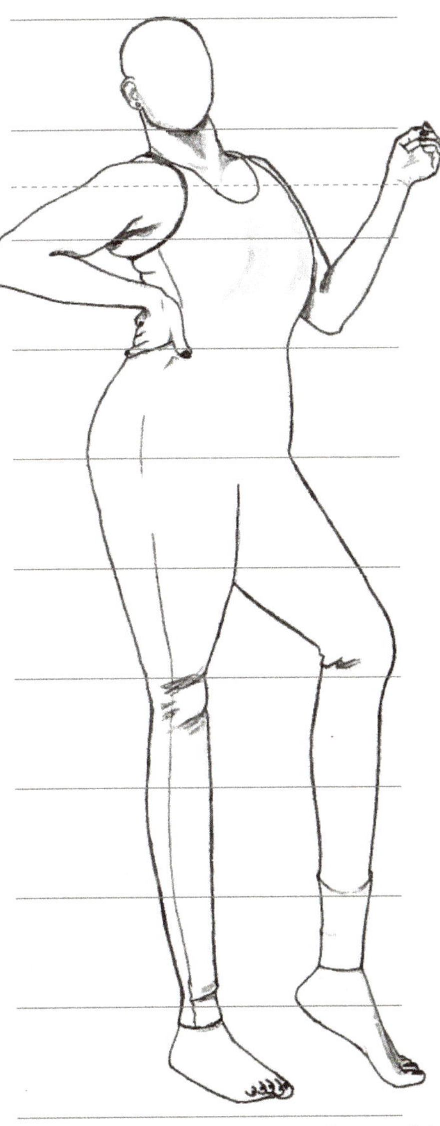

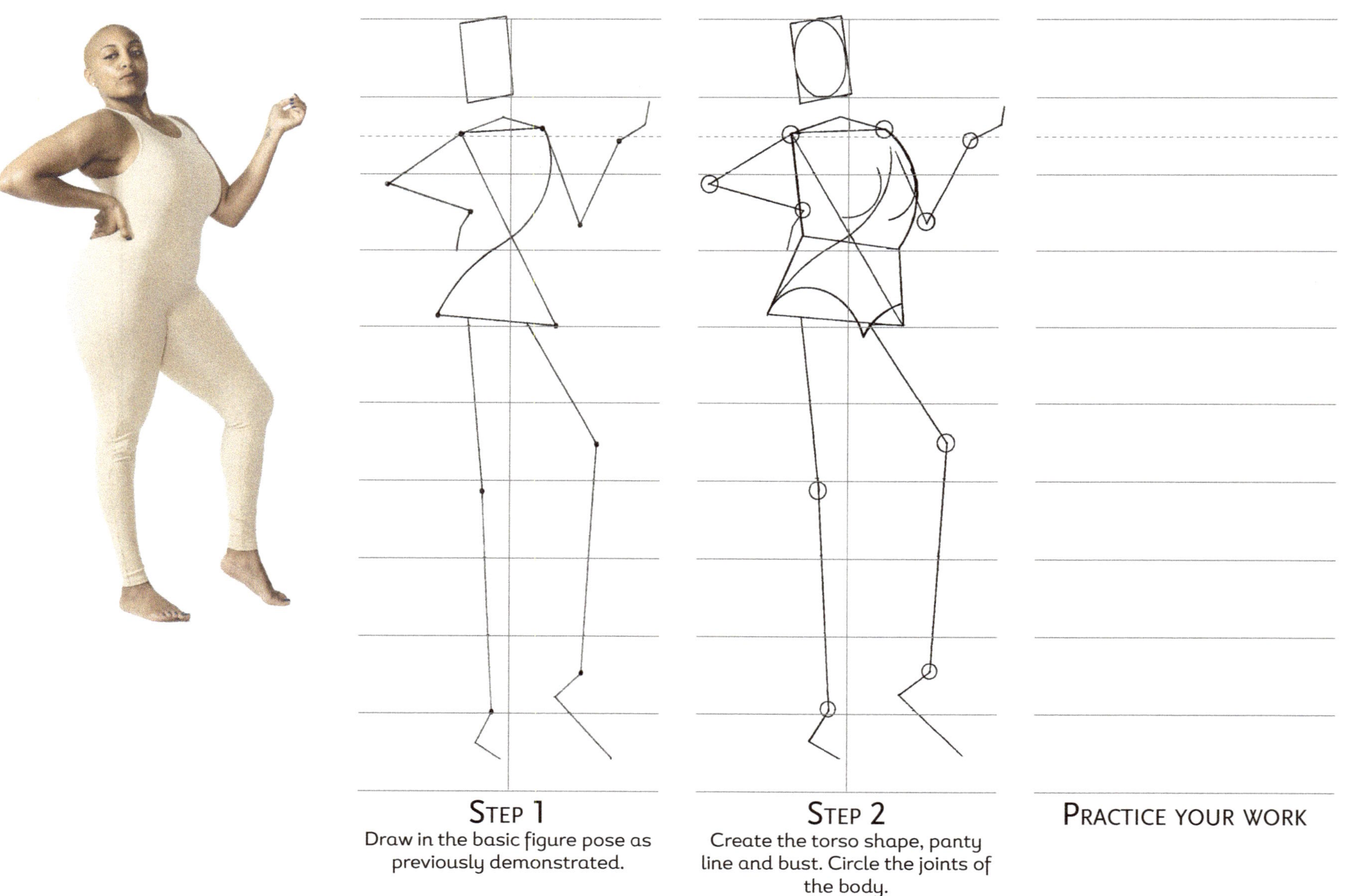

STEP 1

Draw in the basic figure pose as previously demonstrated.

STEP 2

Create the torso shape, panty line and bust. Circle the joints of the body.

PRACTICE YOUR WORK

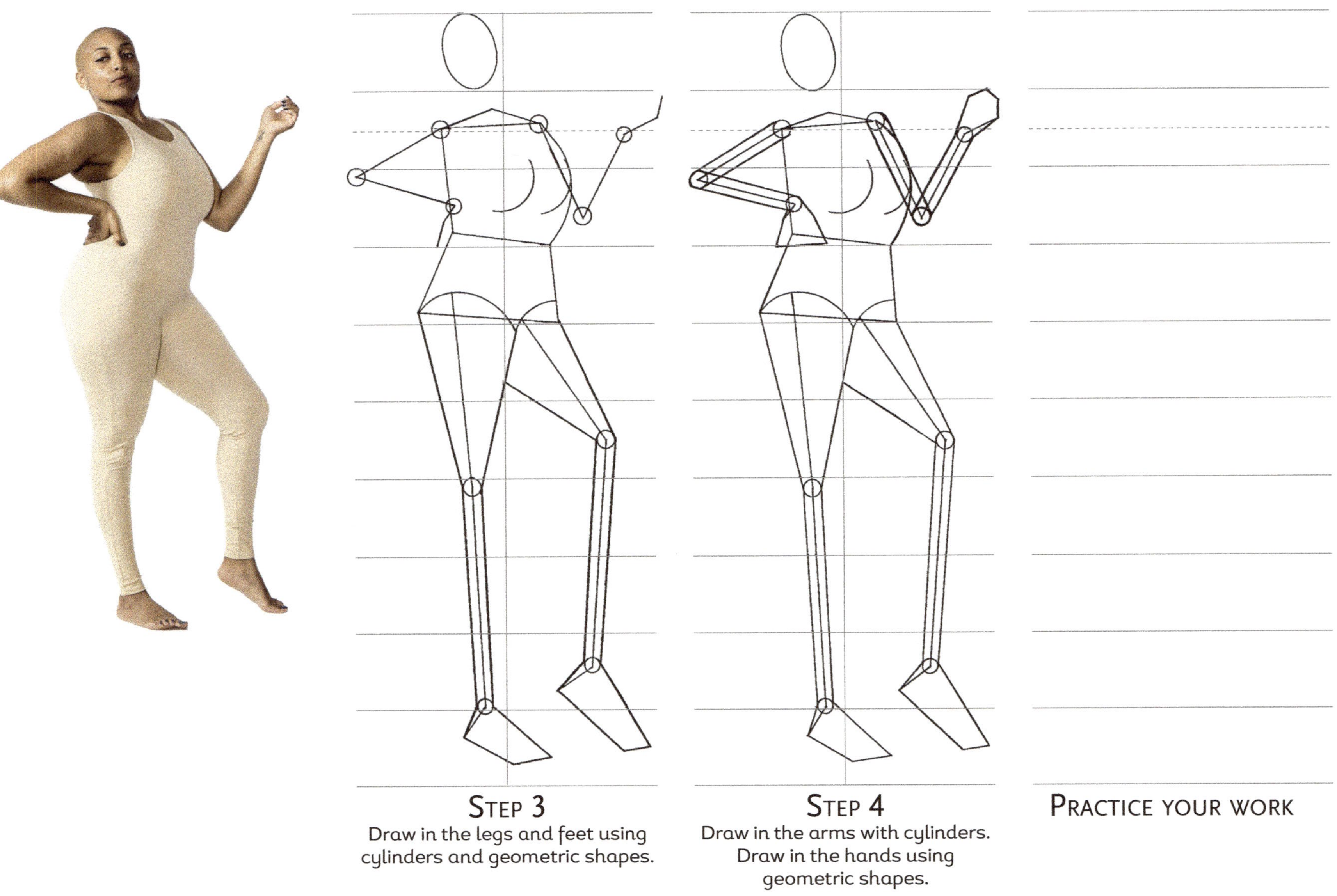

STEP 3

Draw in the legs and feet using cylinders and geometric shapes.

STEP 4

Draw in the arms with cylinders. Draw in the hands using geometric shapes.

PRACTICE YOUR WORK

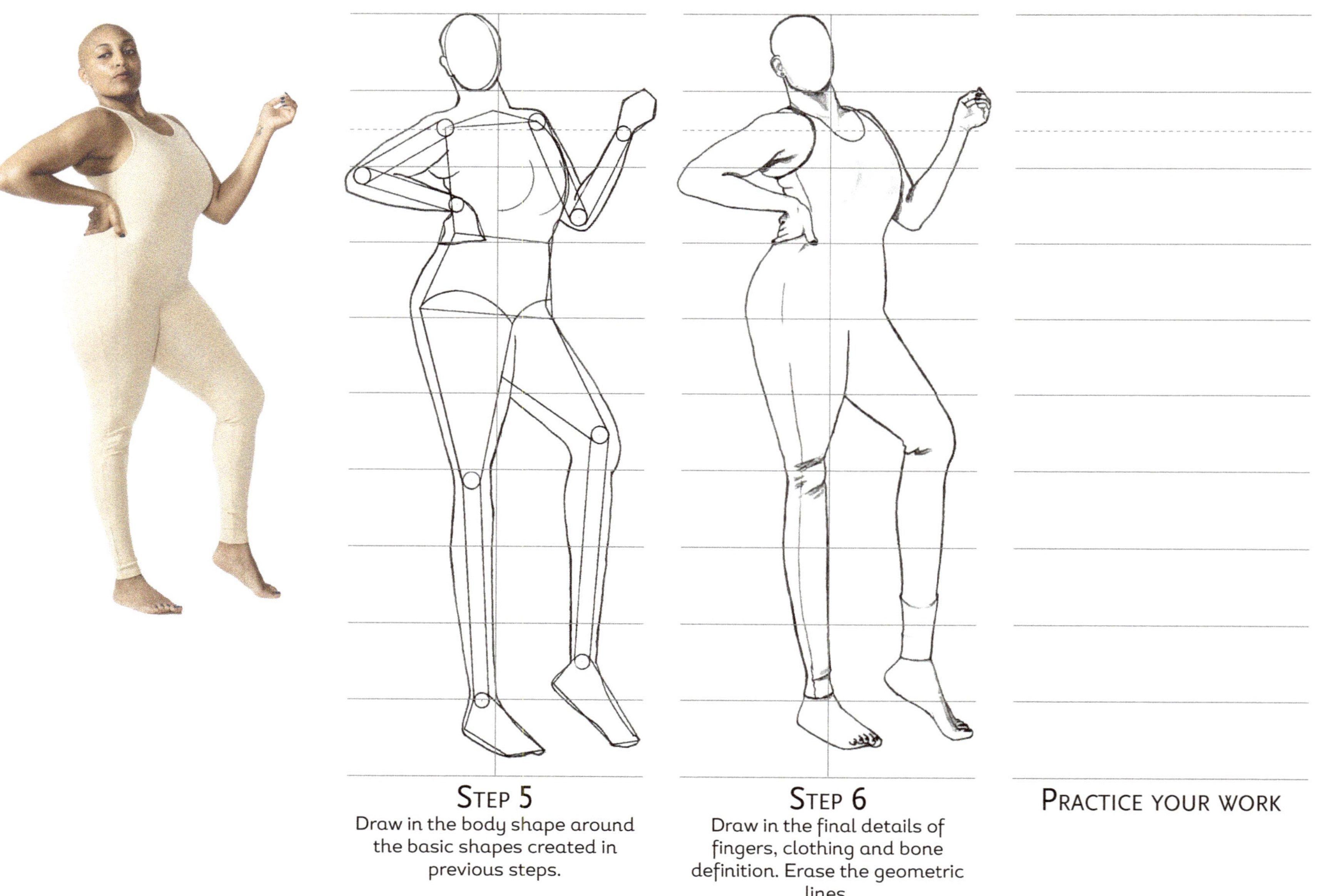

STEP 5

Draw in the body shape around the basic shapes created in previous steps.

STEP 6

Draw in the final details of fingers, clothing and bone definition. Erase the geometric lines.

PRACTICE YOUR WORK

FRONT VIEW - POSE 2

This simple movement pose is slightly turned, changing the perspective of the front leg. Note the tilt of the hips and shoulders, as well as the position of both knees and ankles.

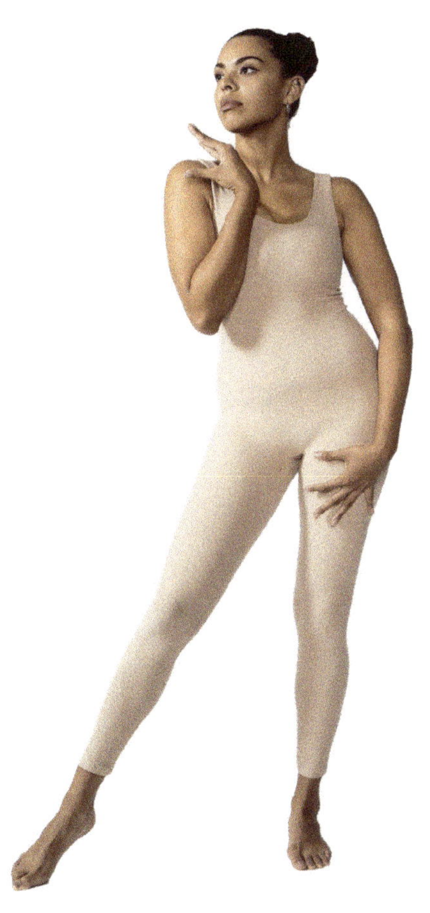

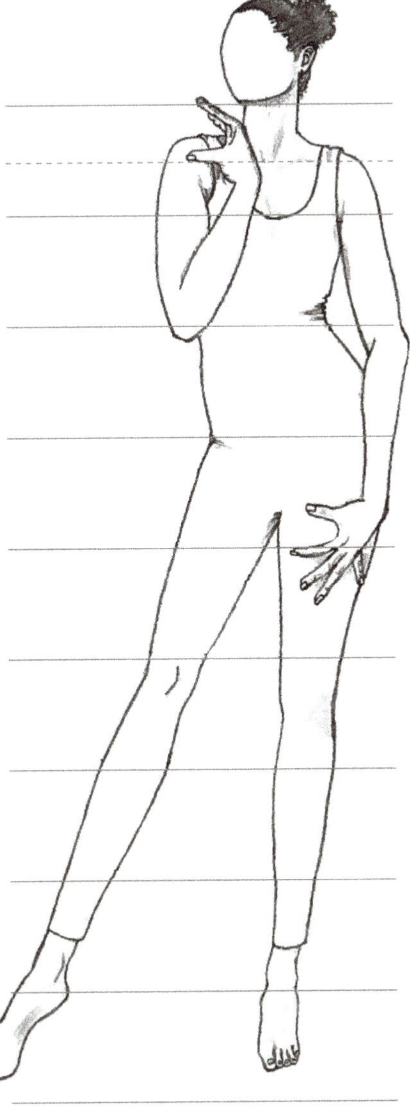

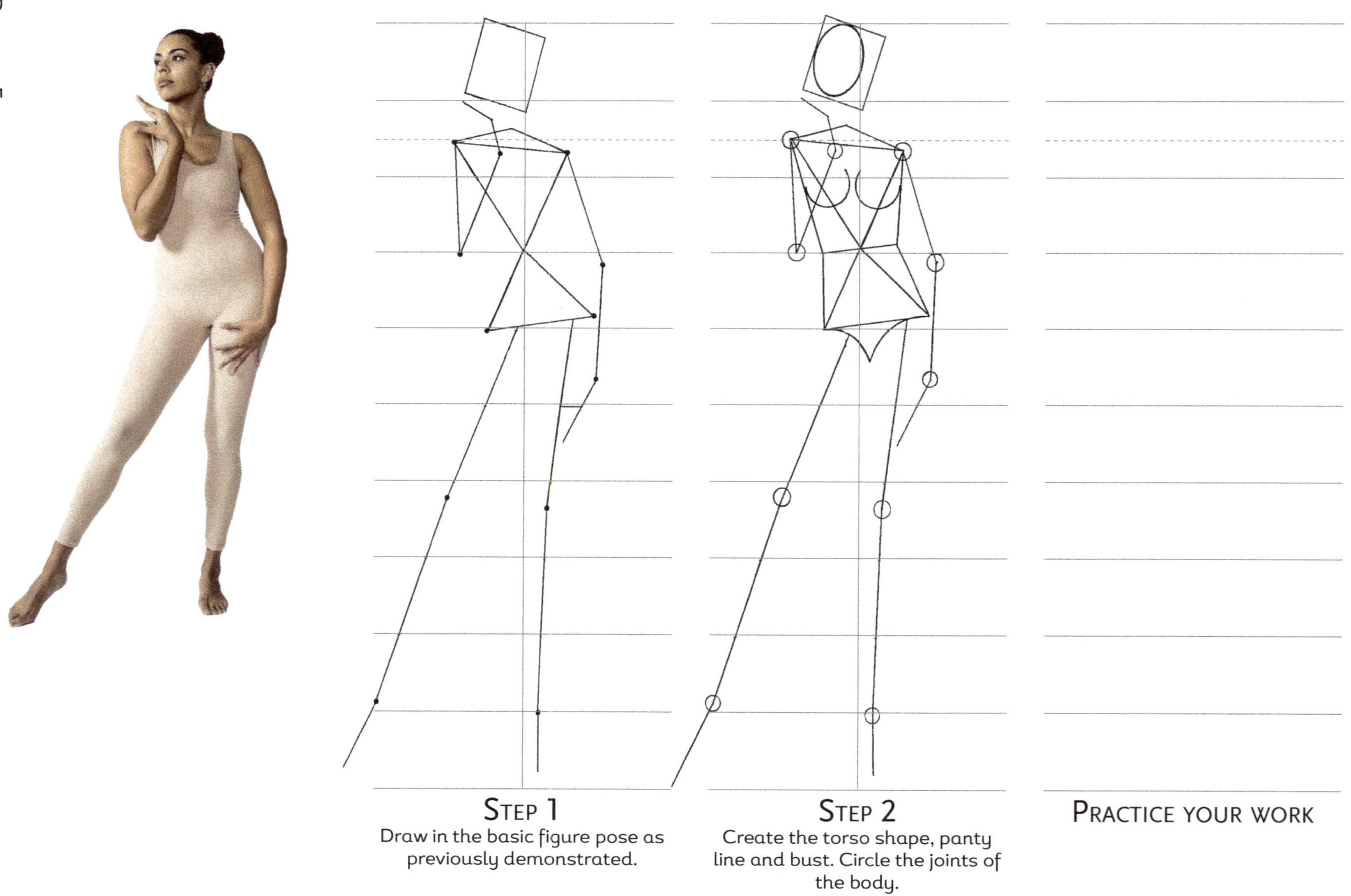

STEP 1

Draw in the basic figure pose as previously demonstrated.

STEP 2

Create the torso shape, panty line and bust. Circle the joints of the body.

PRACTICE YOUR WORK

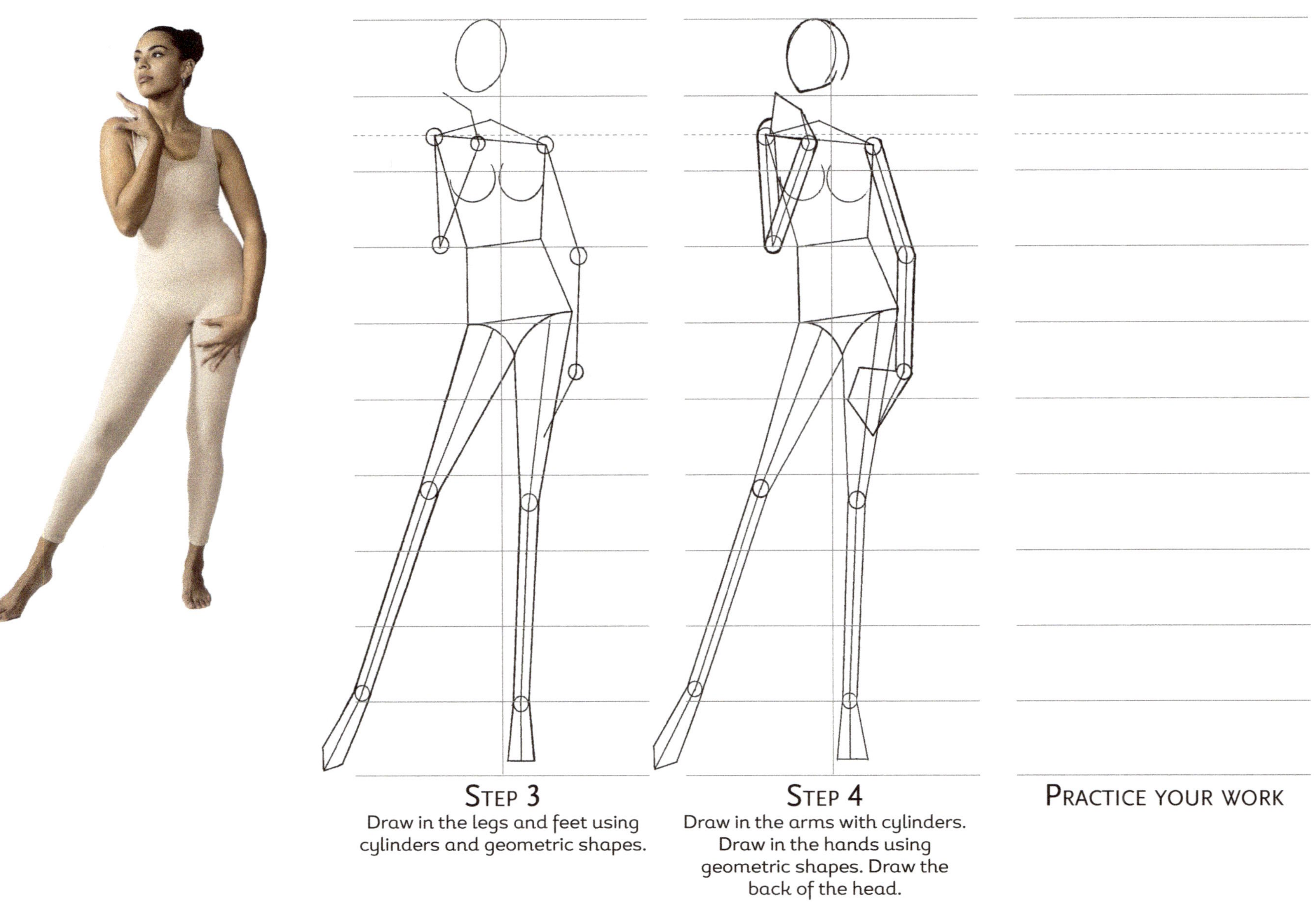

STEP 3

Draw in the legs and feet using cylinders and geometric shapes.

STEP 4

Draw in the arms with cylinders. Draw in the hands using geometric shapes. Draw the back of the head.

PRACTICE YOUR WORK

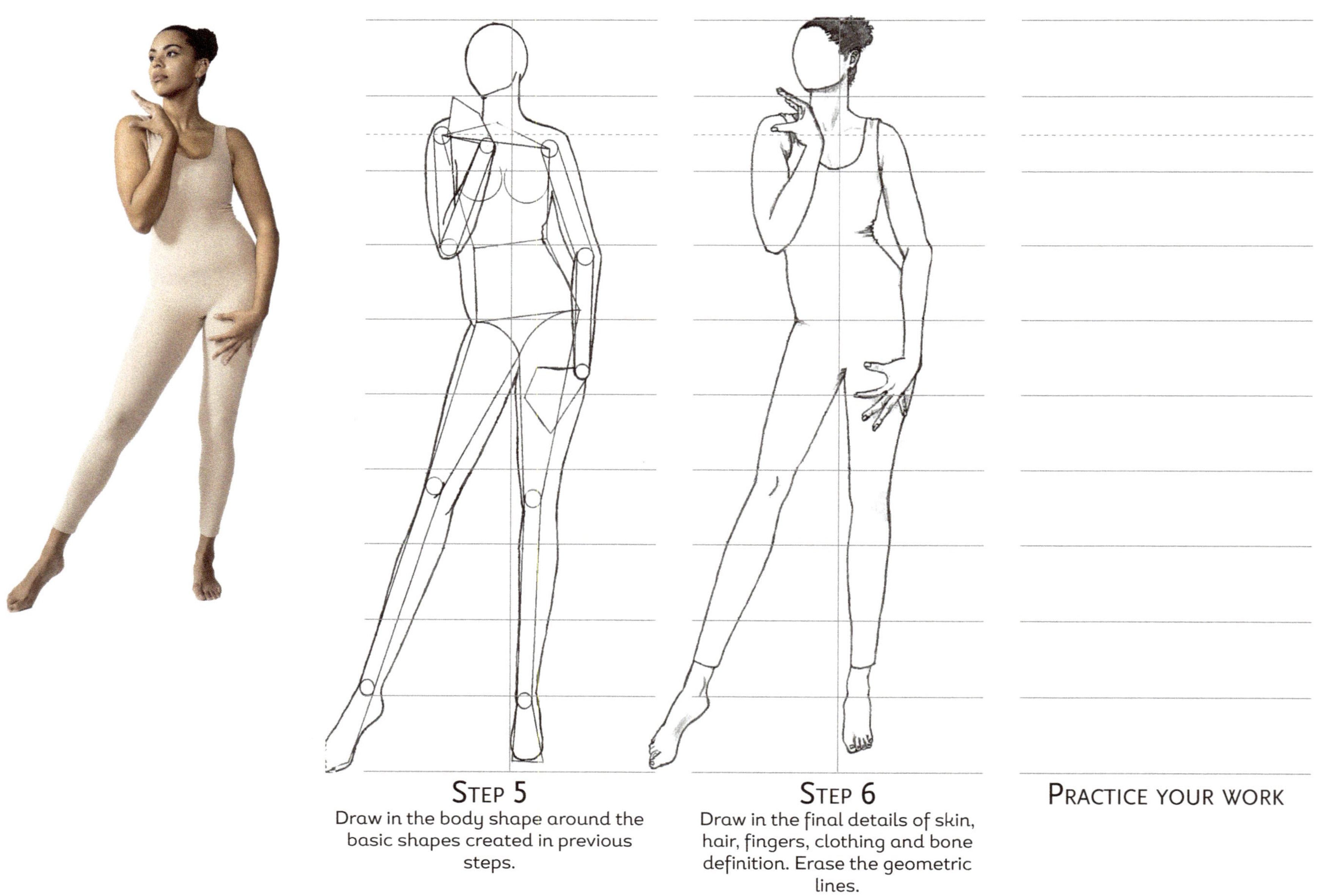

STEP 5

Draw in the body shape around the basic shapes created in previous steps.

STEP 6

Draw in the final details of skin, hair, fingers, clothing and bone definition. Erase the geometric lines.

PRACTICE YOUR WORK

BACK 3/4 TURN - POSE 3

This simple movement pose combines a straight upper back with a 3/4 turned hip. Note the change in the perspective, one leg is in front of the other, as well as the tilt of the hips.

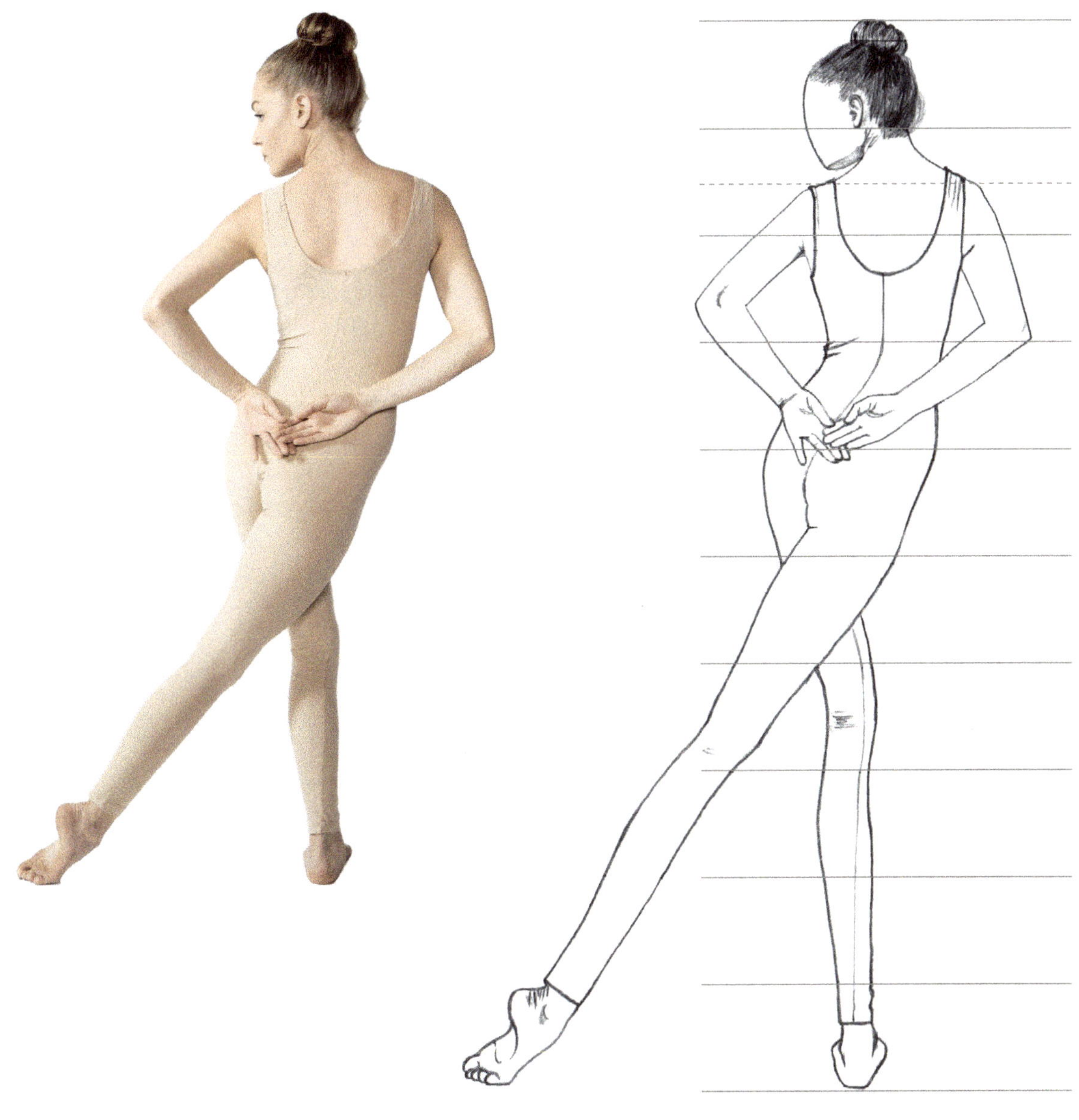

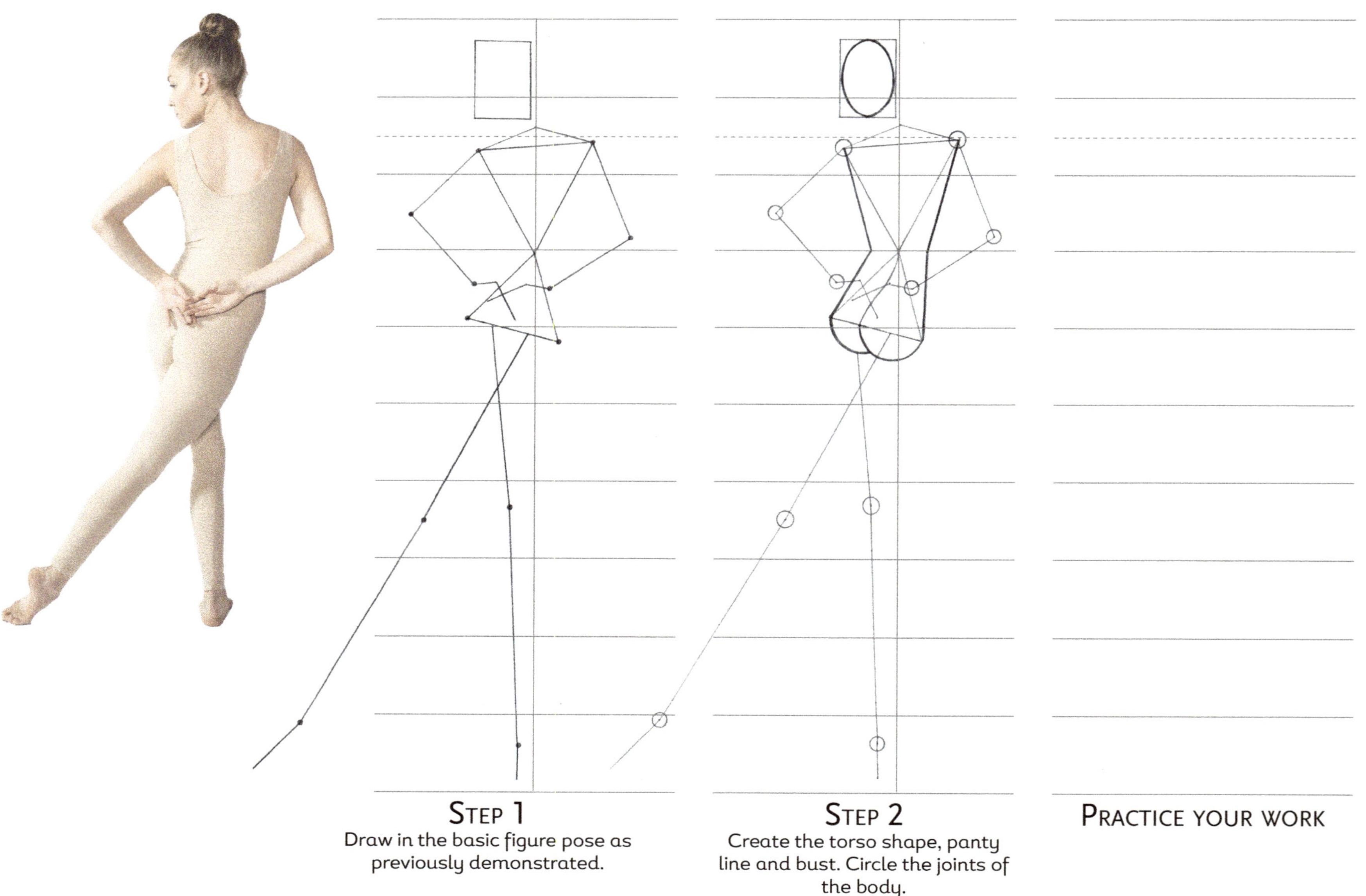

STEP 1
Draw in the basic figure pose as previously demonstrated.

STEP 2
Create the torso shape, panty line and bust. Circle the joints of the body.

PRACTICE YOUR WORK

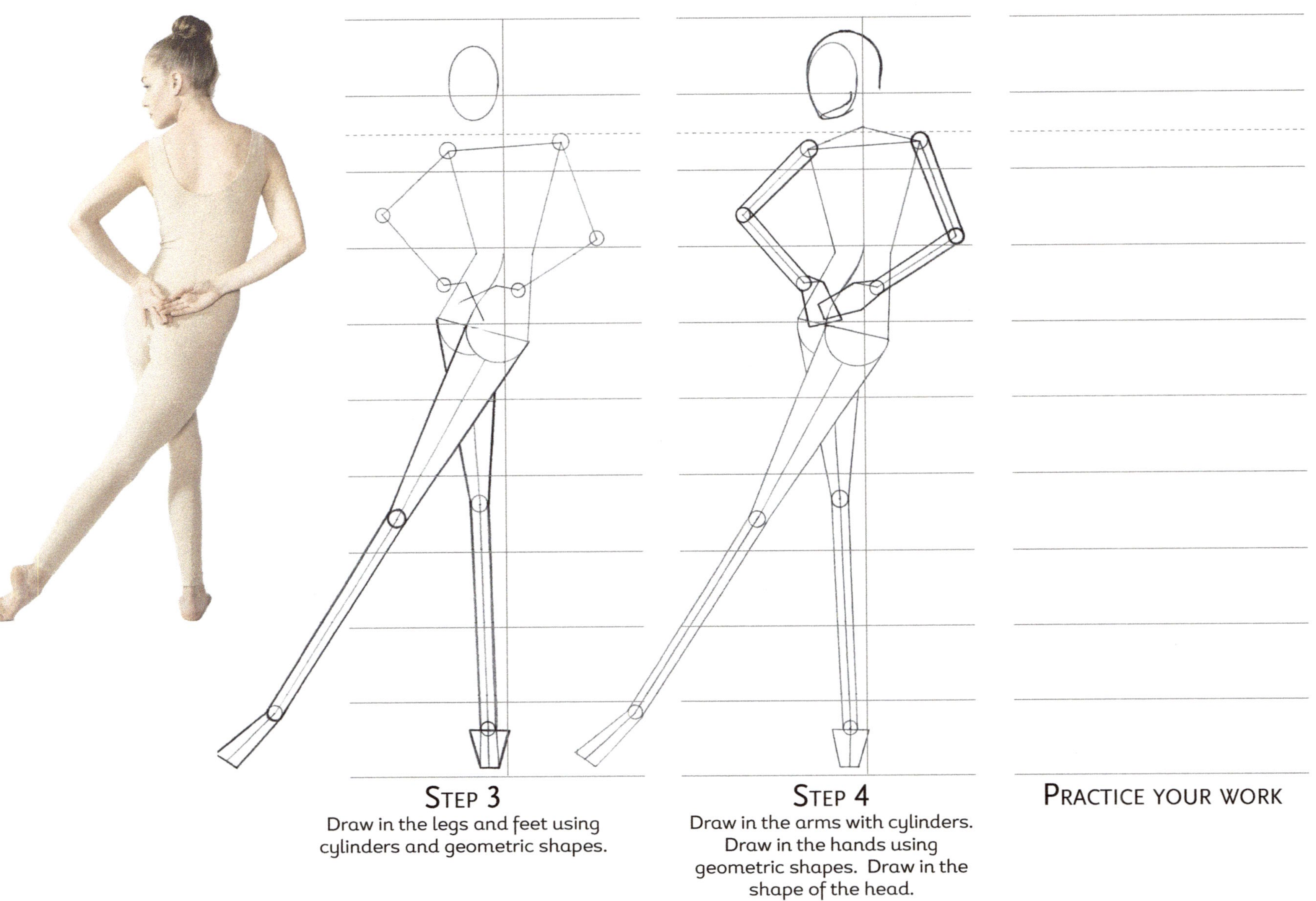

Step 3

Draw in the legs and feet using cylinders and geometric shapes.

Step 4

Draw in the arms with cylinders. Draw in the hands using geometric shapes. Draw in the shape of the head.

Practice your work

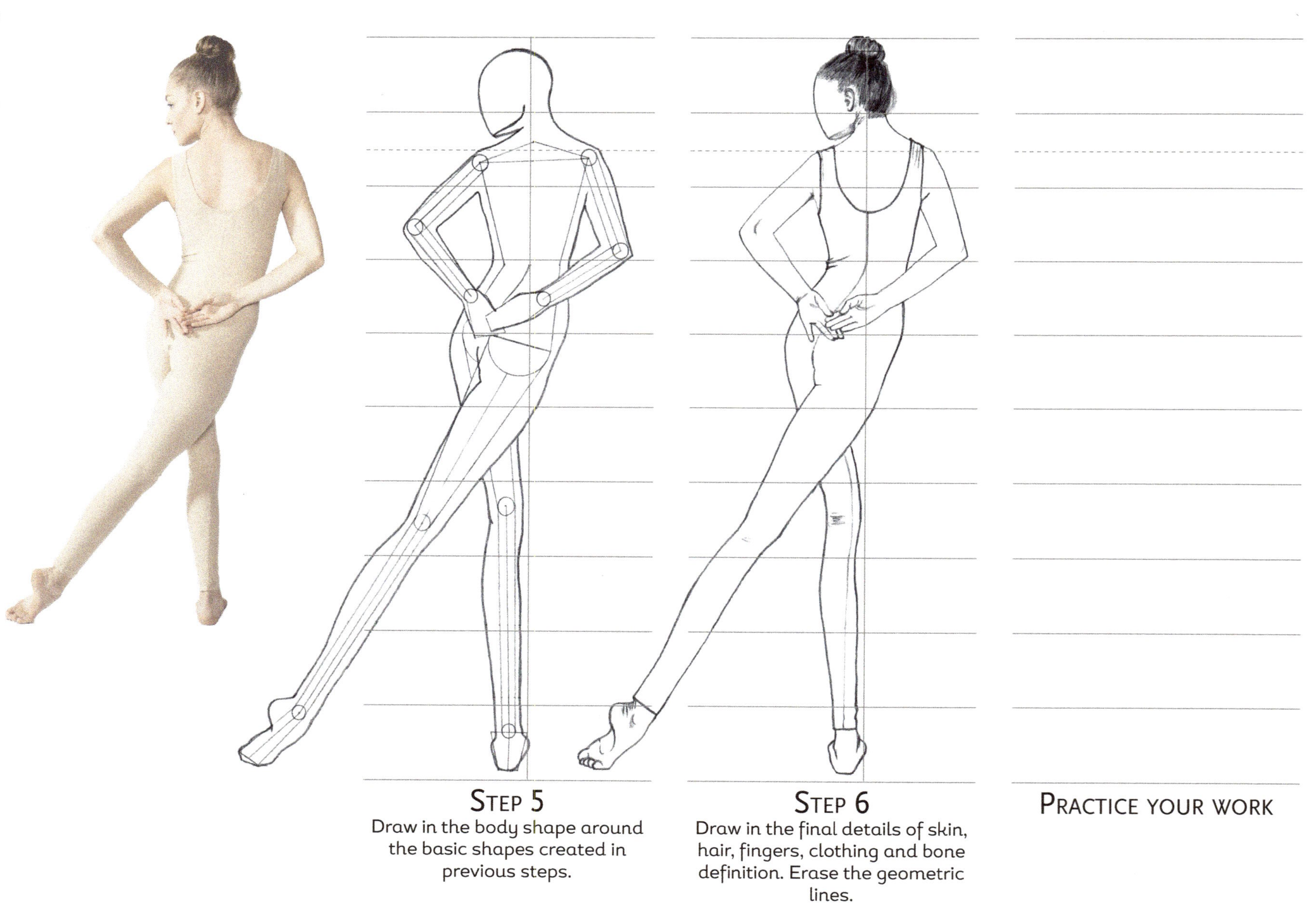

STEP 5

Draw in the body shape around the basic shapes created in previous steps.

STEP 6

Draw in the final details of skin, hair, fingers, clothing and bone definition. Erase the geometric lines.

PRACTICE YOUR WORK

3/4 TURN - POSE 4

The simple pose is a typical 3/4 view fashion pose. The hip line, while tilted physically, is drawn straight based on the perspective angle of the body. Note the turn of the chest and the elongated perspective of the front leg.

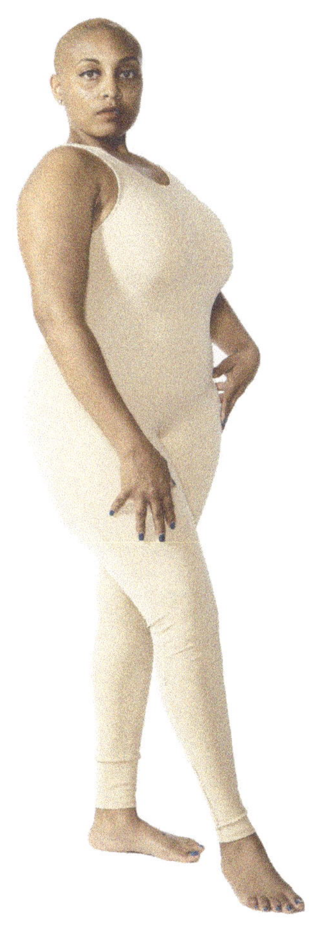

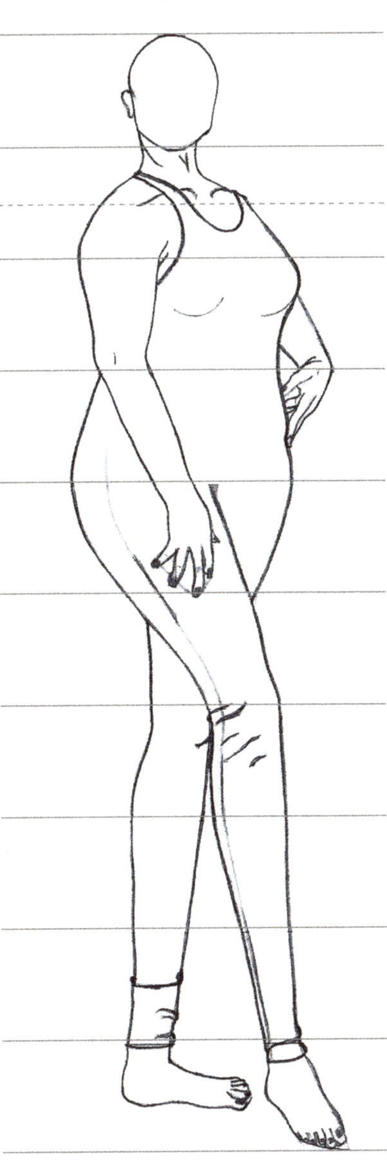

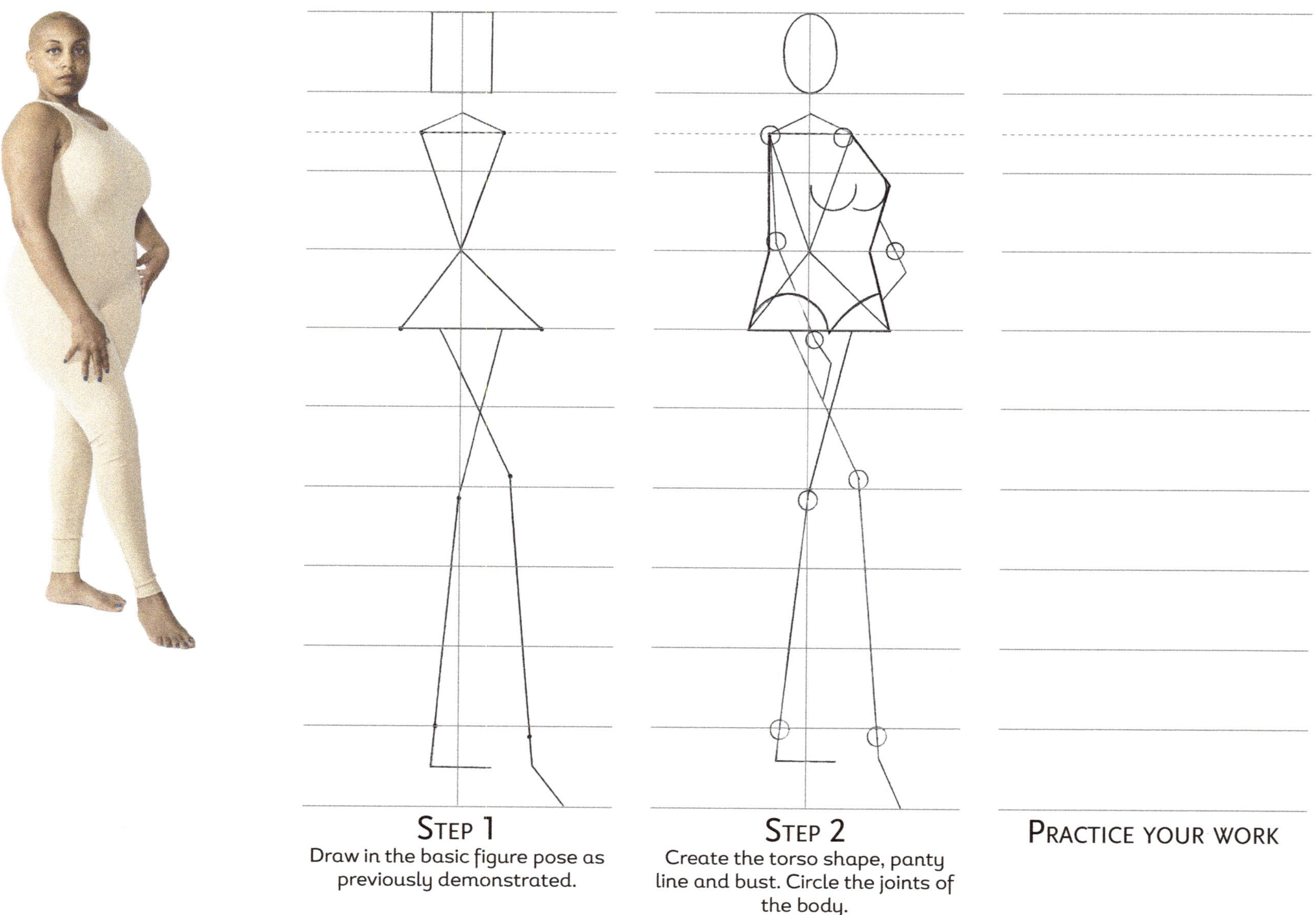

STEP 1

Draw in the basic figure pose as previously demonstrated.

STEP 2

Create the torso shape, panty line and bust. Circle the joints of the body.

PRACTICE YOUR WORK

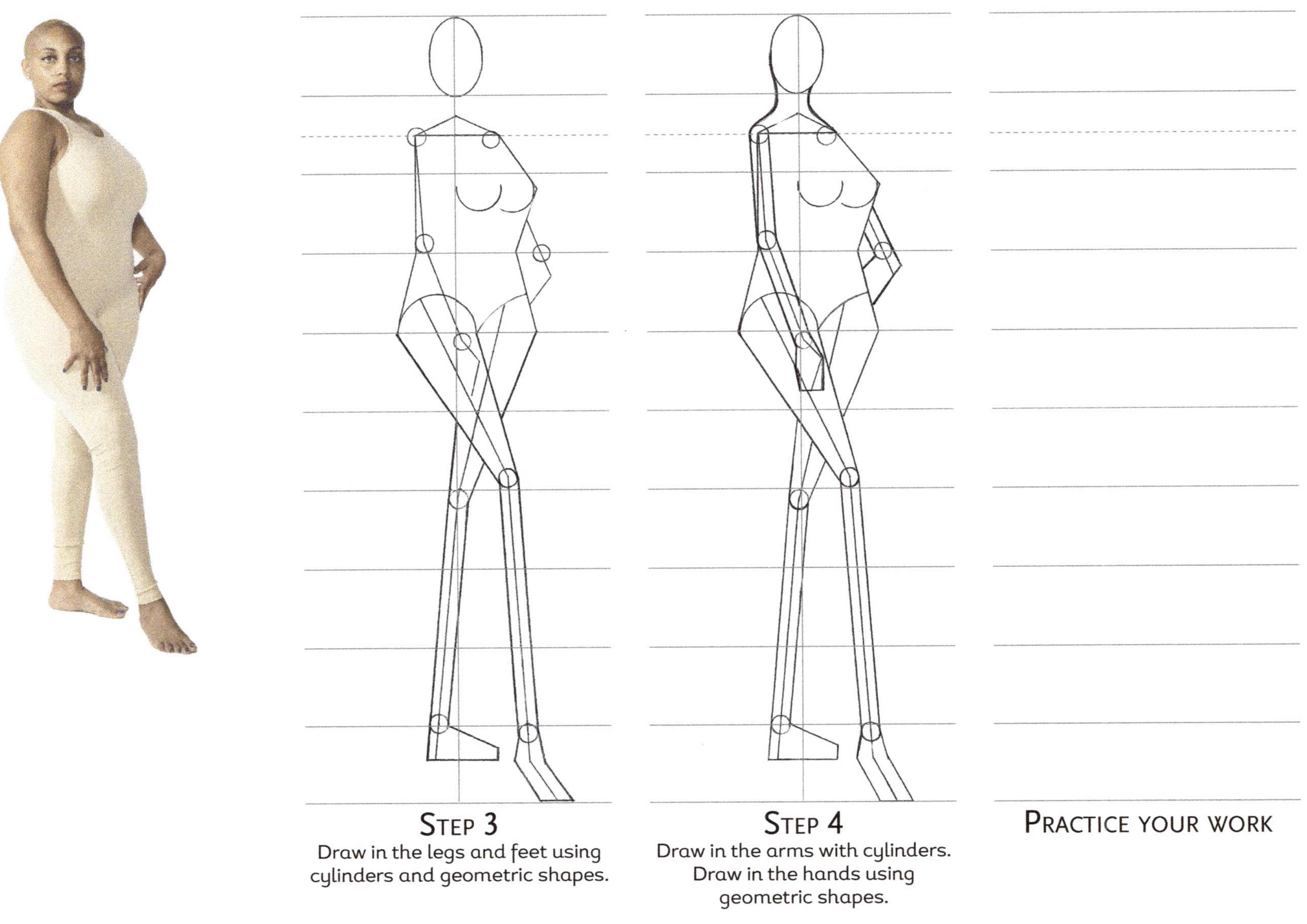

Step 3

Draw in the legs and feet using cylinders and geometric shapes.

Step 4

Draw in the arms with cylinders. Draw in the hands using geometric shapes.

Practice your work

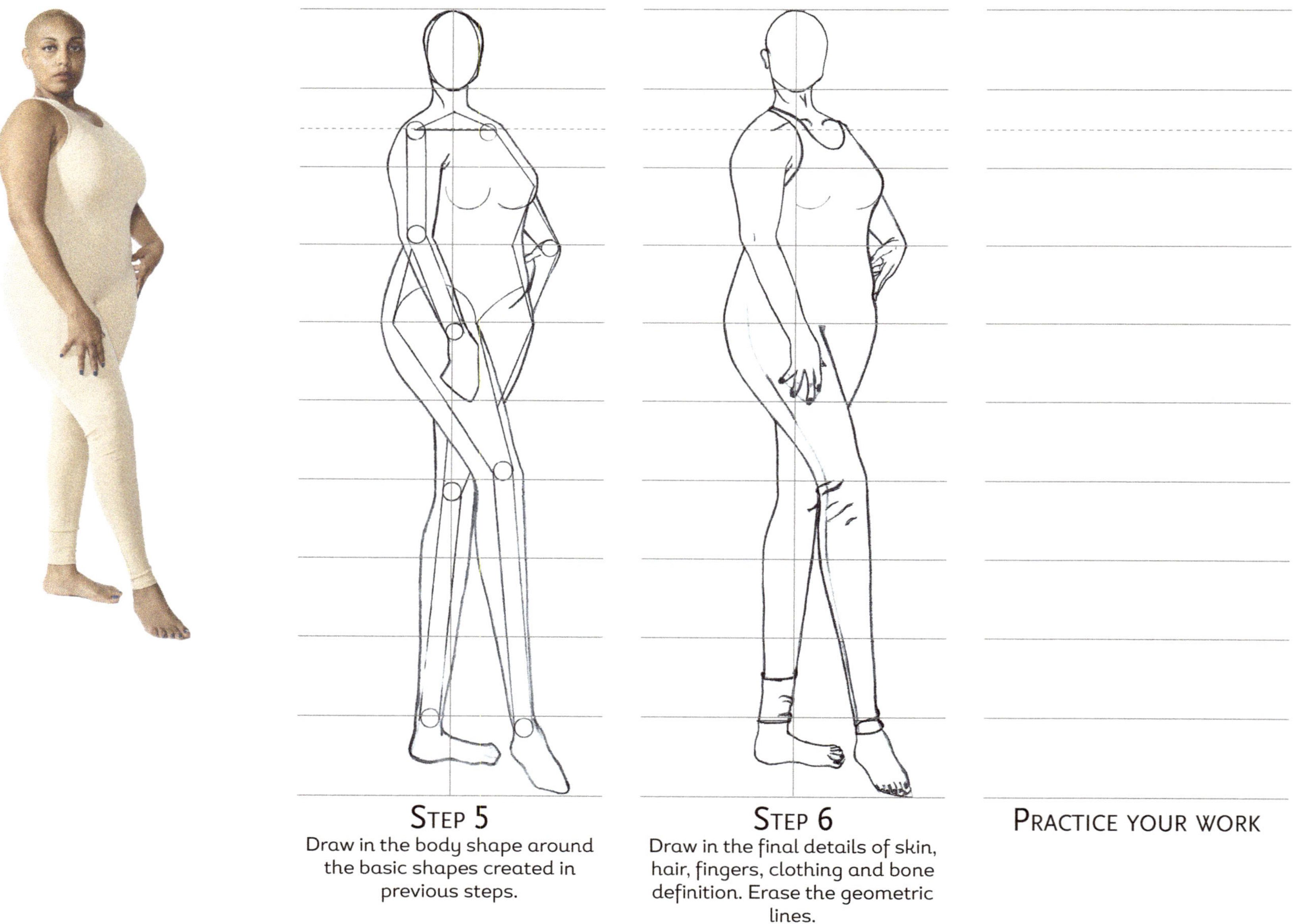

Step 5

Draw in the body shape around the basic shapes created in previous steps.

Step 6

Draw in the final details of skin, hair, fingers, clothing and bone definition. Erase the geometric lines.

PRACTICE SIMPLE MOVEMENT

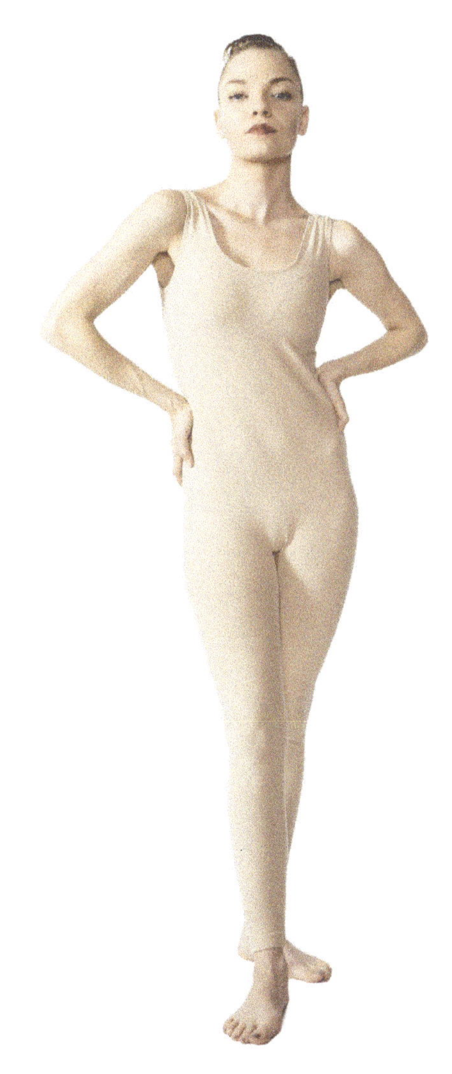

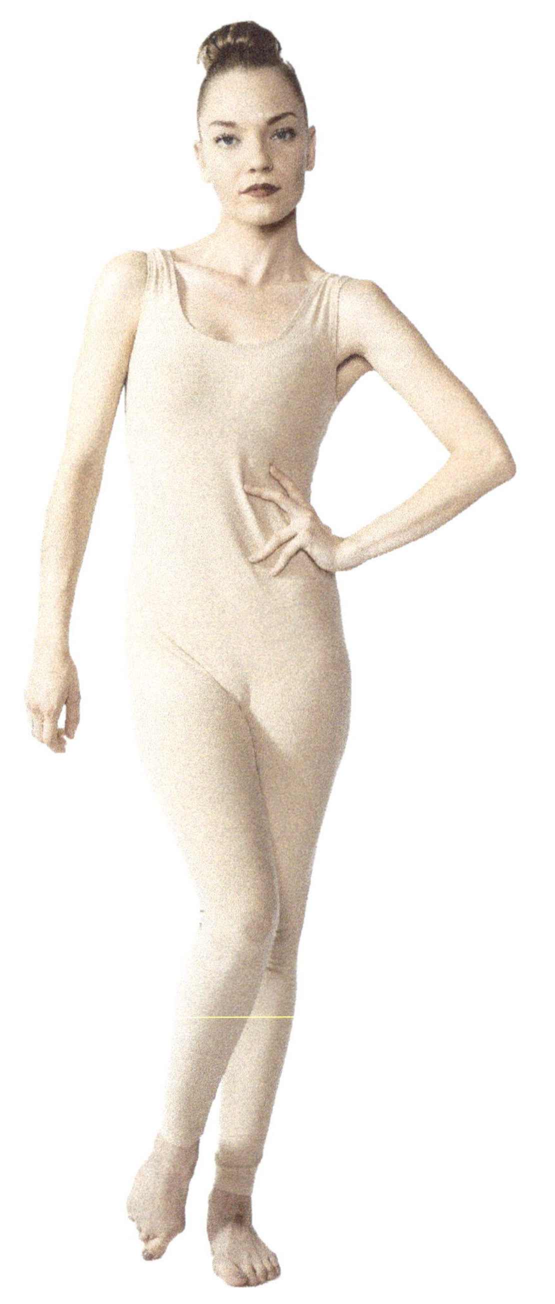

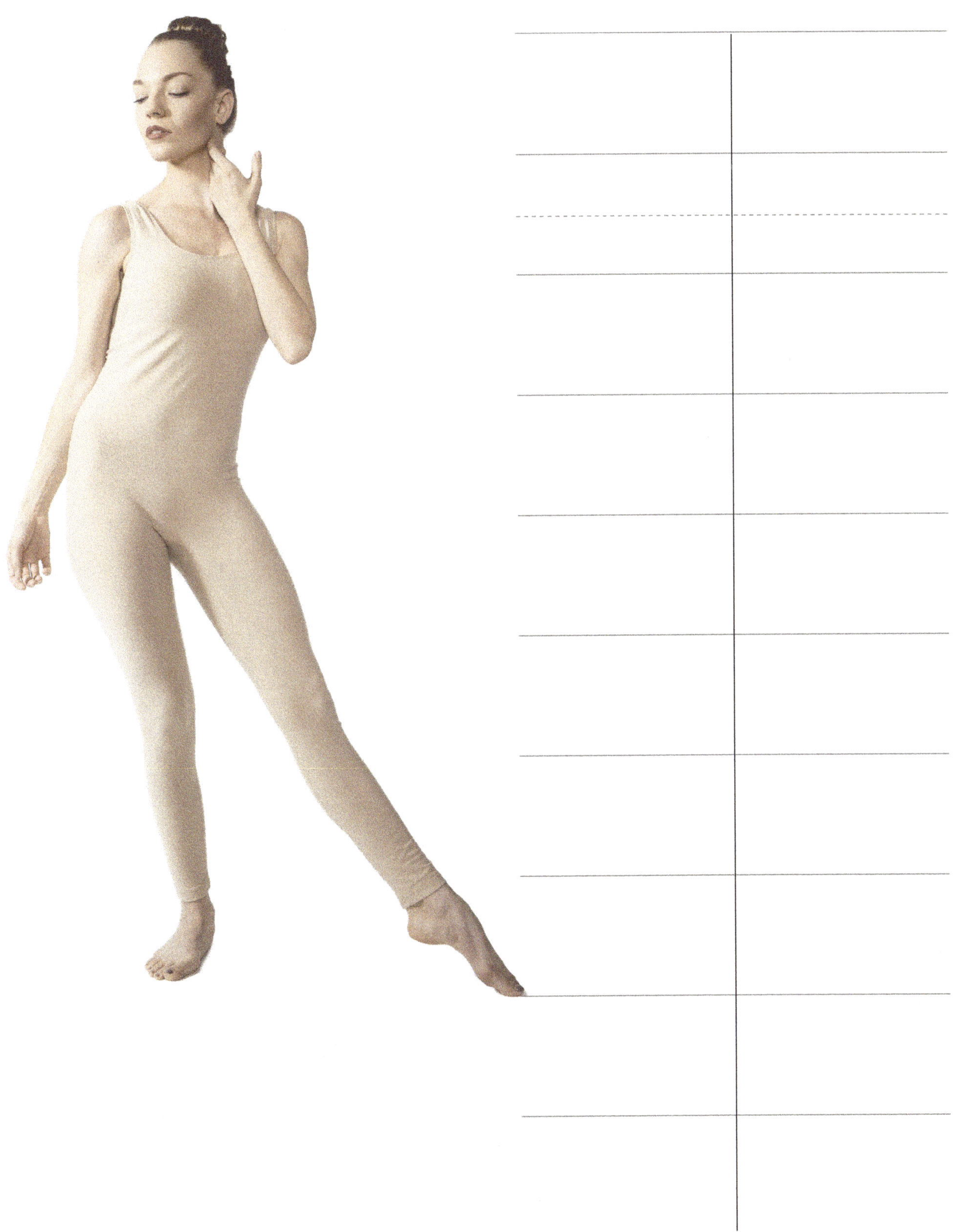

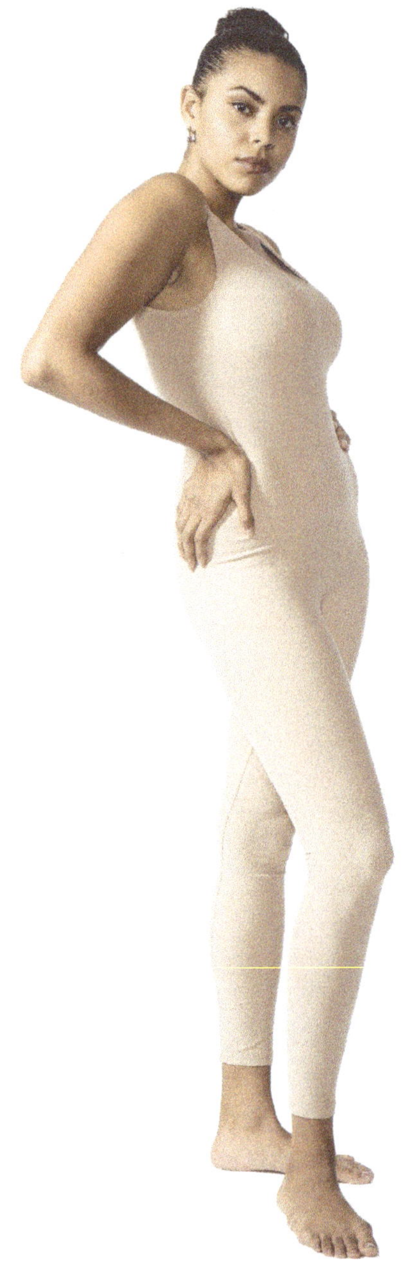

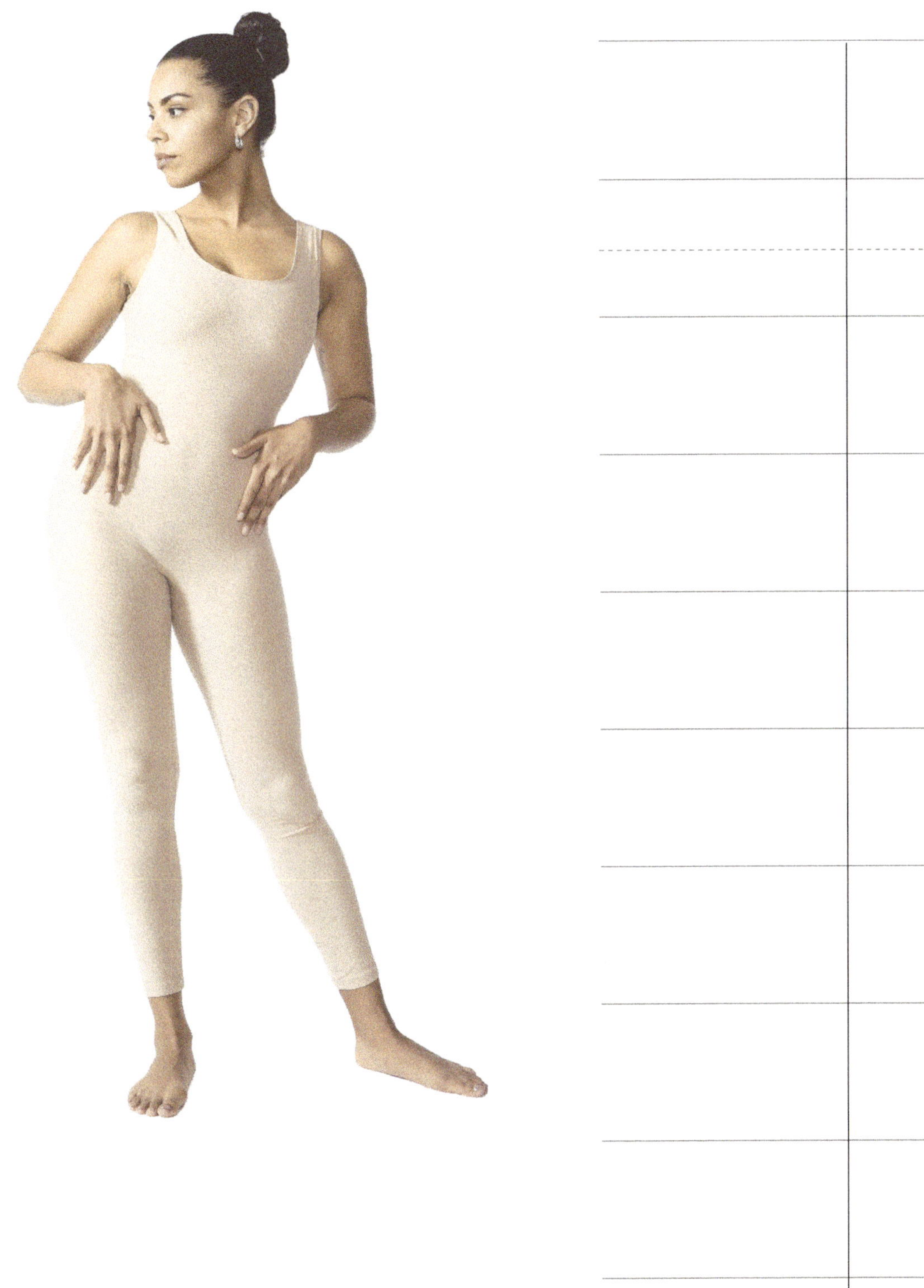

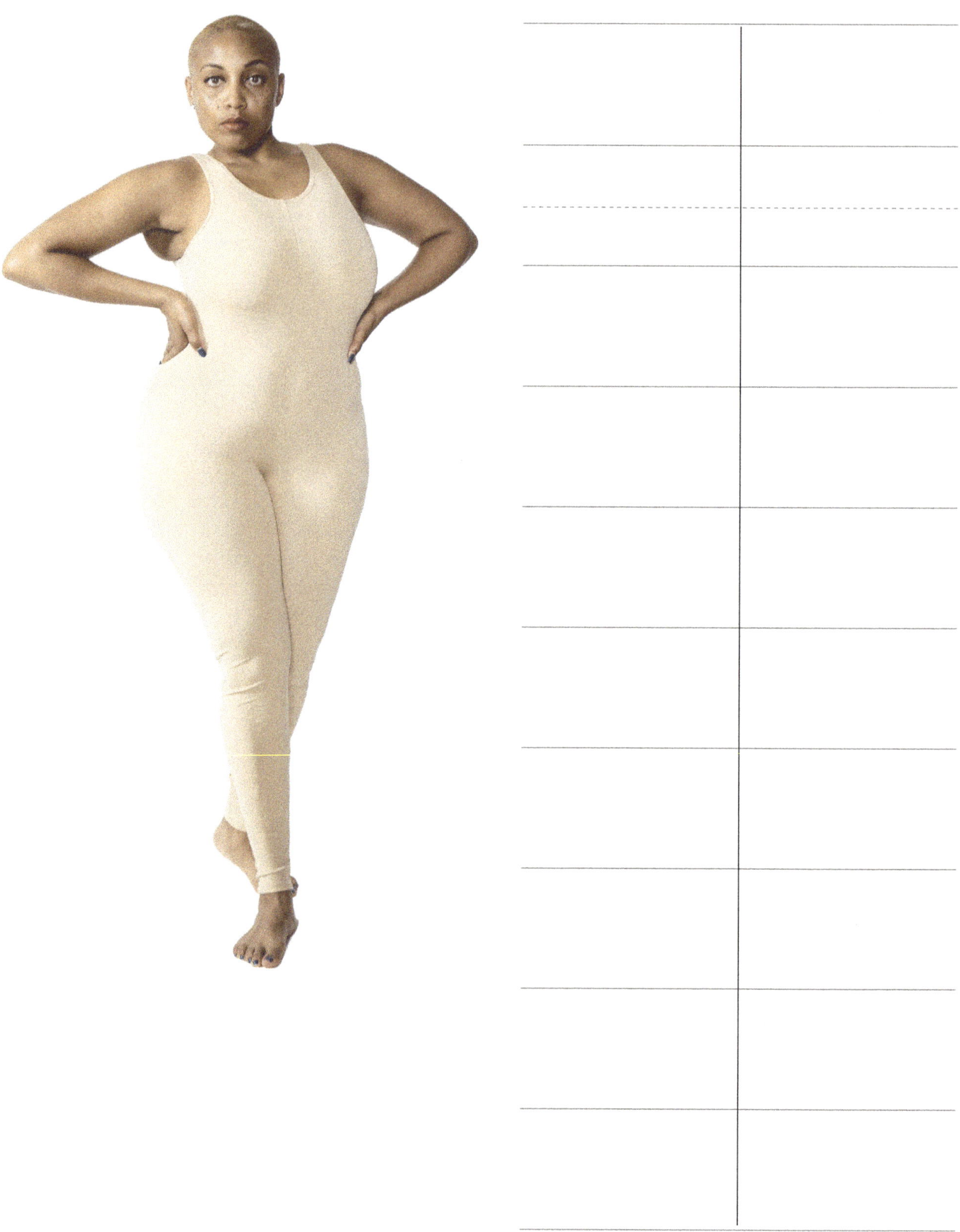

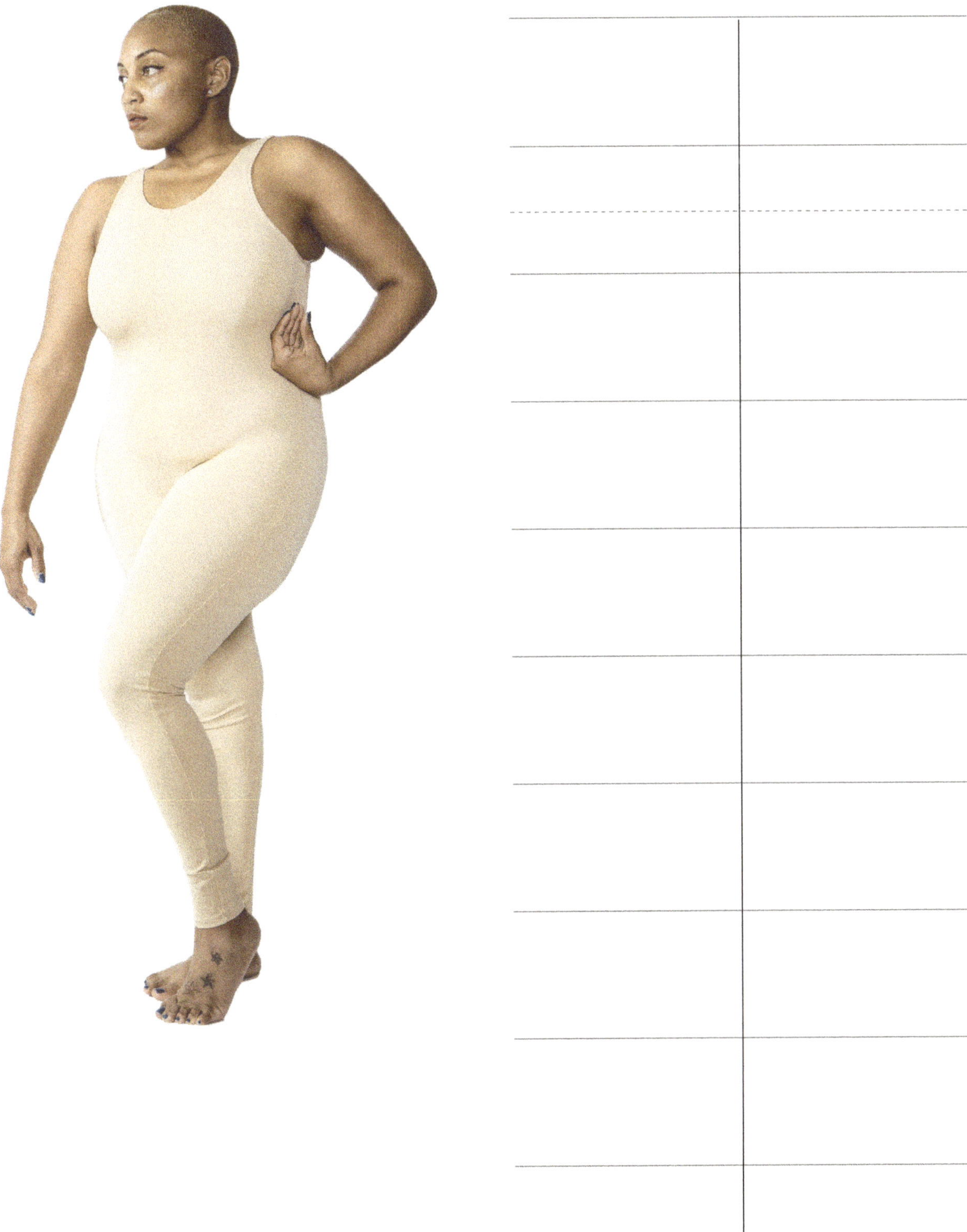

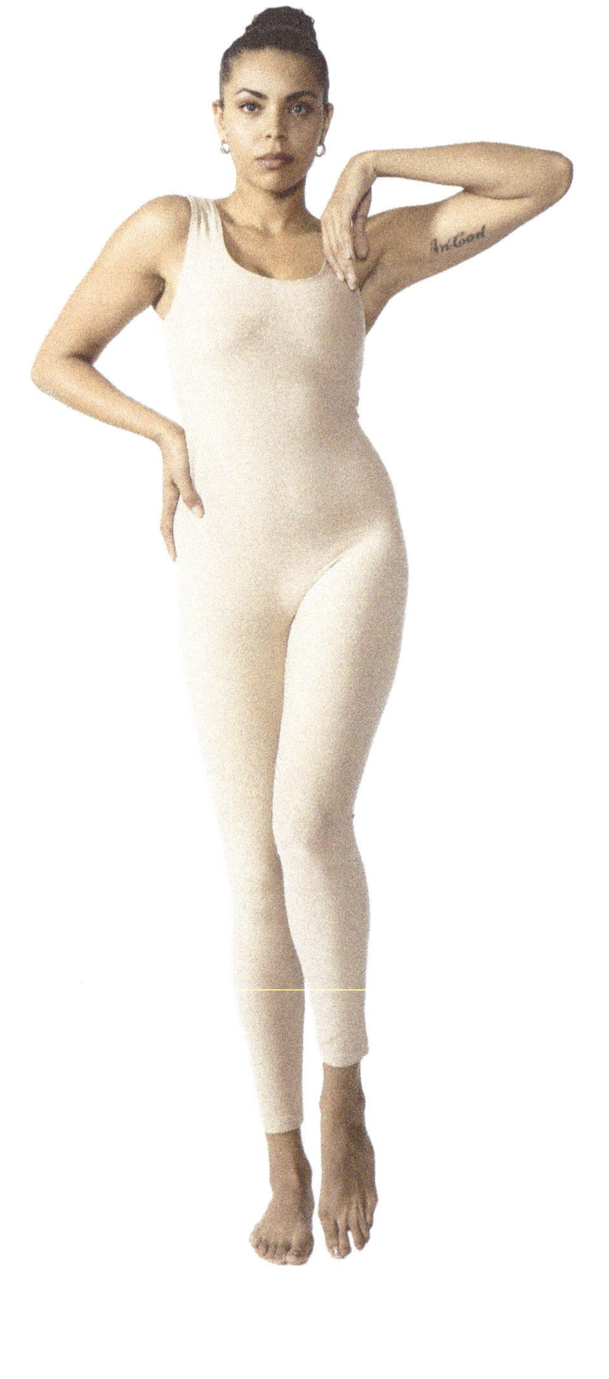

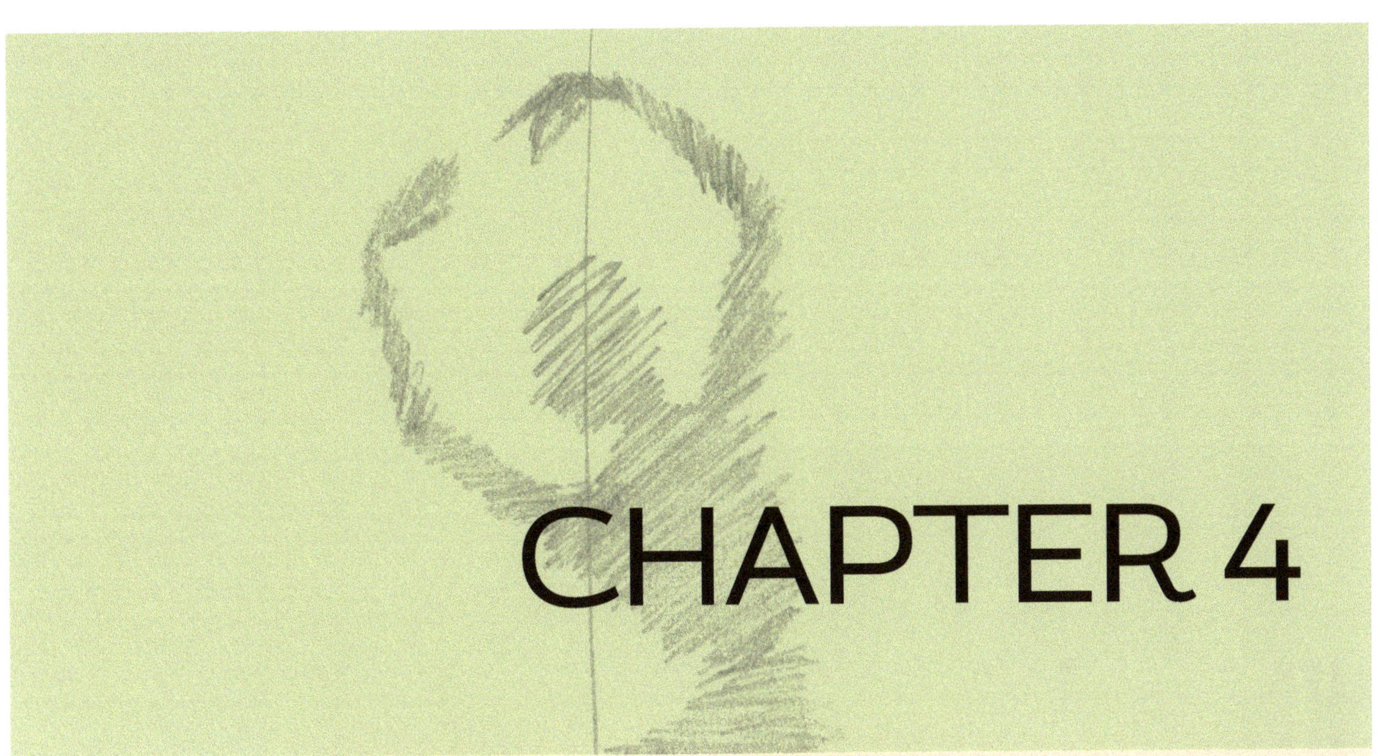

CHAPTER 4

Extreme Movements

EXTREME MOVEMENT POSE 1

Not all poses are easy to illustrate. In the following exercises, the body shape contours and bends in different angles. The 10 head figure is more complicated to elongate. In this exercise, the head and neck are bent at the shoulder point and the extension of the body is altered.

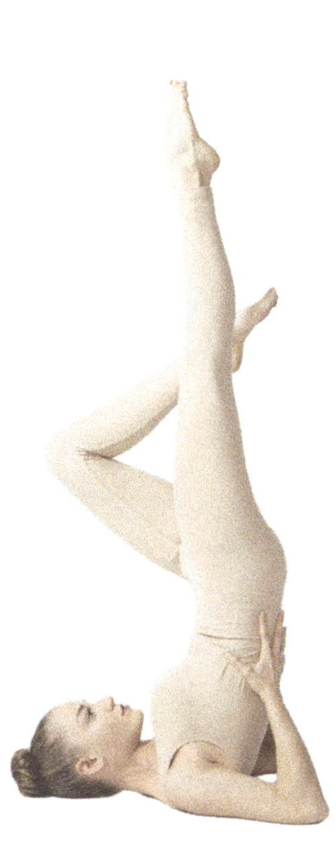

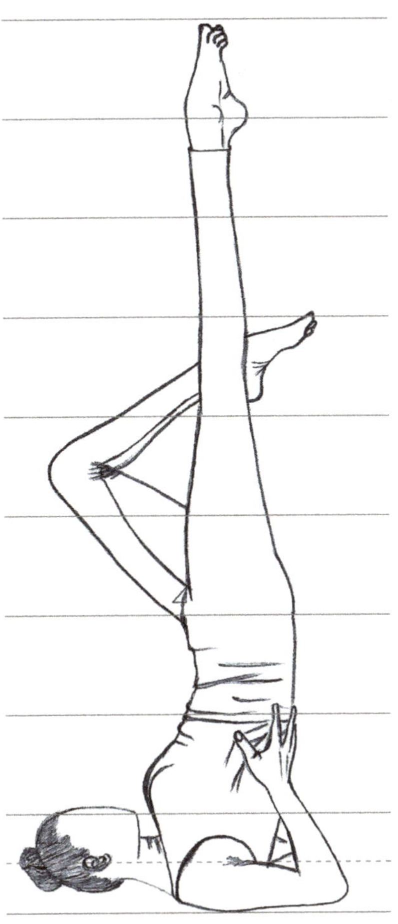

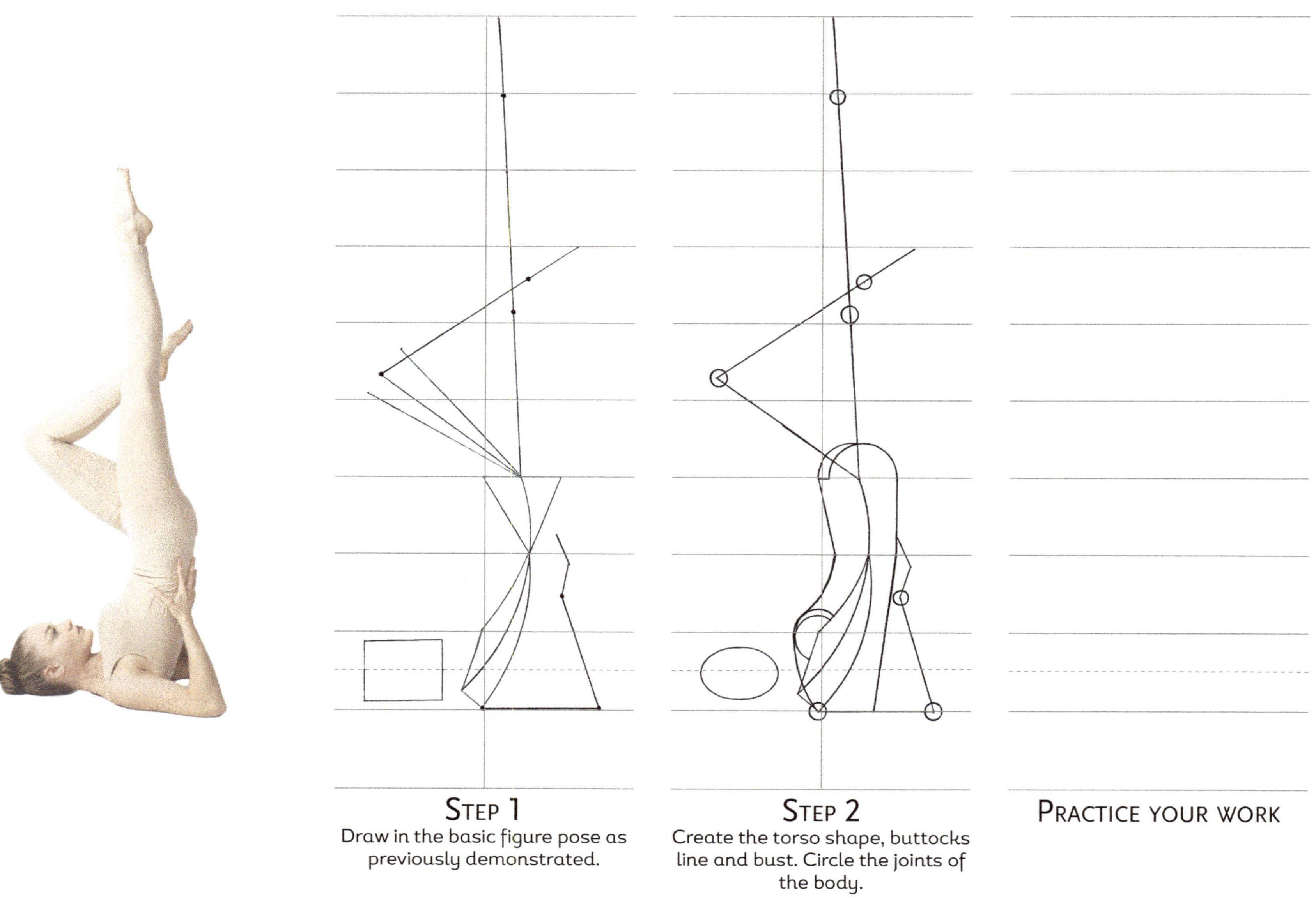

STEP 1

Draw in the basic figure pose as previously demonstrated.

STEP 2

Create the torso shape, buttocks line and bust. Circle the joints of the body.

PRACTICE YOUR WORK

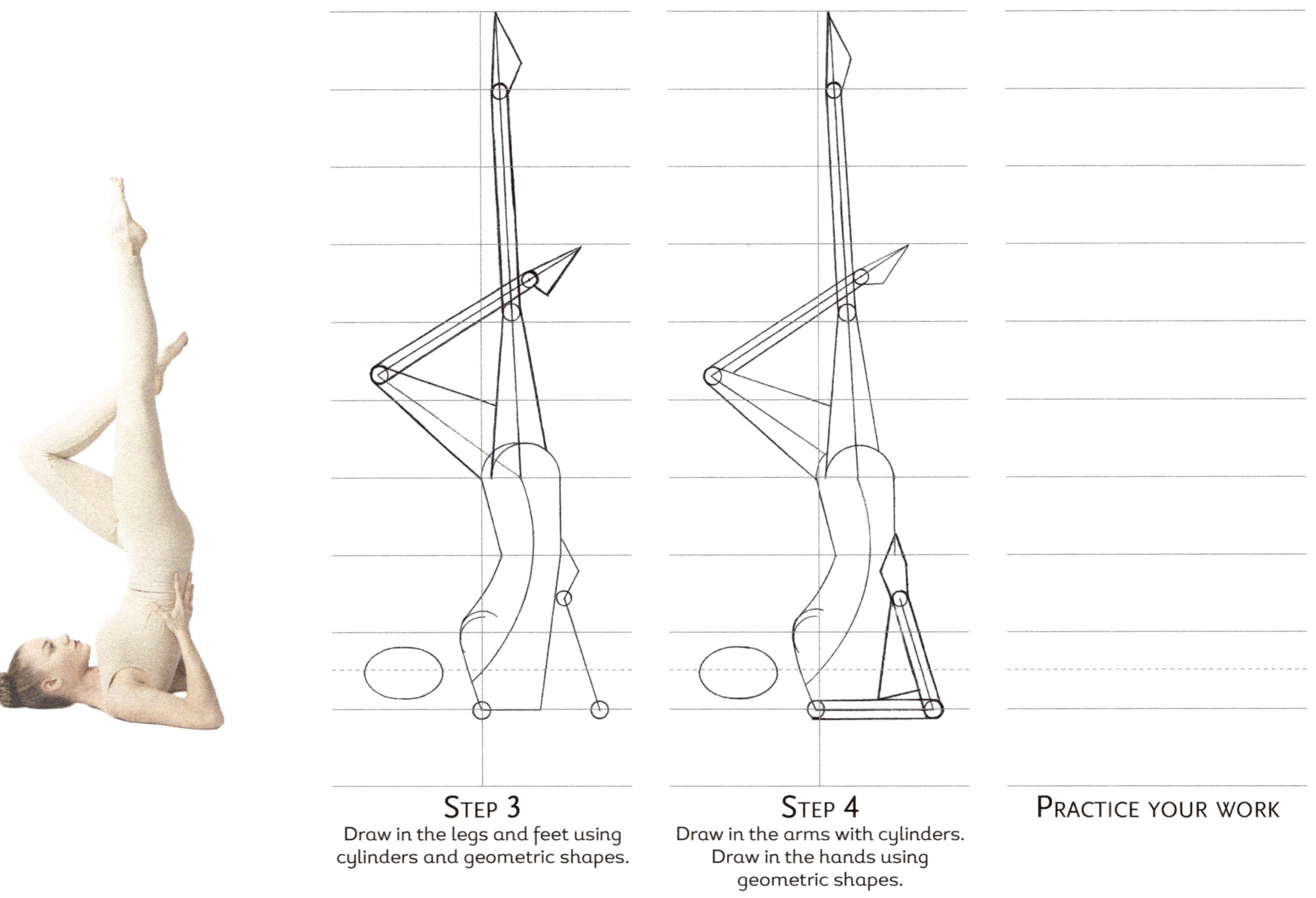

Step 3

Draw in the legs and feet using cylinders and geometric shapes.

Step 4

Draw in the arms with cylinders. Draw in the hands using geometric shapes.

Practice your work

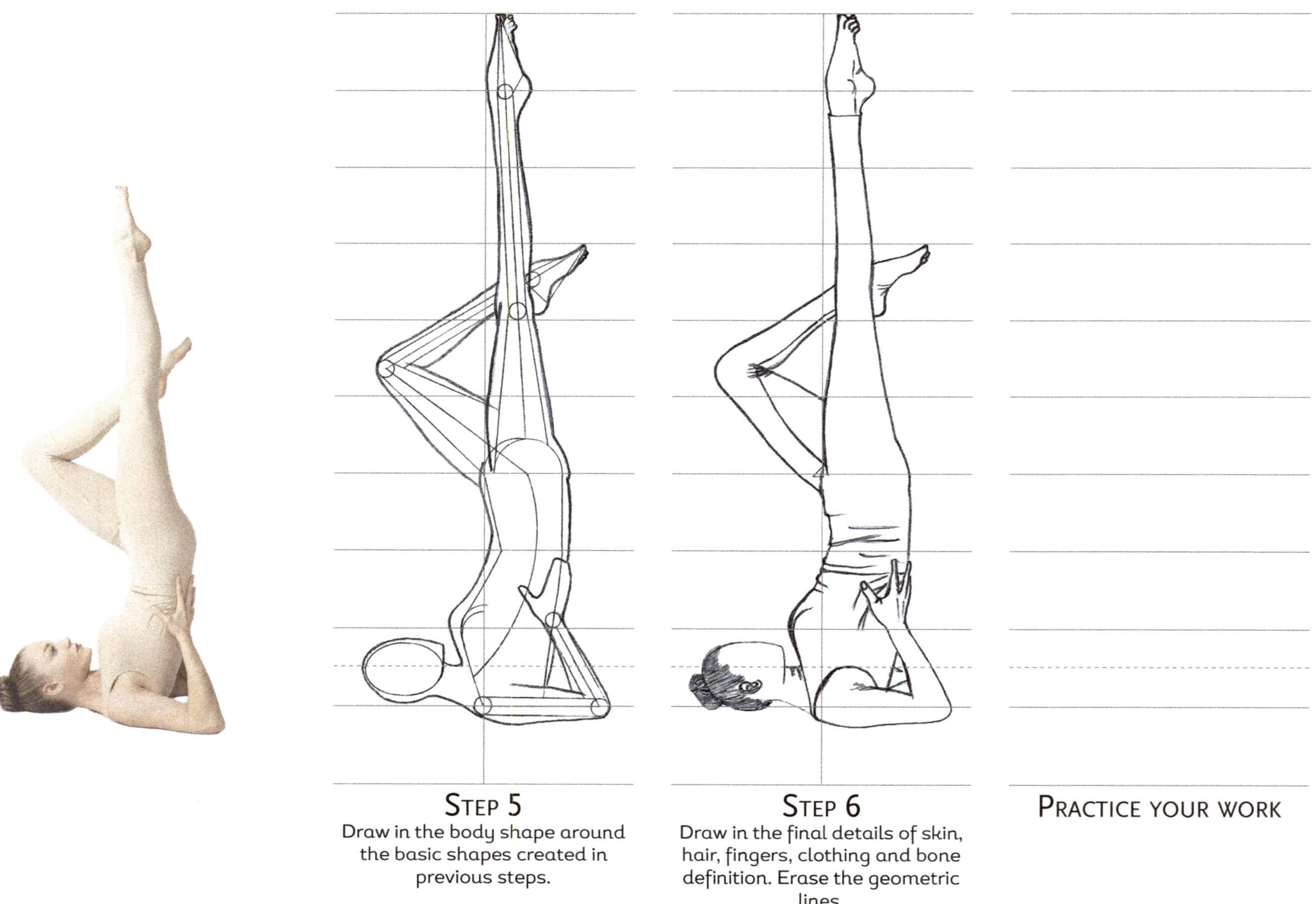

STEP 5

Draw in the body shape around the basic shapes created in previous steps.

STEP 6

Draw in the final details of skin, hair, fingers, clothing and bone definition. Erase the geometric lines.

PRACTICE YOUR WORK

EXTREME MOVEMENT POSE 2

In this exercise, the model is bent with her knees at hip level, shortening the position of the lower portion of the body. In addition her neck is leaning down to shoulder level. The lower legs and torso are extended.

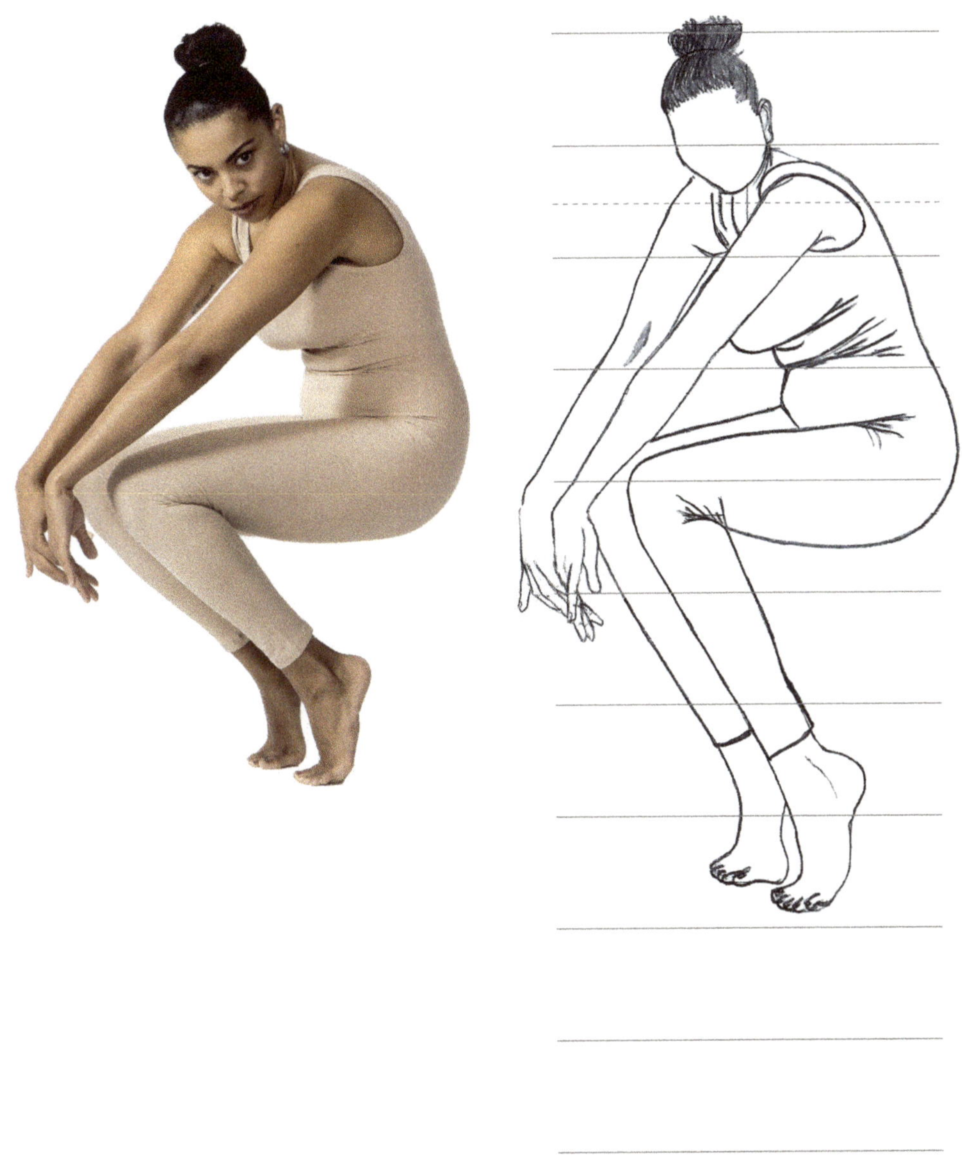

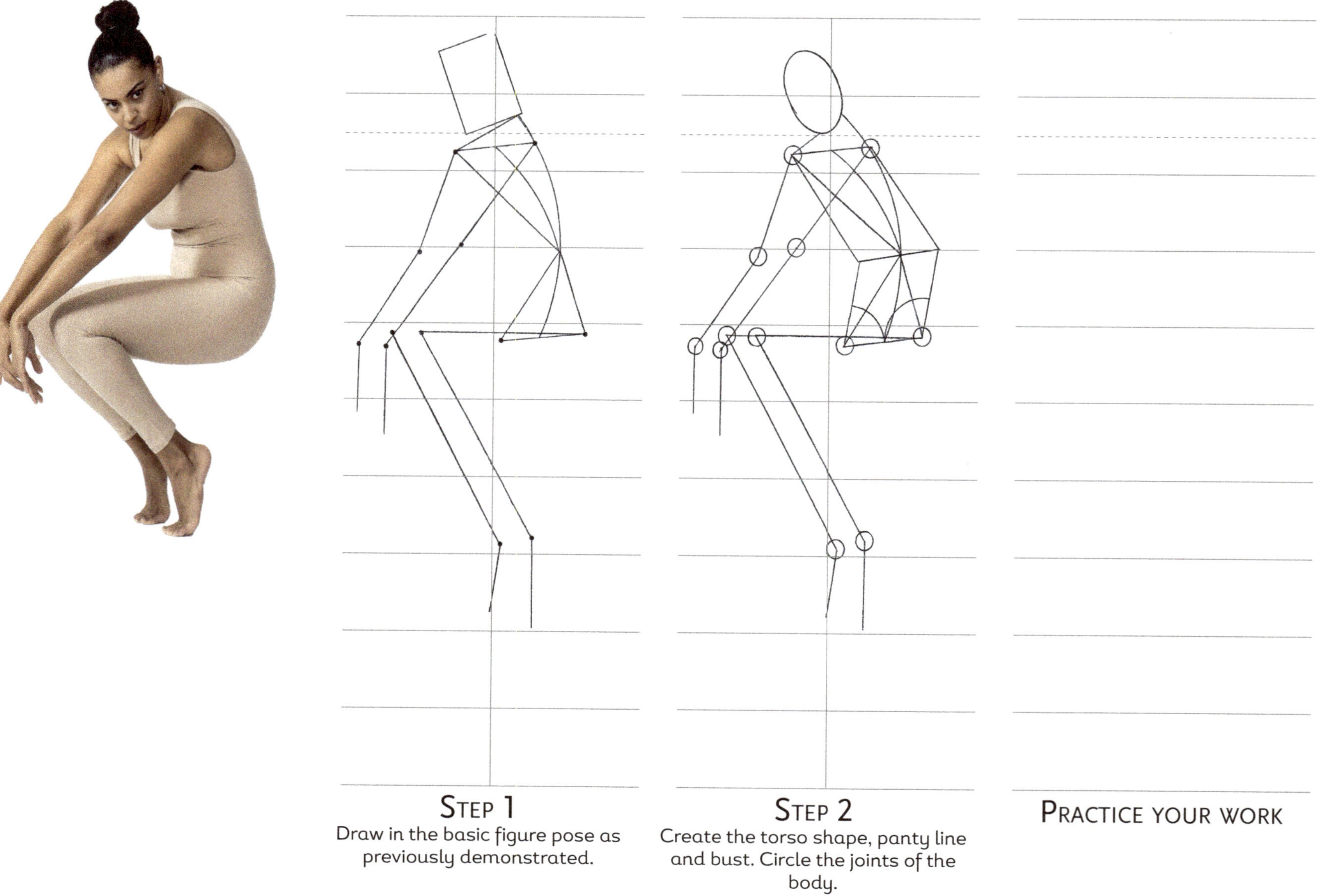

STEP 1

Draw in the basic figure pose as previously demonstrated.

STEP 2

Create the torso shape, panty line and bust. Circle the joints of the body.

PRACTICE YOUR WORK

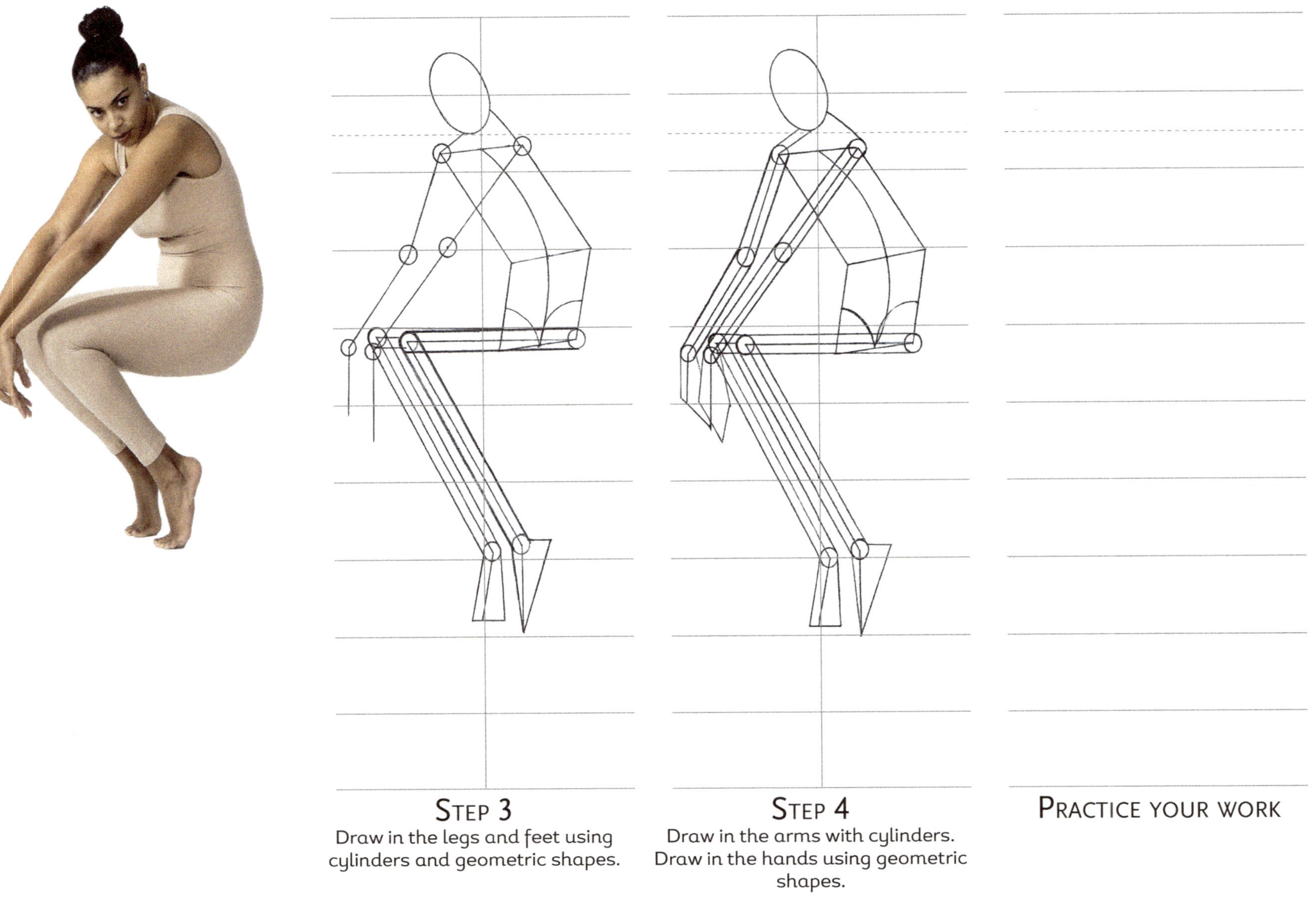

STEP 3

Draw in the legs and feet using cylinders and geometric shapes.

STEP 4

Draw in the arms with cylinders. Draw in the hands using geometric shapes.

PRACTICE YOUR WORK

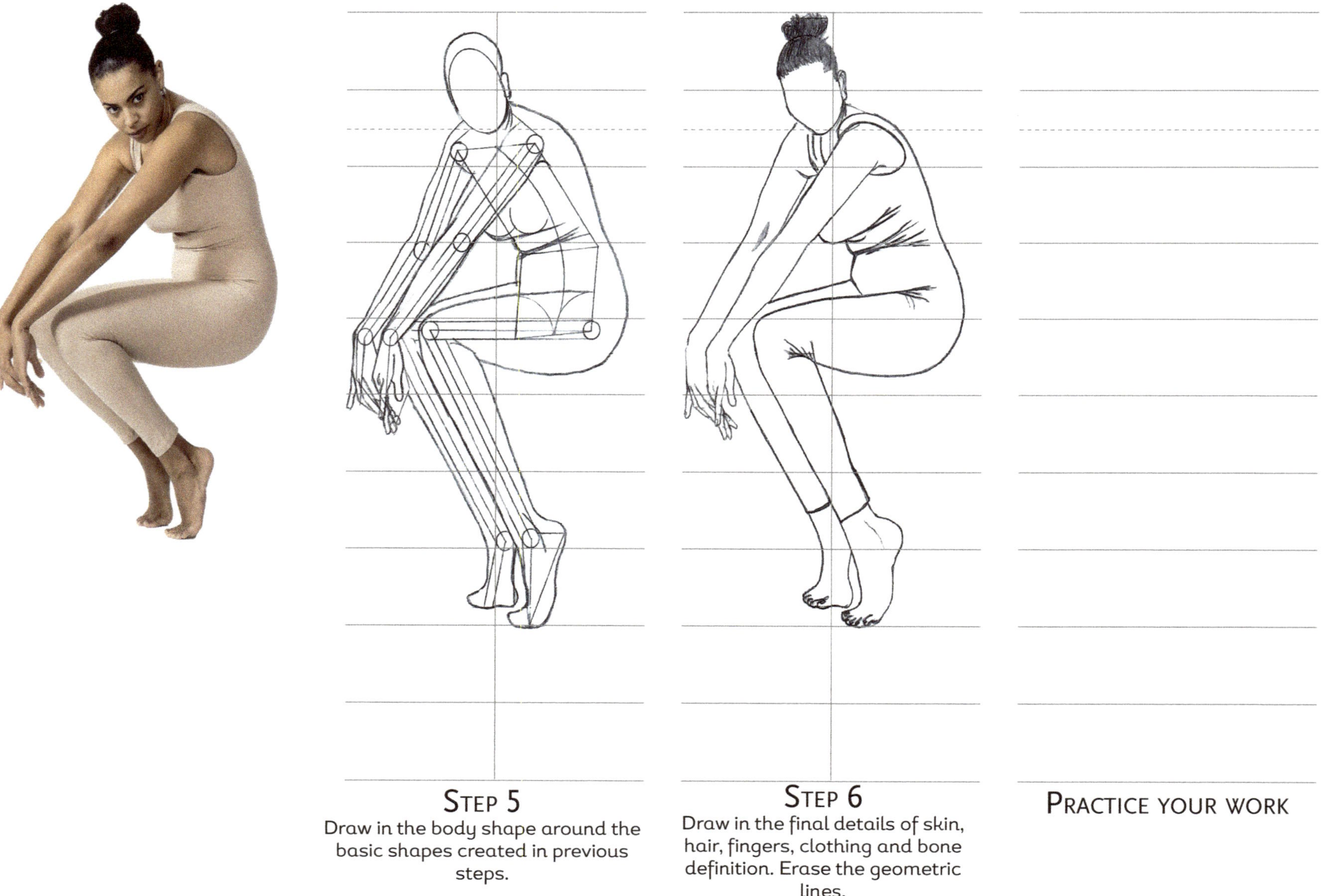

Step 5

Draw in the body shape around the basic shapes created in previous steps.

Step 6

Draw in the final details of skin, hair, fingers, clothing and bone definition. Erase the geometric lines.

Practice your work

Extreme Movement Pose 3

A model that is not upright, also poses a challenge. Begin this illustration in the same manner, but mark the center line further down from the center of the grid. Reposition the body with the head starting between lines 3 and 4 from the right side of the paper.

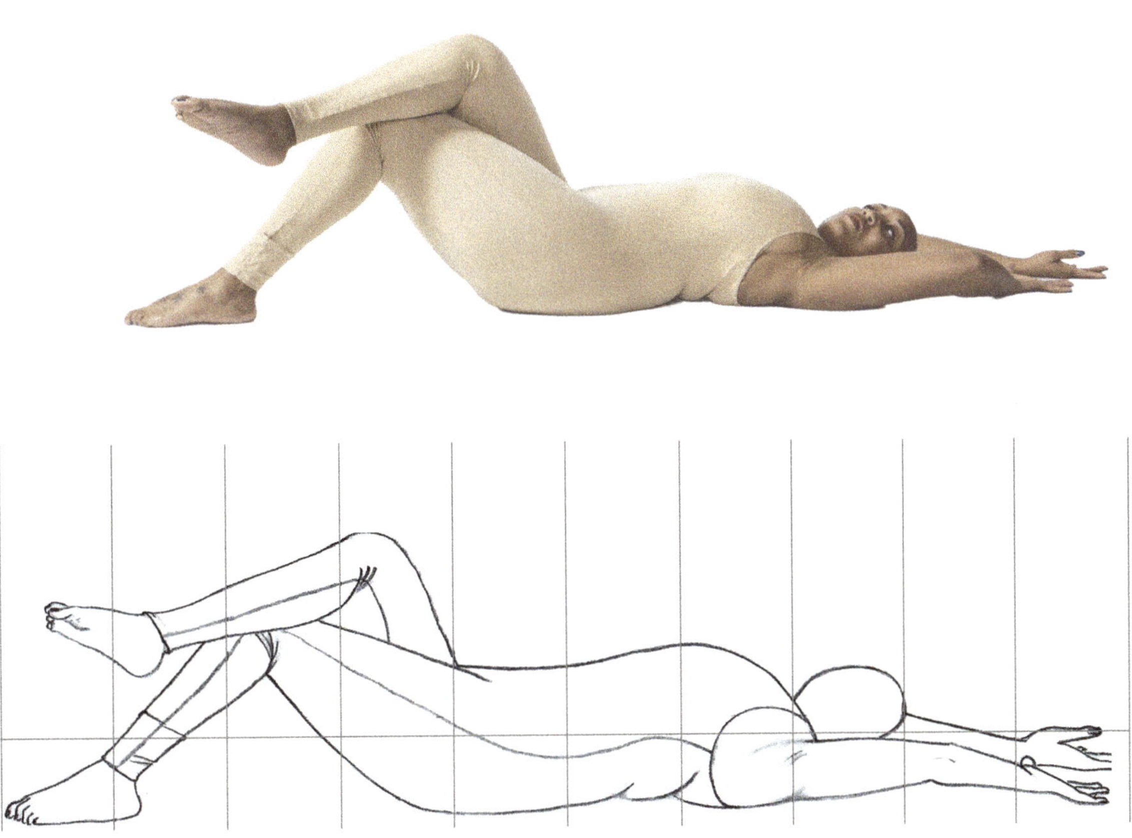

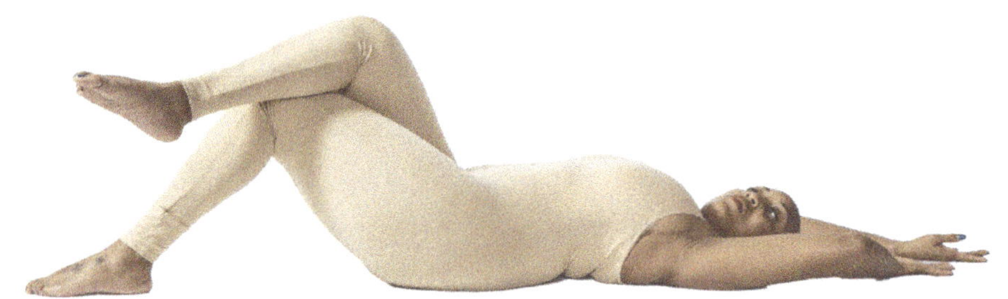

Step 1

Draw in the basic figure pose as previously demonstrated.

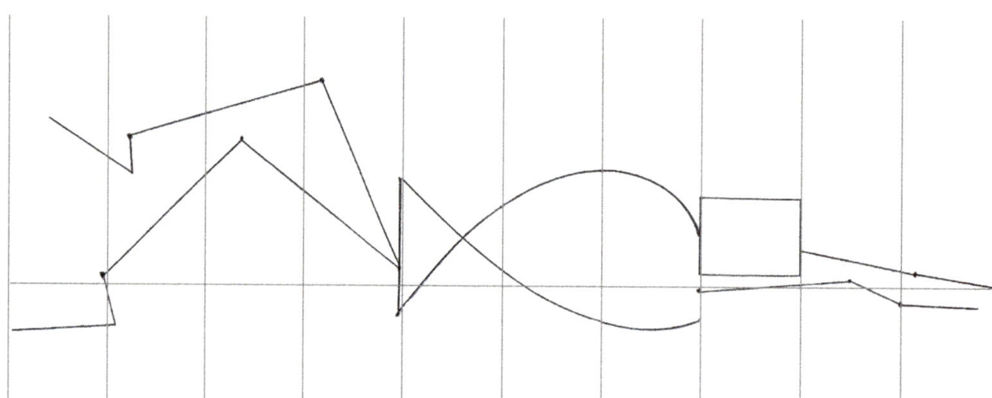

Step 2

Create the torso shape, panty line and bust. Circle the joints of the body.

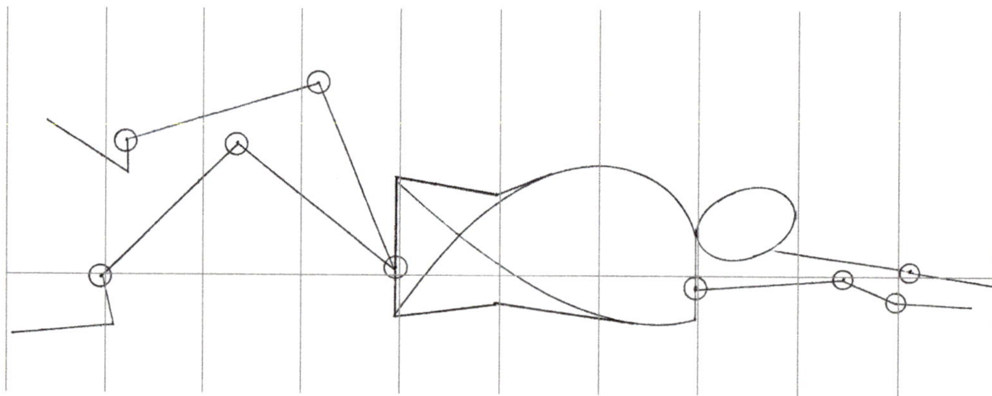

Practice

your work

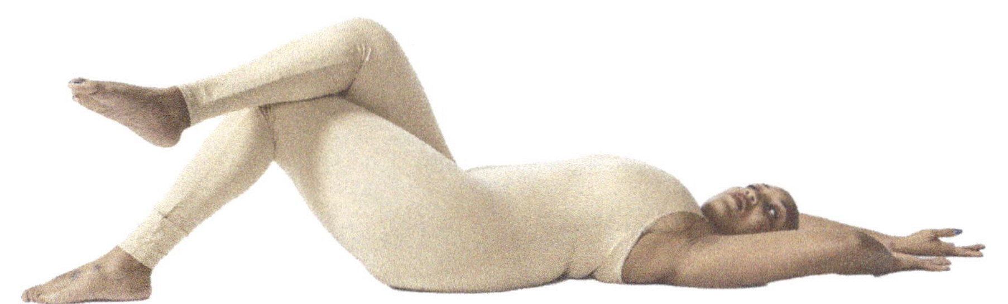

STEP 3

Draw in the legs and feet using cylinders and geometric shapes.

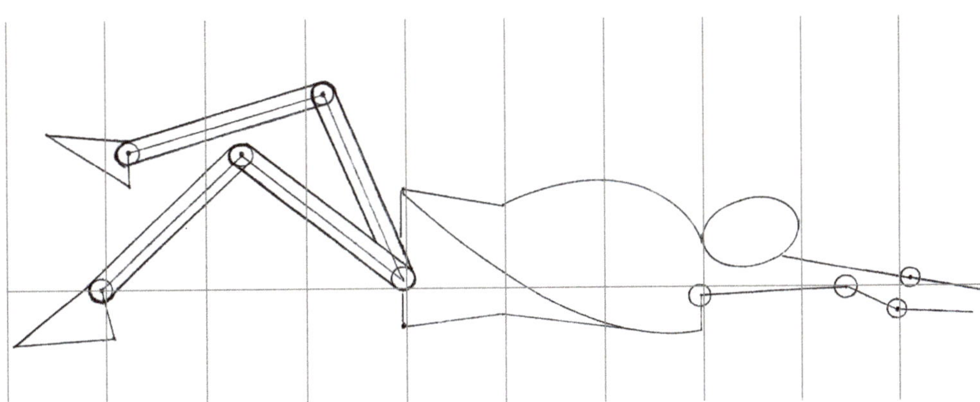

STEP 4

Draw in the arms with cylinders. Draw in the hands using geometric shapes.

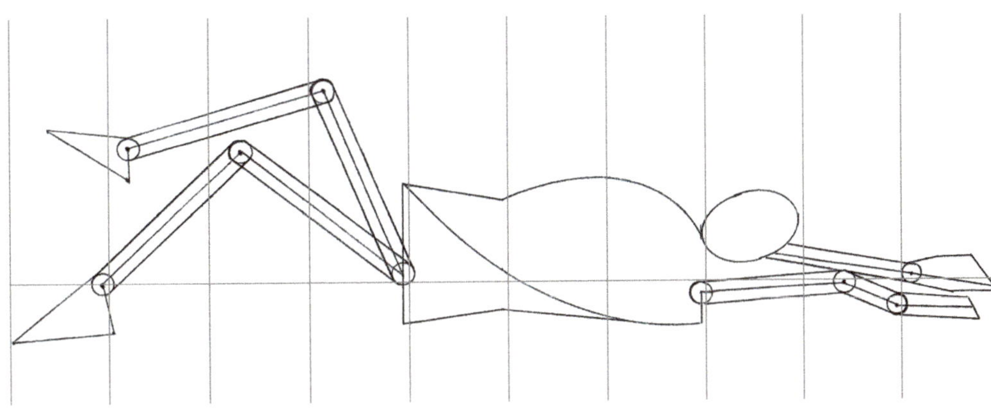

PRACTICE

YOUR WORK

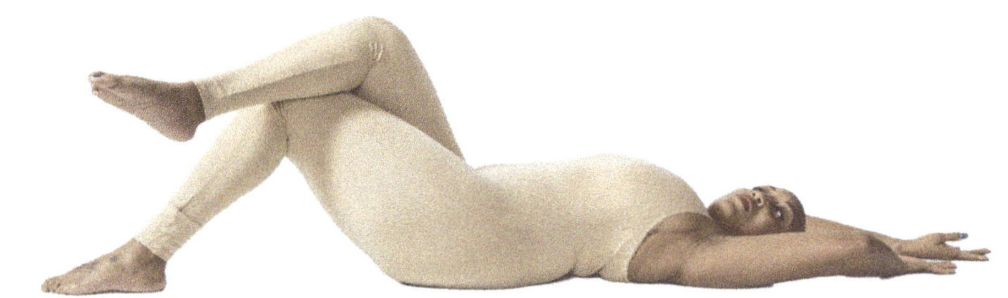

Step 5

Draw in the body shape around the basic shapes created in previous steps.

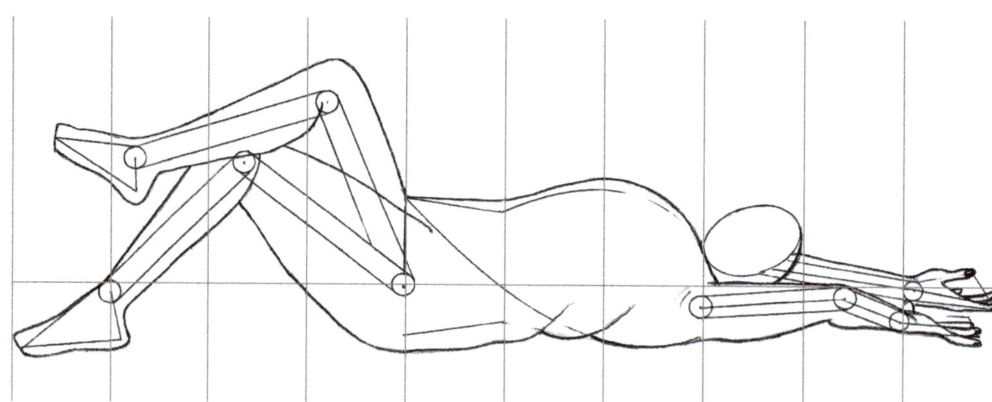

Step 6

Draw in the final details of skin, hair, fingers, clothing and bone definition. Erase the geometric lines.

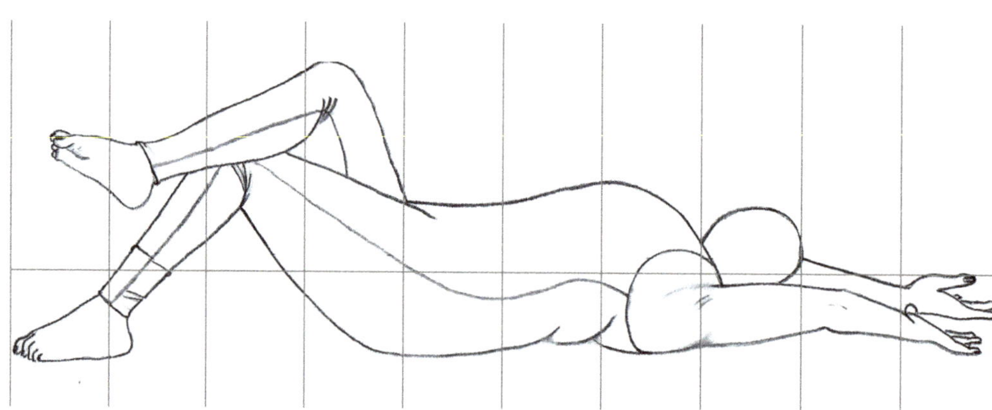

Practice

your work

PRACTICE EXTREME MOVEMENTS

Practice illustrating the following poses. Note the center of balance may shift based on the pose. For more complicated movements, align the shoulder position up to the grid.

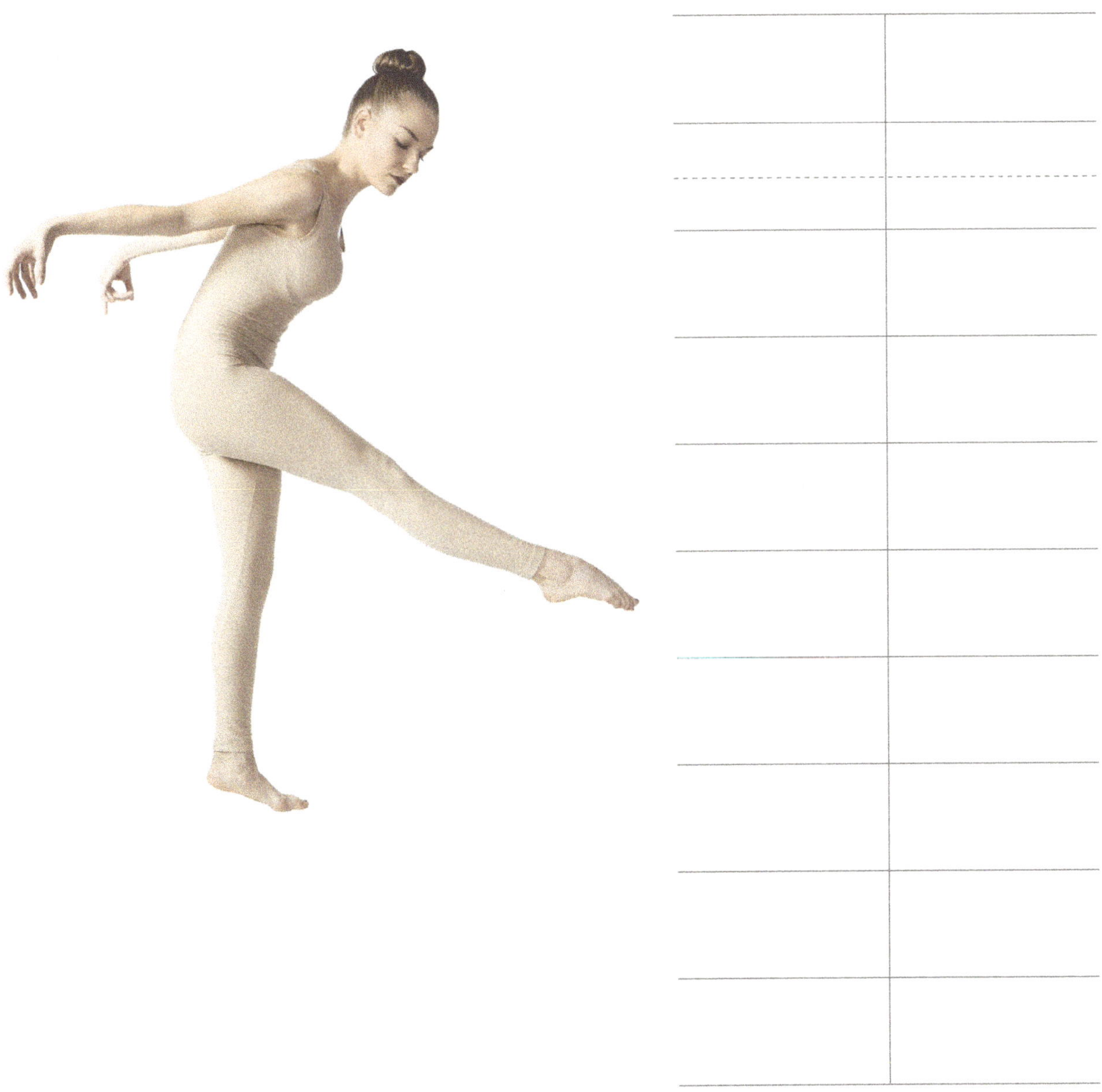

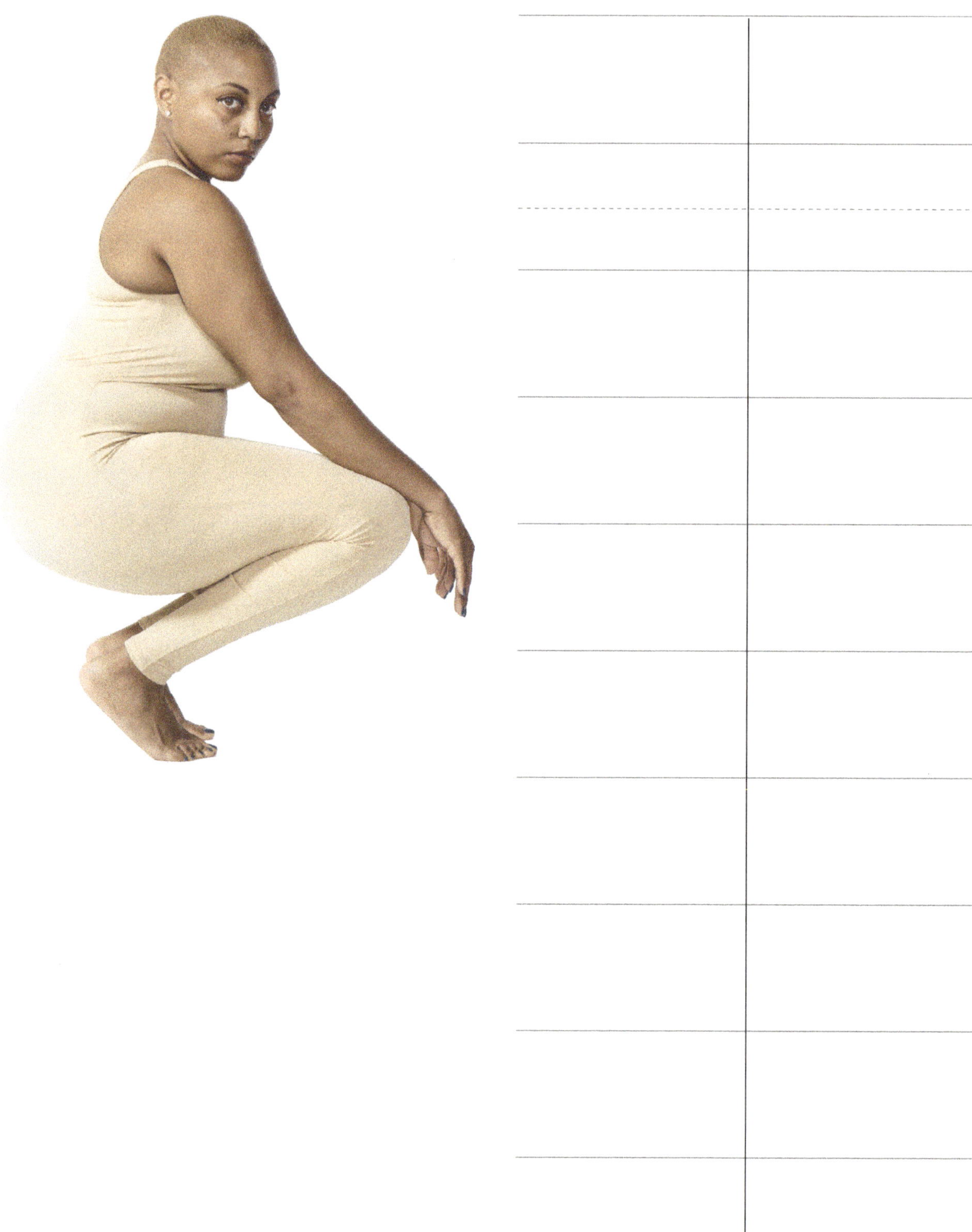

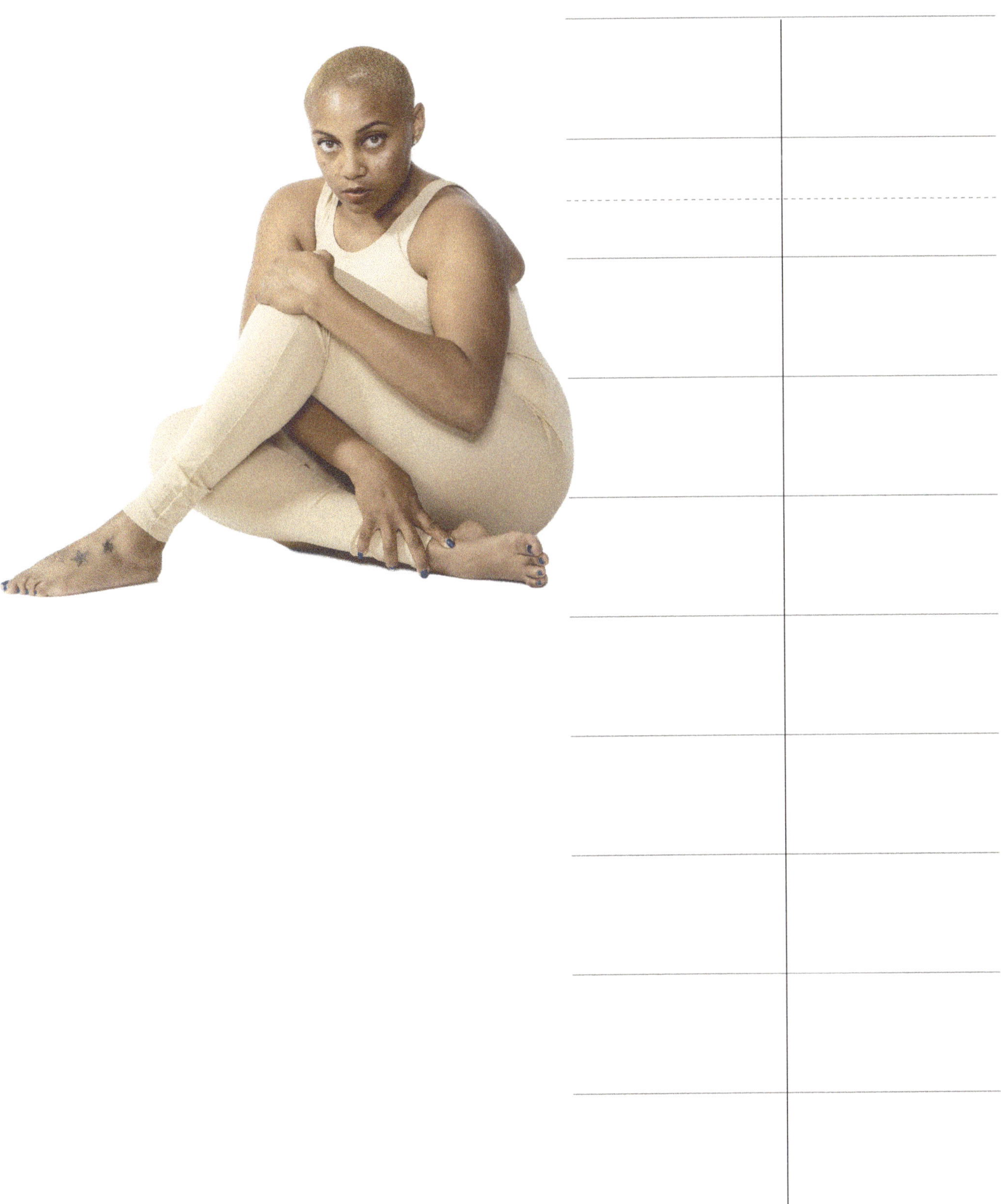

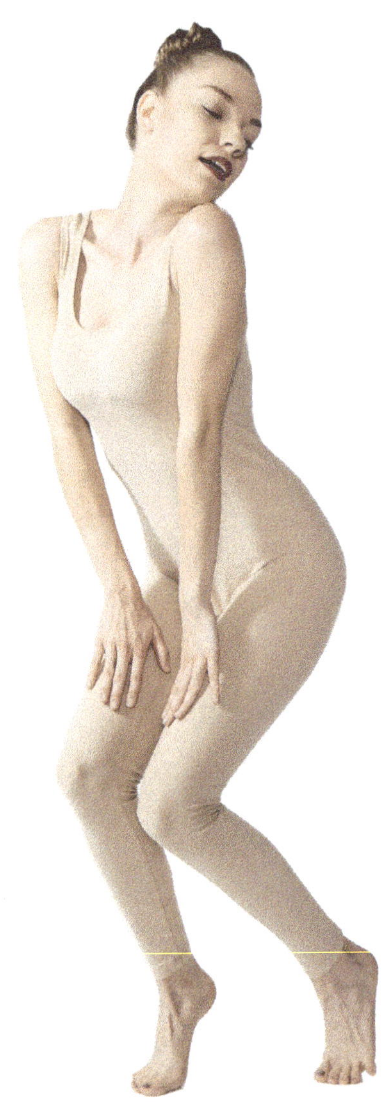

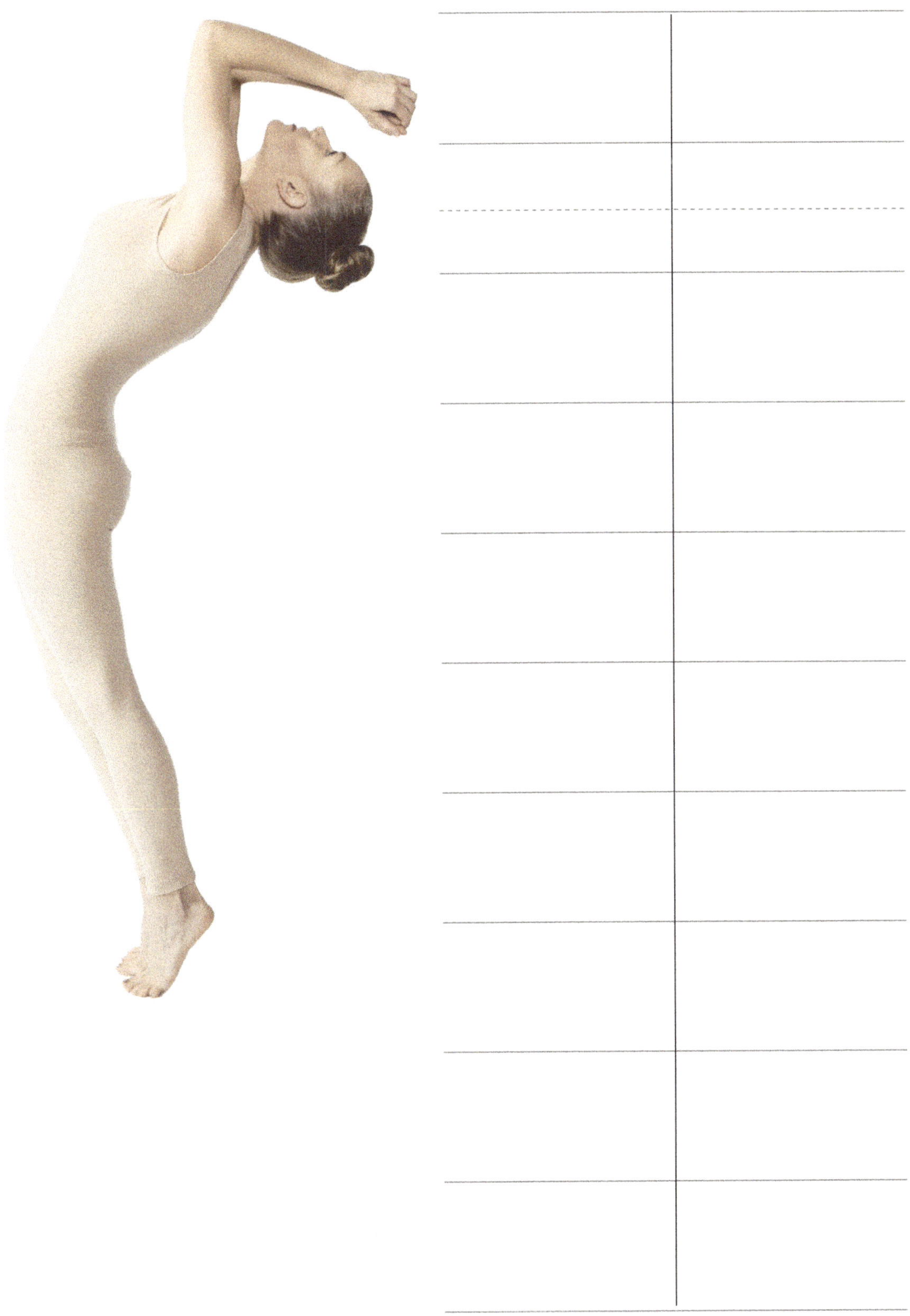

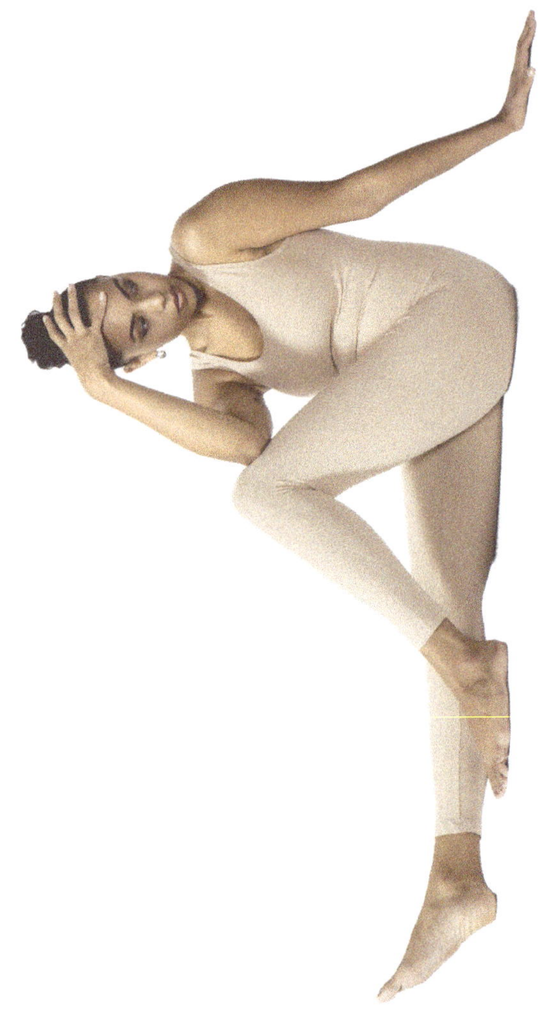

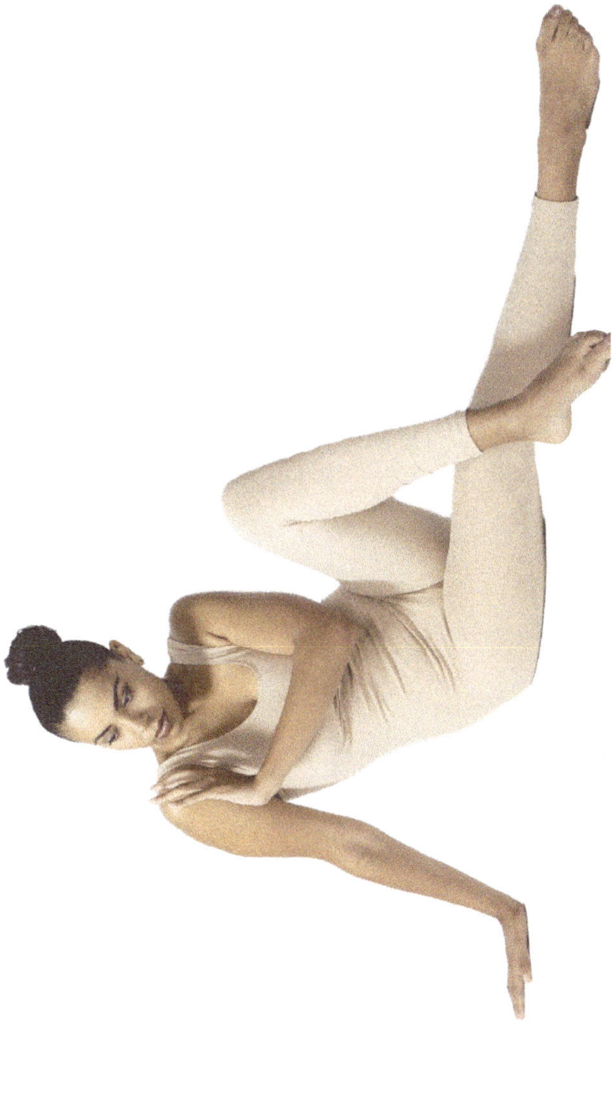

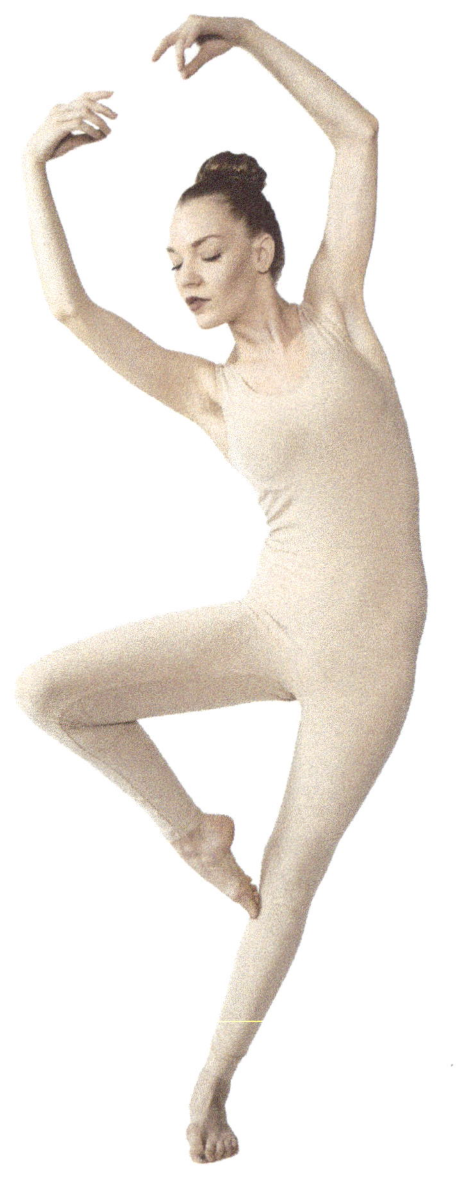

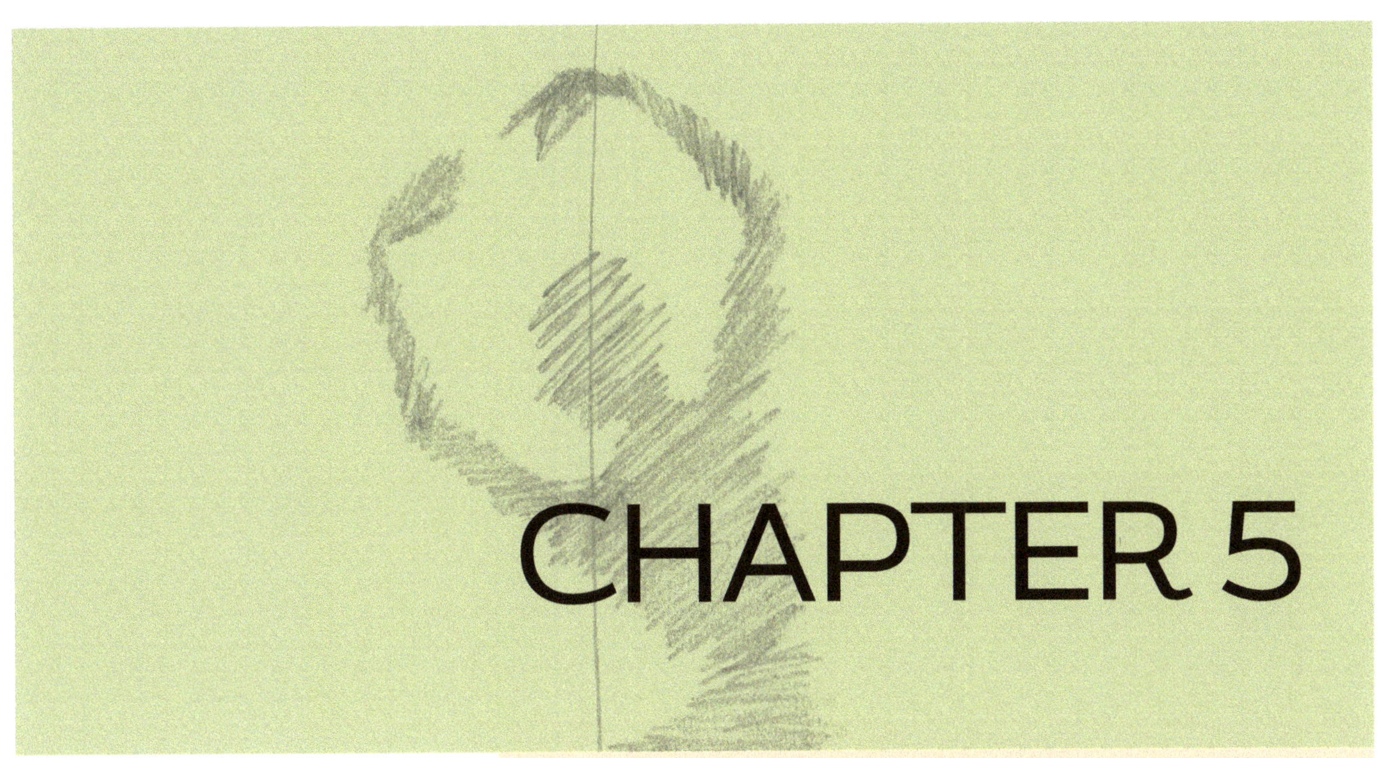

CHAPTER 5

Hand Poses

HAND POSES

Illustrating hands can be as complex as the full fashion figure. Illustrations in this chapter demonstrate various hand positions and perspectives.

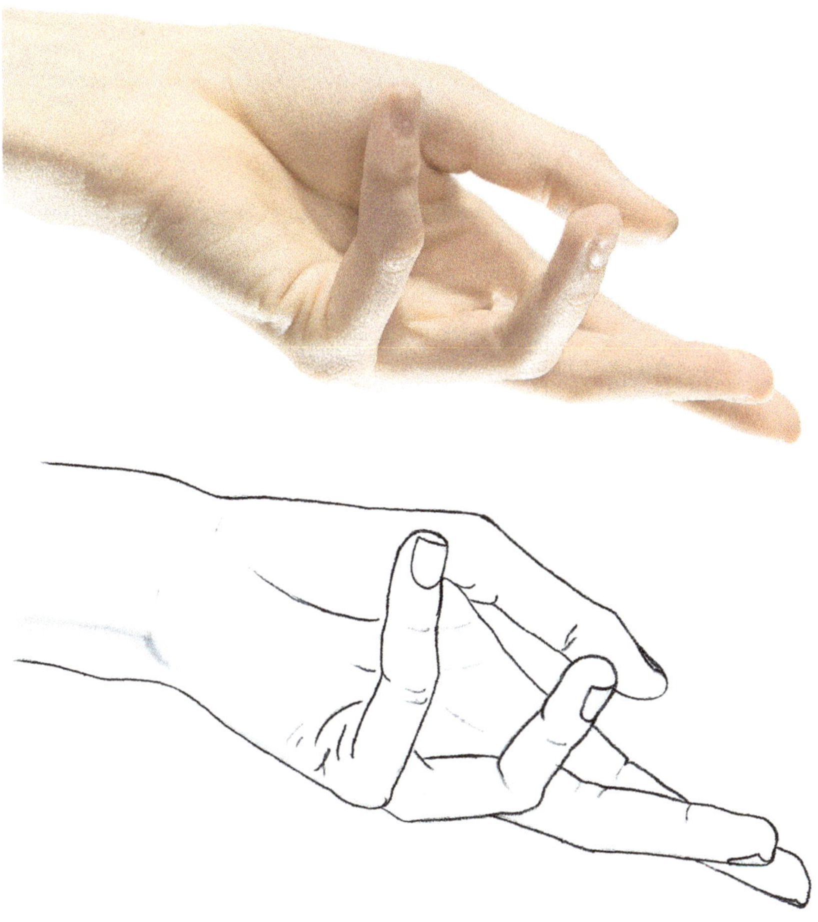

POSE 1

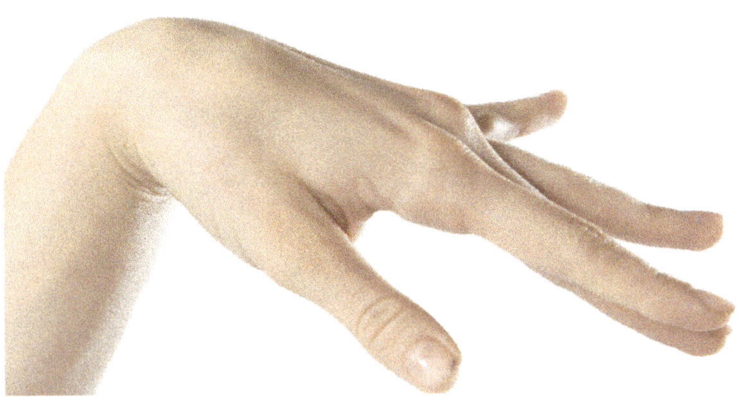

STEP 1

Draw lines for the bones of the hand. Draw lines for the fingers and circle the joints of the fingers.

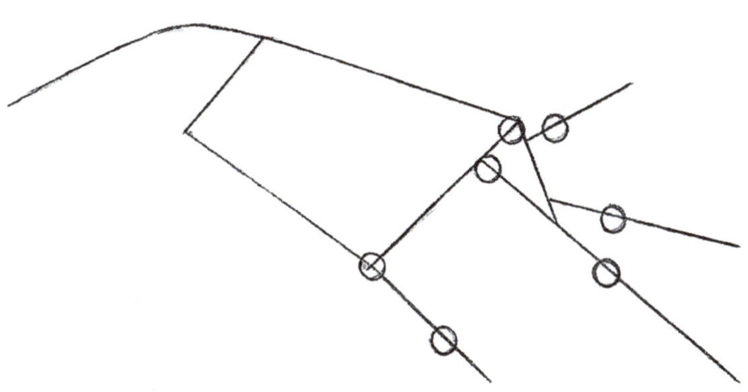

PRACTICE

YOUR WORK

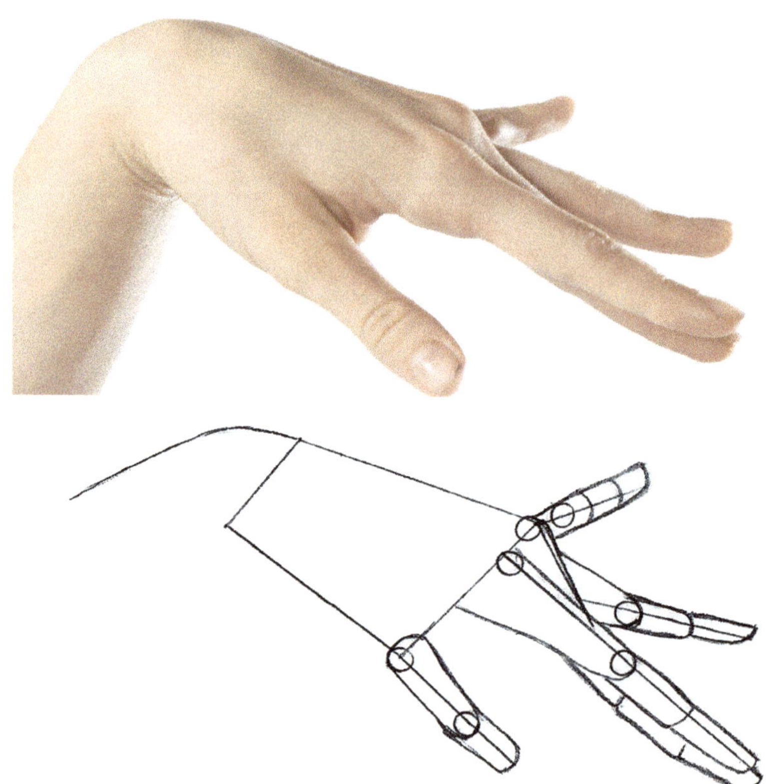

STEP 2

Draw in the shape of the hand and fingers using geometric shapes.

PRACTICE

YOUR WORK

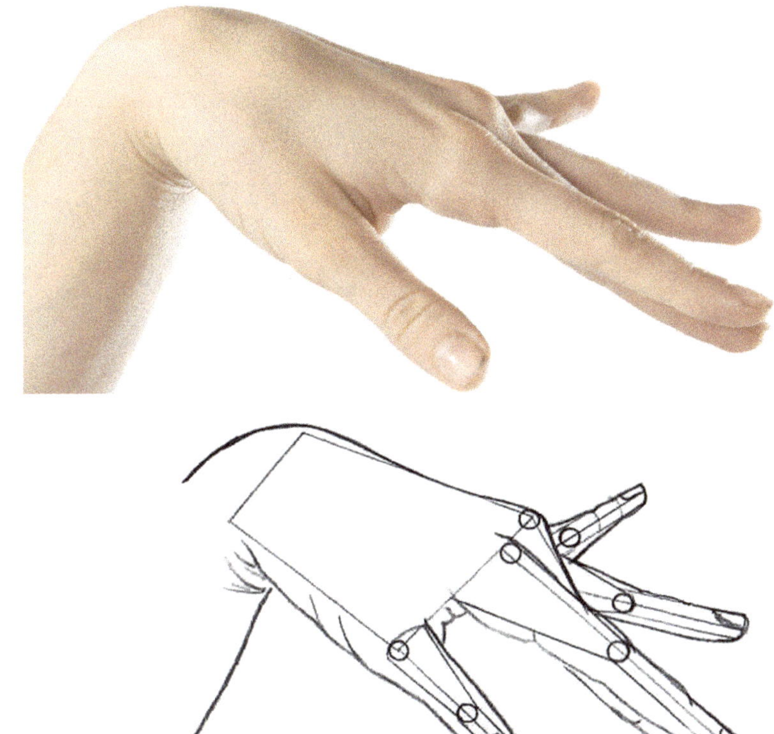

STEP 3

Draw the outline of the hand and fingers using the basic shapes as your guide.

PRACTICE

YOUR WORK

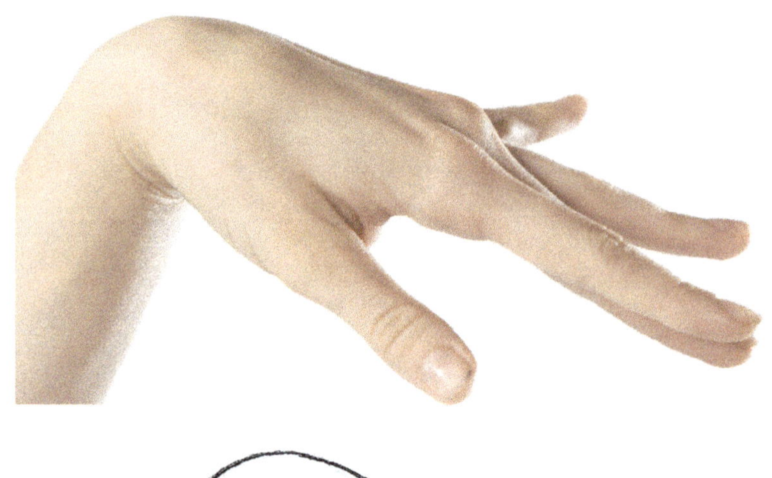

STEP 4

Draw in the details of the skin, nails and bone definition. Erase the geometric lines.

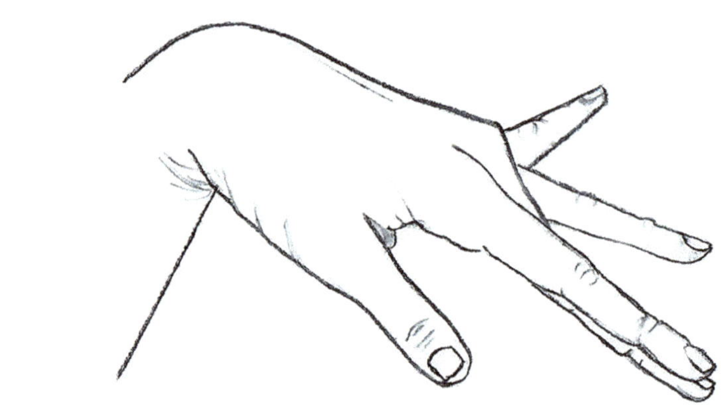

PRACTICE

YOUR WORK

POSE 2

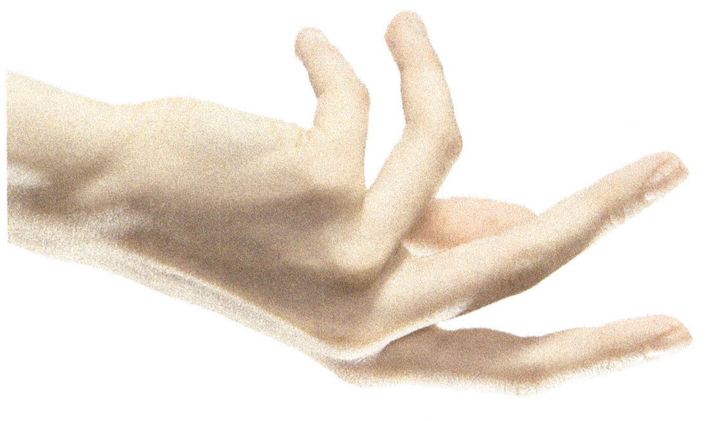

STEP 1

Draw lines for
the bones of
the hand. Draw
lines for the
fingers and
circle the joints
of the fingers.

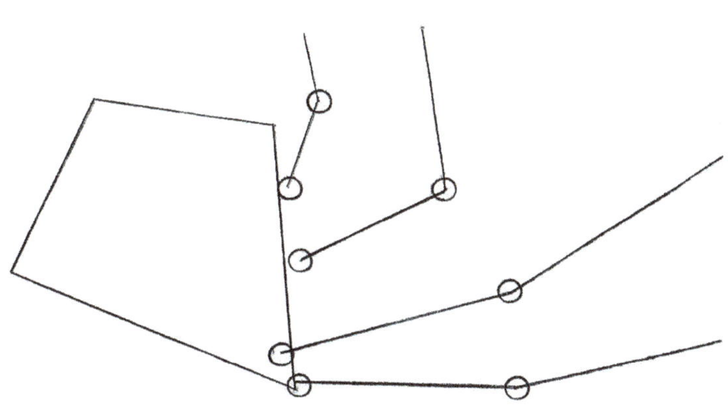

PRACTICE

YOUR WORK

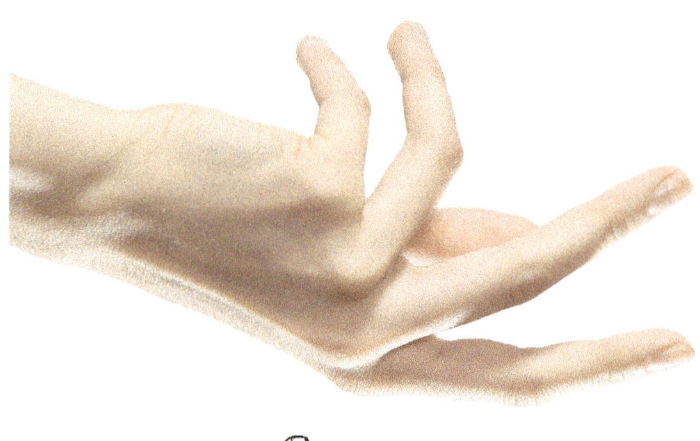

STEP 2

Draw in the shape of the hand and fingers using geometric shapes.

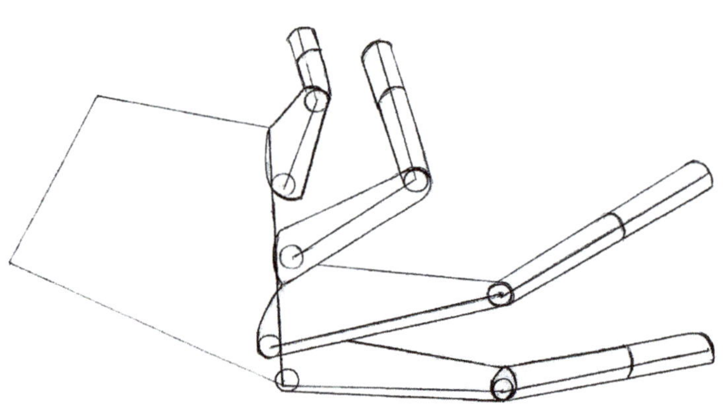

PRACTICE

YOUR WORK

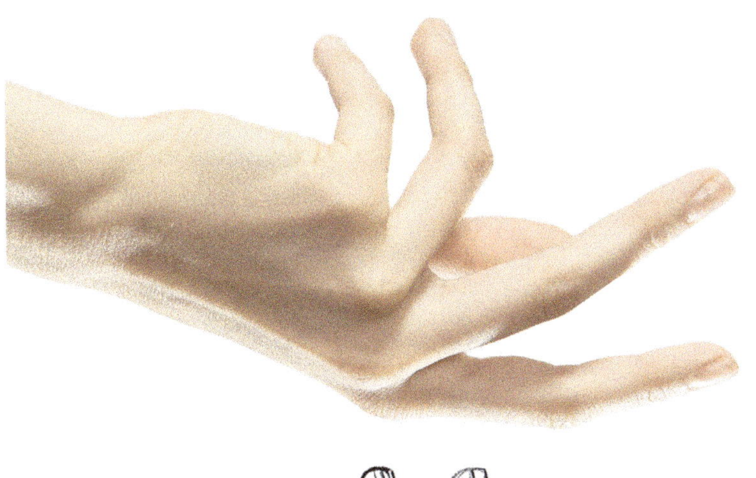

STEP 3

Draw the outline of the hand and fingers using the basic shapes as your guide.

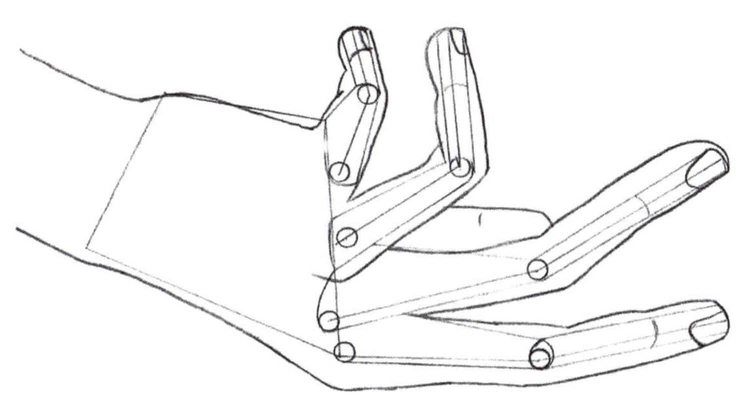

PRACTICE
YOUR WORK

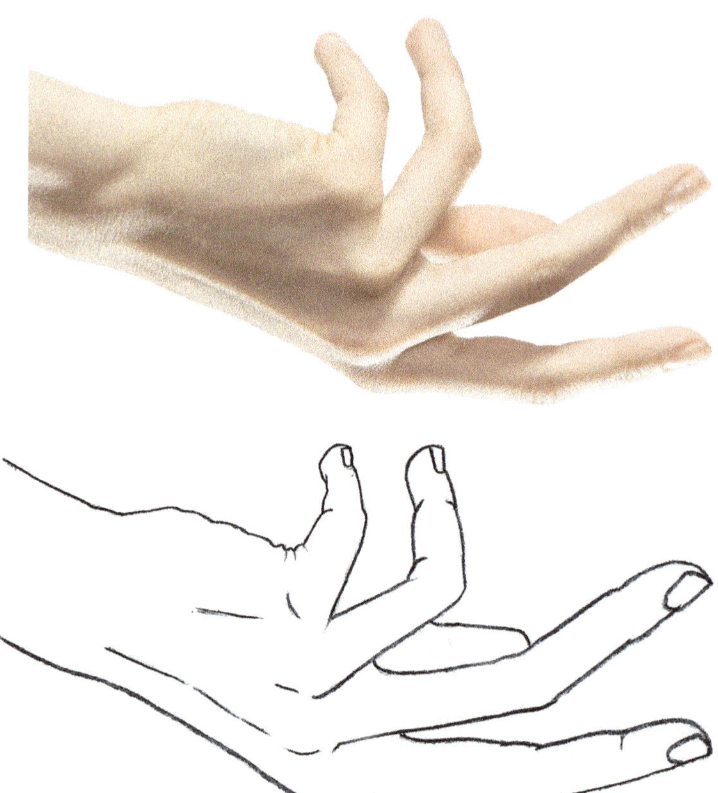

STEP 4

Draw in the
details of the
skin, nails and
bone definition.
Erase the
geometric lines.

PRACTICE

YOUR WORK

POSE 3

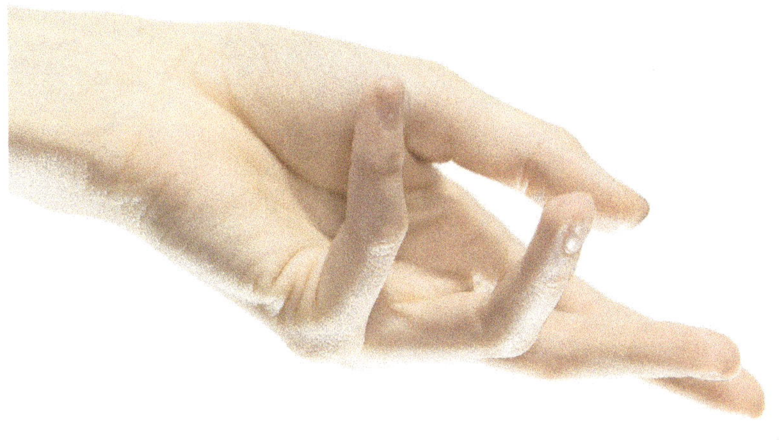

STEP 1

Draw lines for the bones of the hand. Draw lines for the fingers and circle the joints of the fingers.

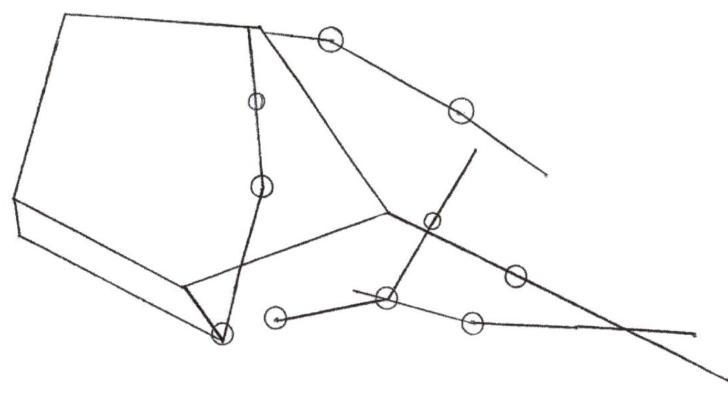

PRACTICE

YOUR WORK

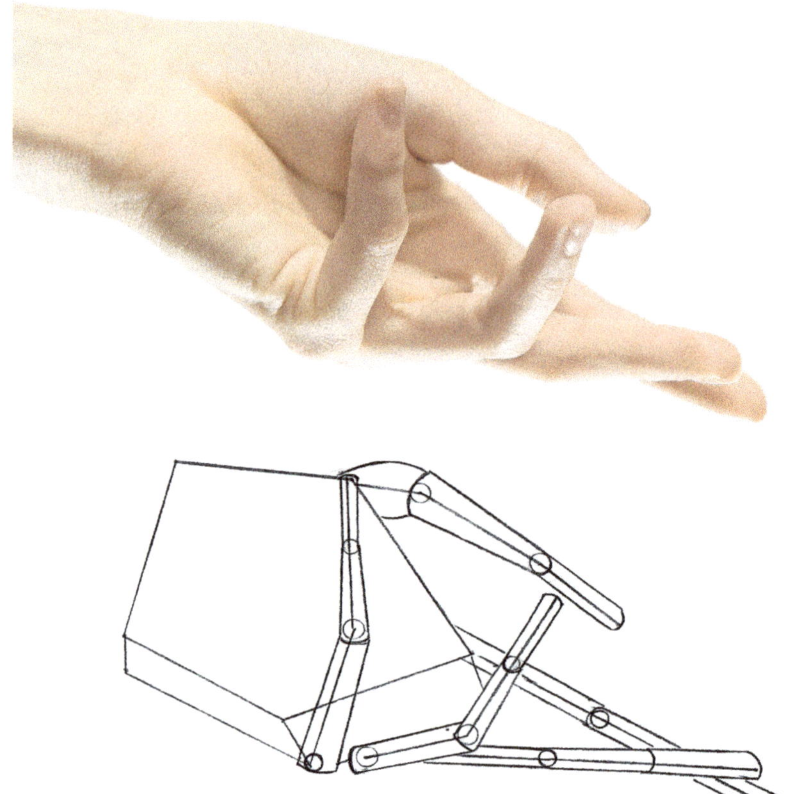

Step 2

Draw in the shape of the hand and fingers using geometric shapes.

Practice

your work

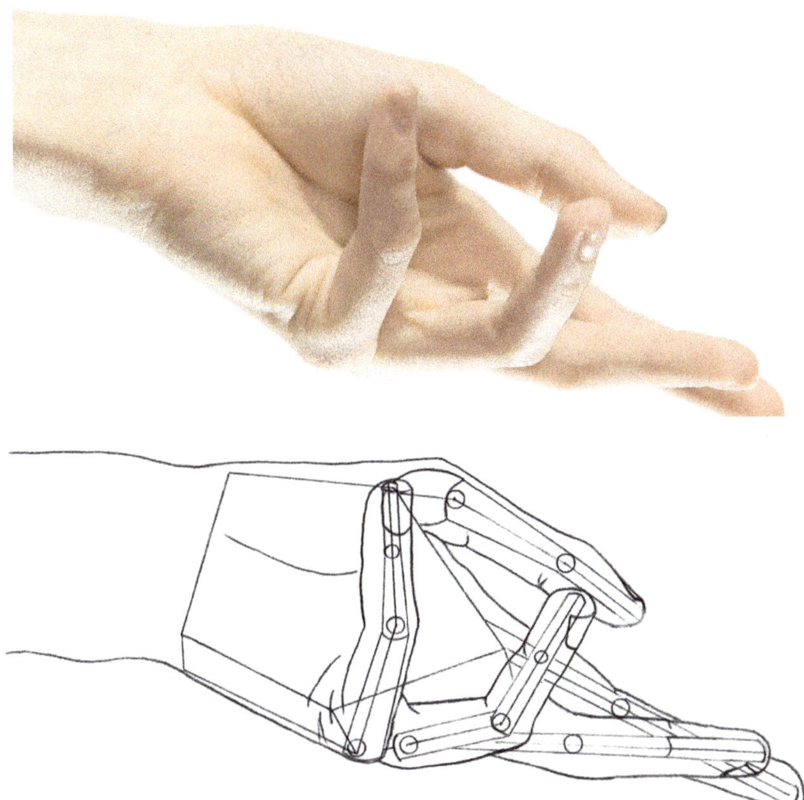

STEP 3
Draw the outline of the hand and fingers using the basic shapes as your guide.

PRACTICE
YOUR WORK

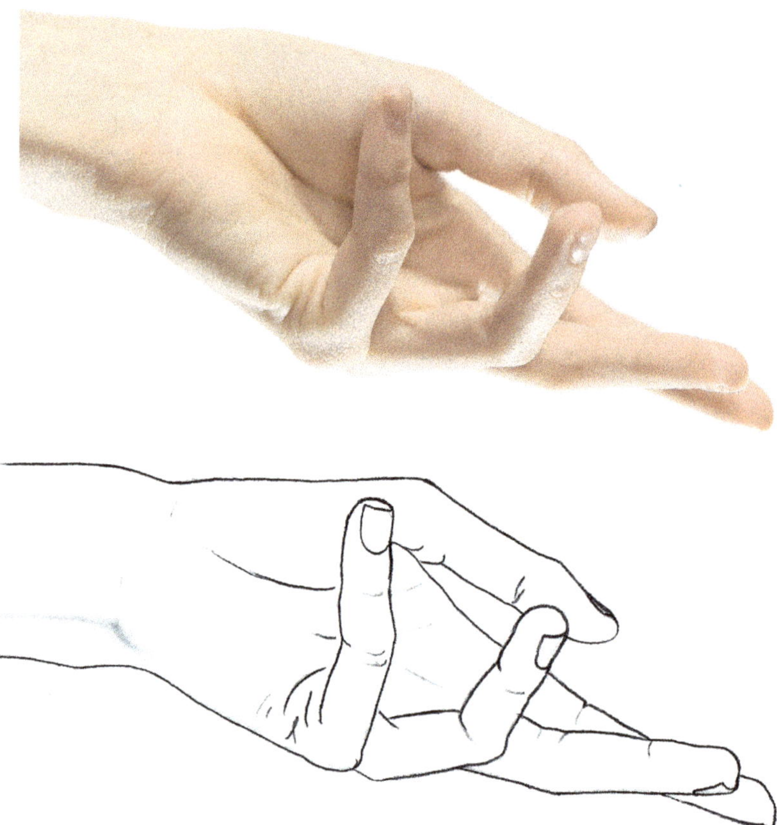

STEP 4

Draw in the
details of the
skin, nails and
bone definition.
Erase the
geometric lines.

PRACTICE

YOUR WORK

PRACTICE POSES

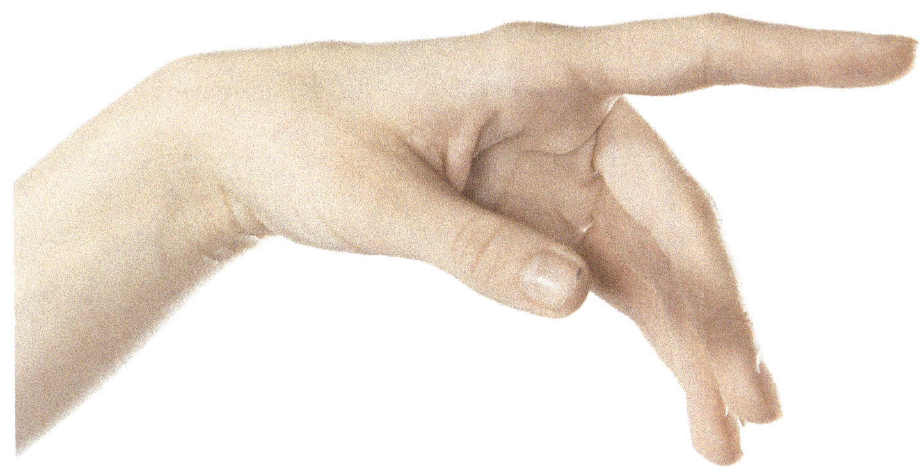

PRACTICE
YOUR WORK

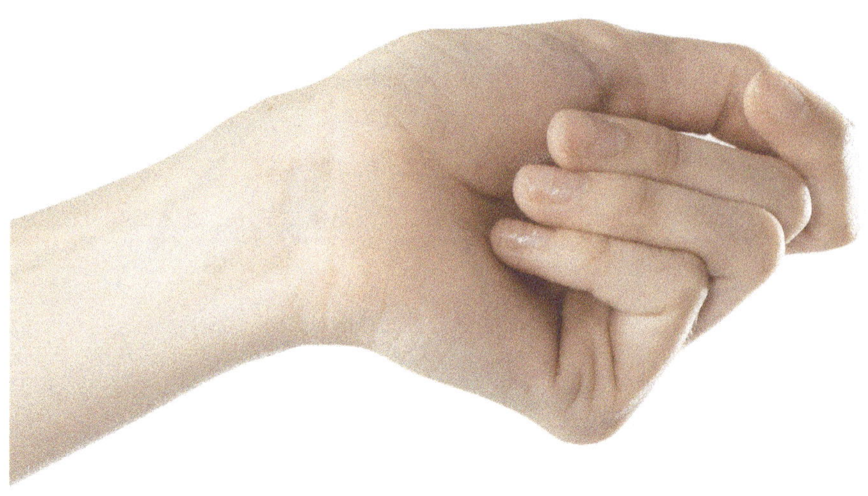

PRACTICE
YOUR WORK

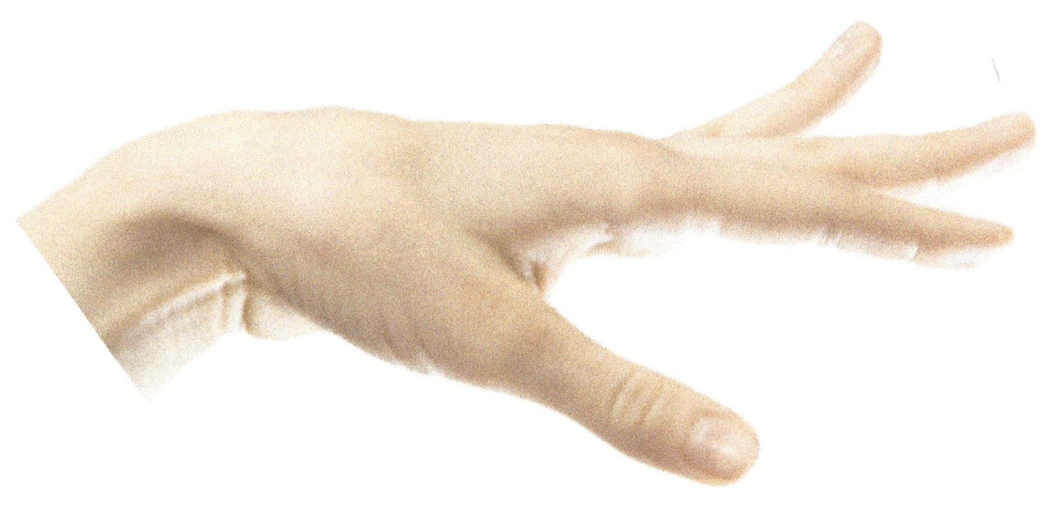

PRACTICE
YOUR WORK

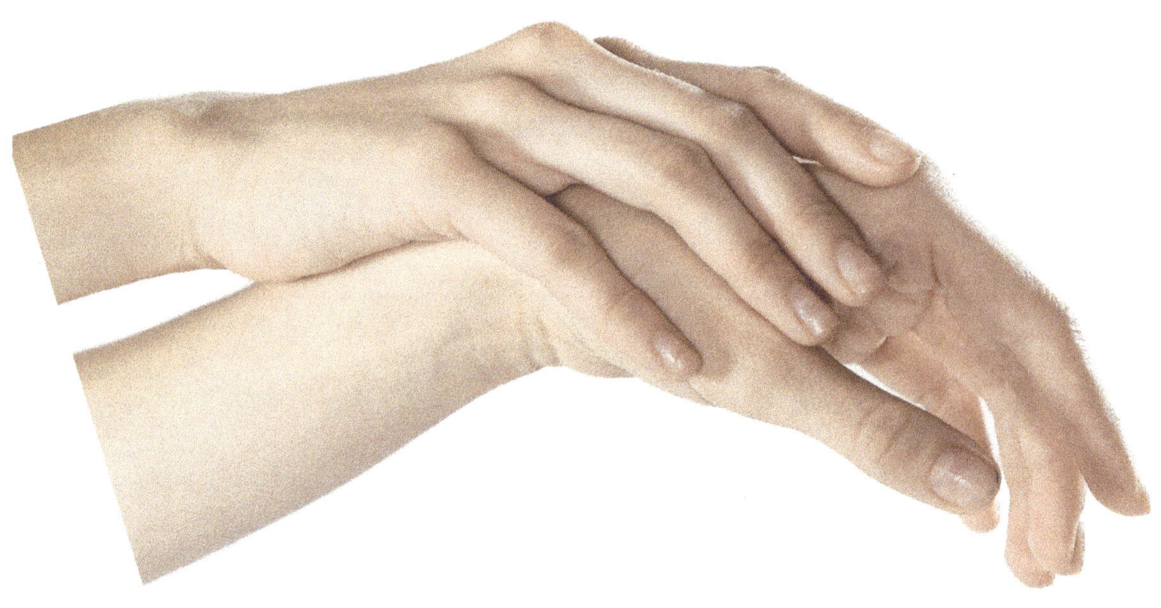

Practice
your work

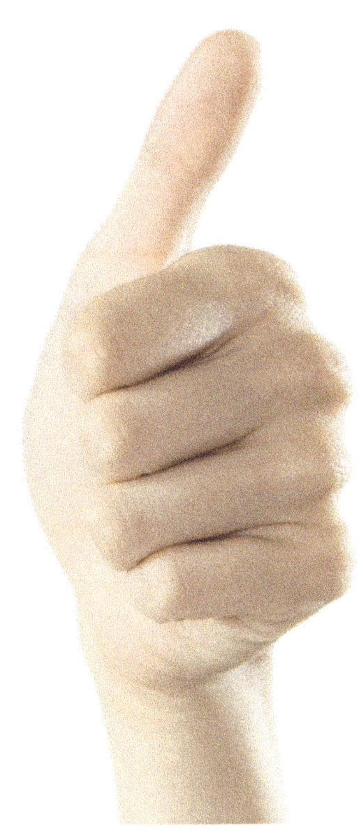

PRACTICE
YOUR WORK

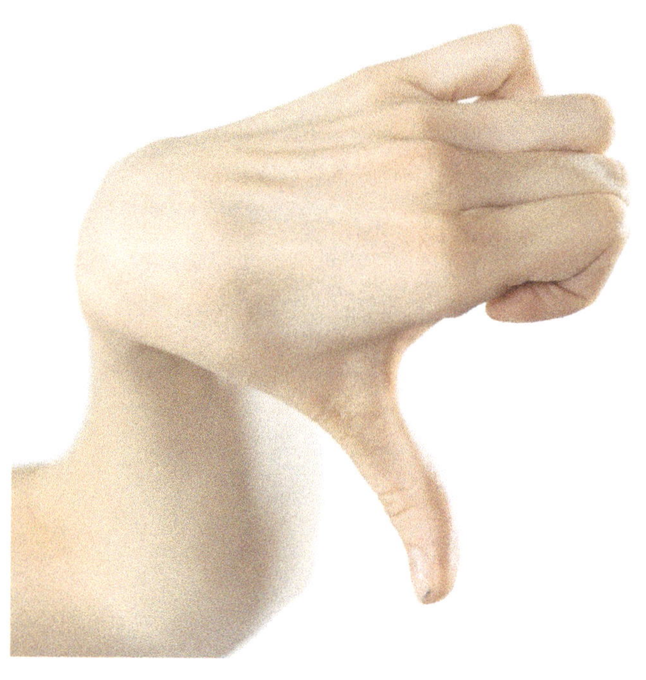

PRACTICE
YOUR WORK

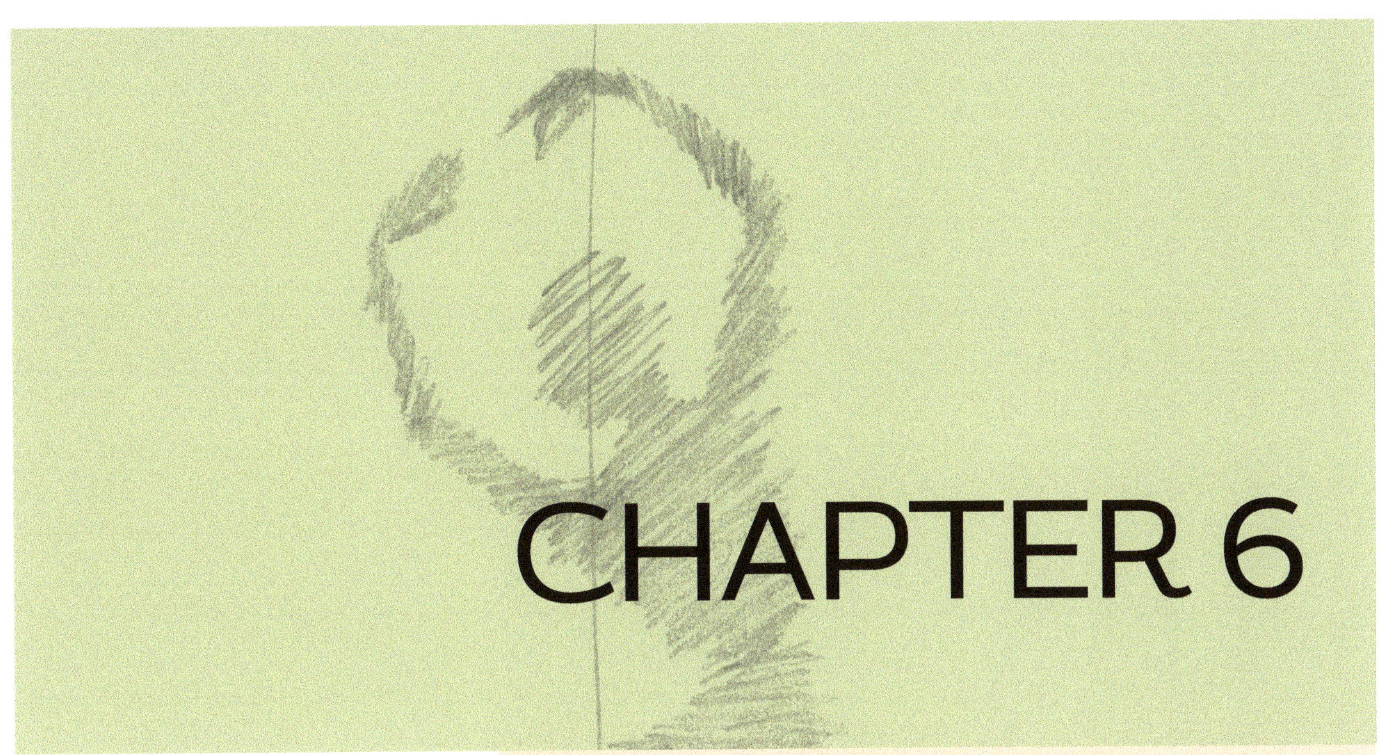

CHAPTER 6

Feet Poses

FEET POSES

Illustrating the feet are not always required for fashion illustration, as most feet are depicted with shoes. The following exercises demonstrate three separate foot poses to assist in the transition of the angles and perspective to the foot in general.

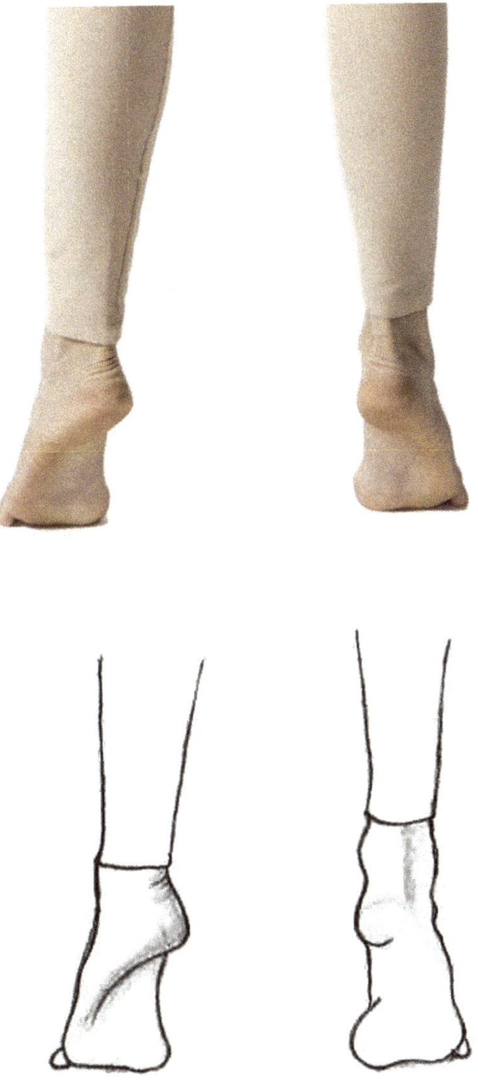

POSE 1

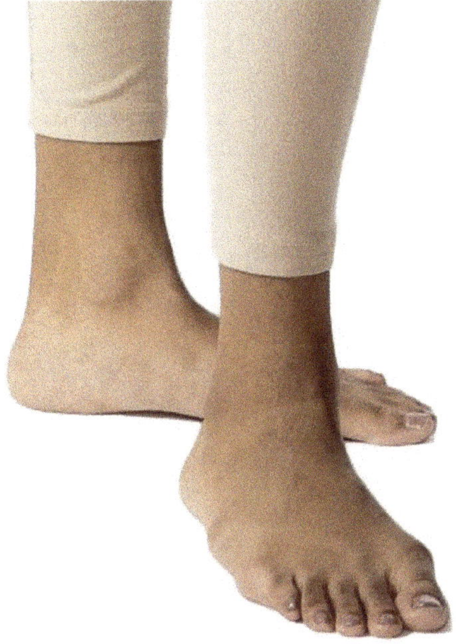

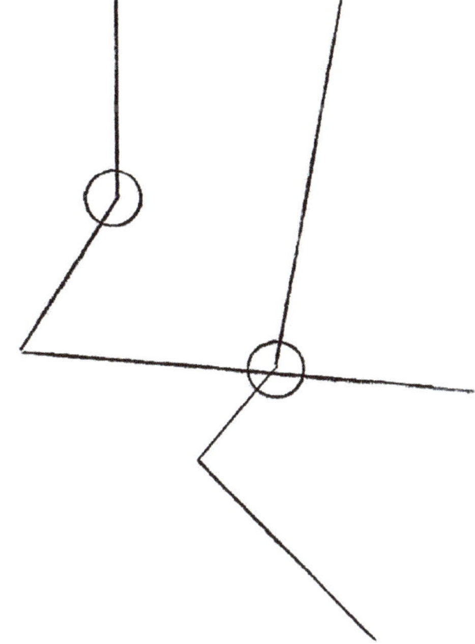

STEP 1

Draw the basic shape of the lower leg and foot.
Circle the joint of the ankle.

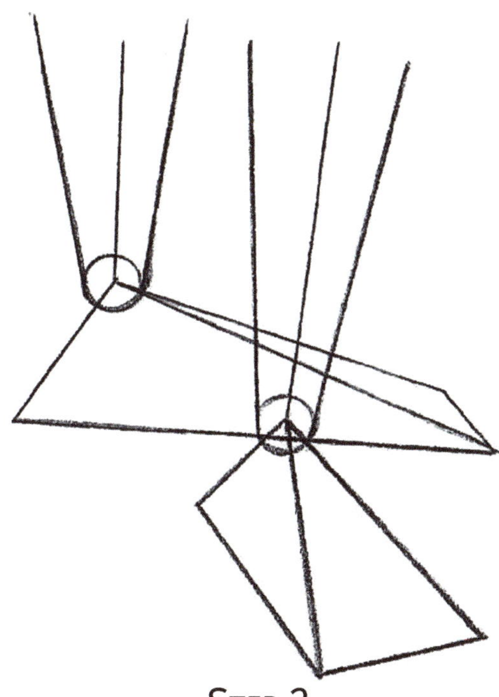

STEP 2

Draw in the shape of the legs and feet using
geometric shapes.

PRACTICE YOUR WORK

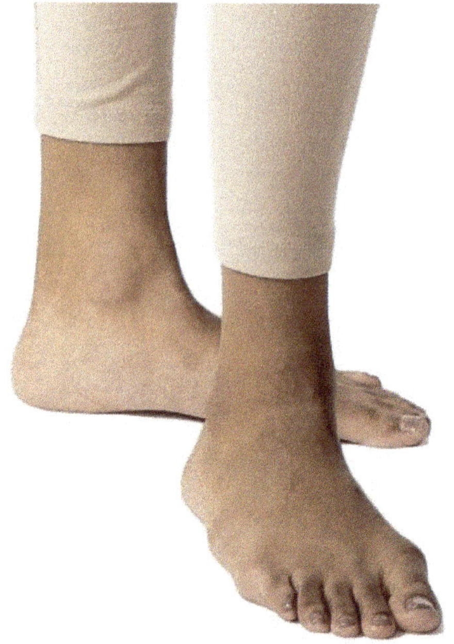

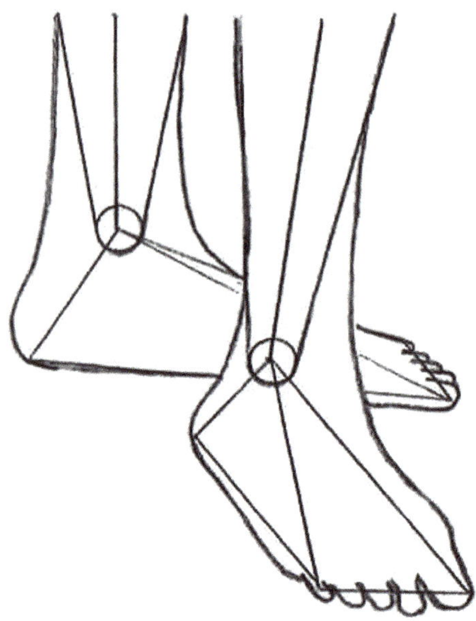

STEP 3

Draw the skin outline using the basic geometric shapes as a guide.

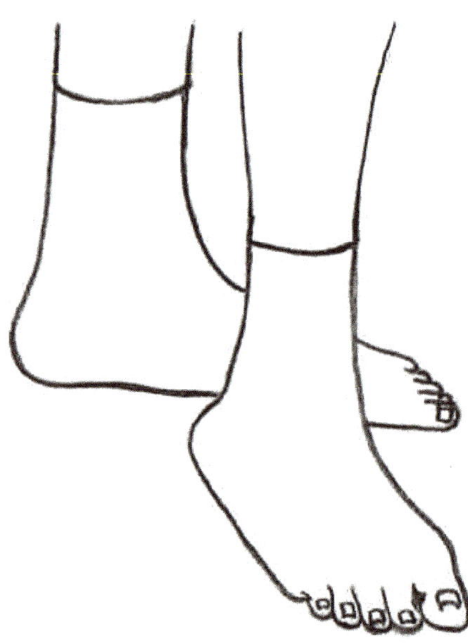

STEP 4

Draw in the details of the nails and skin. Erase the geometric lines.

PRACTICE YOUR WORK

POSE 2

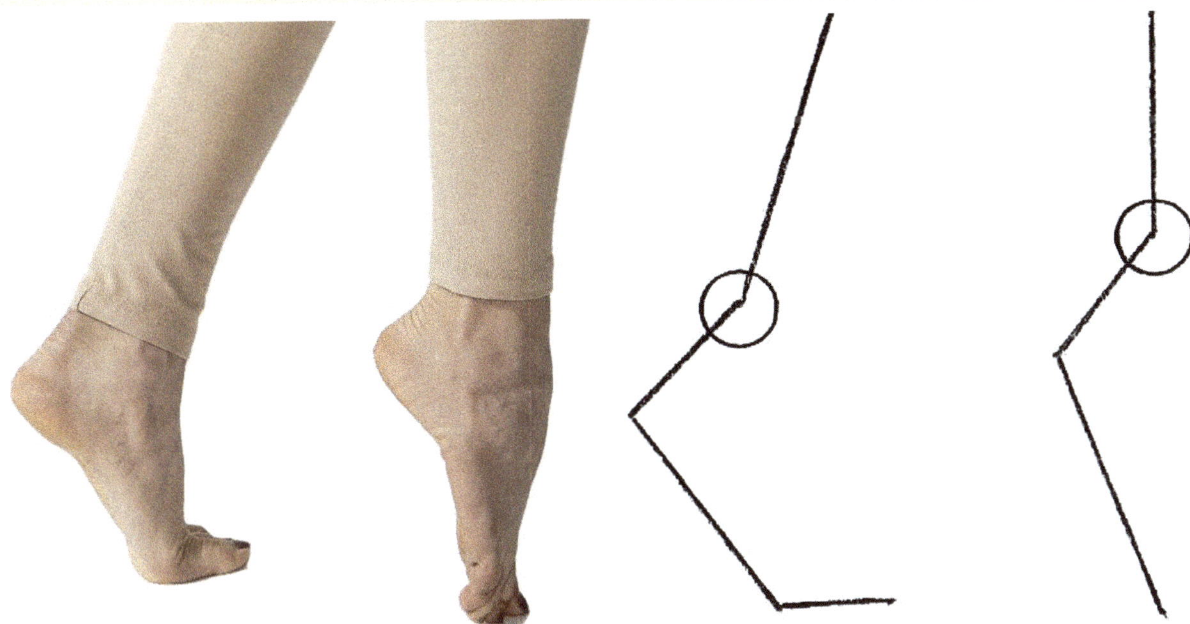

STEP 1
Draw the basic shape of the lower leg and foot.
Circle the joint of the ankle.

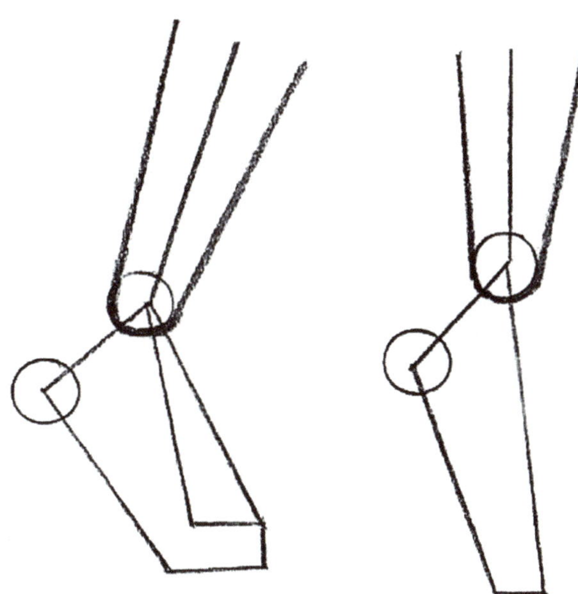

STEP 2
Draw in the shape of the legs and feet using
geometric shapes.

PRACTICE YOUR WORK

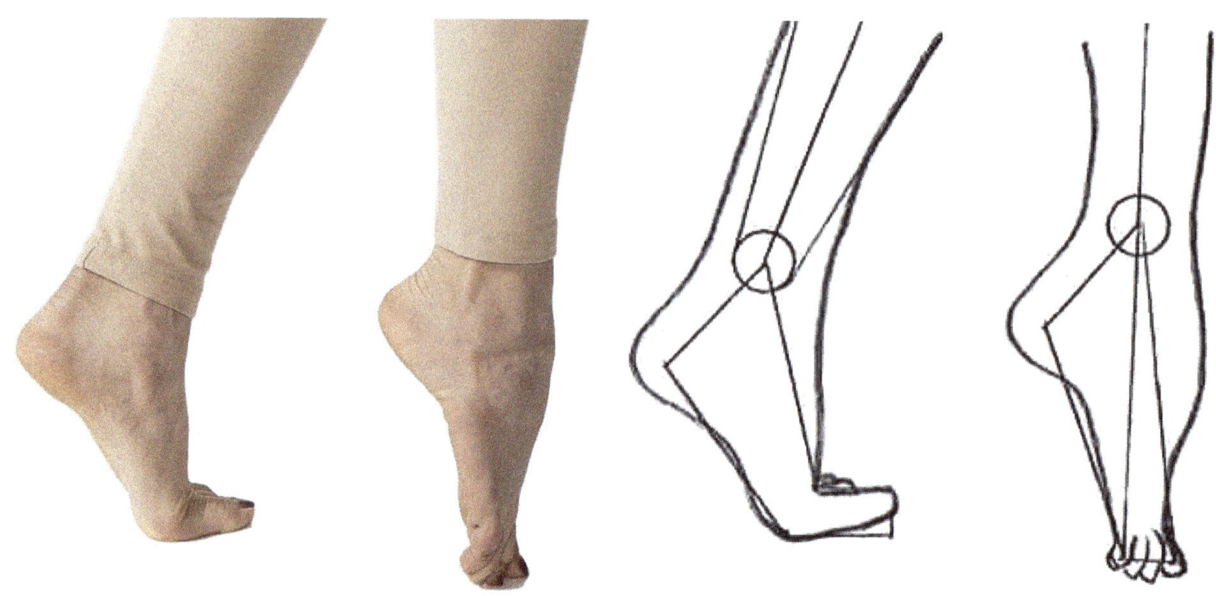

STEP 3

Draw the skin outline using the basic
geometric shapes as a guide.

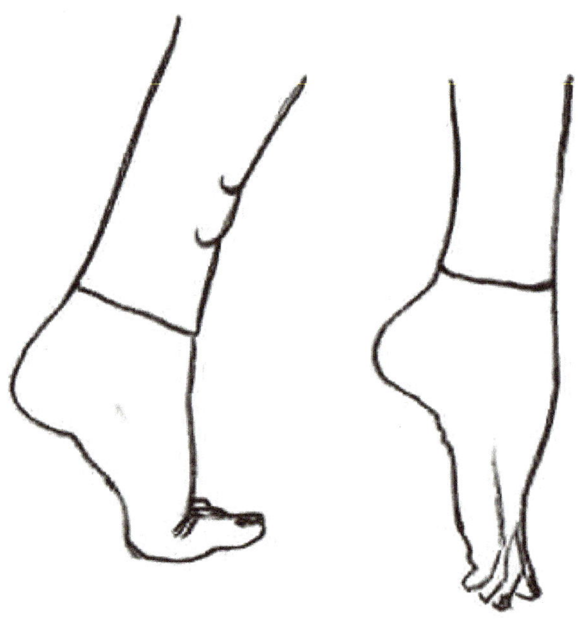

STEP 4

Draw in the details of the nails and skin.
Erase the geometric lines.

PRACTICE YOUR WORK

POSE 3

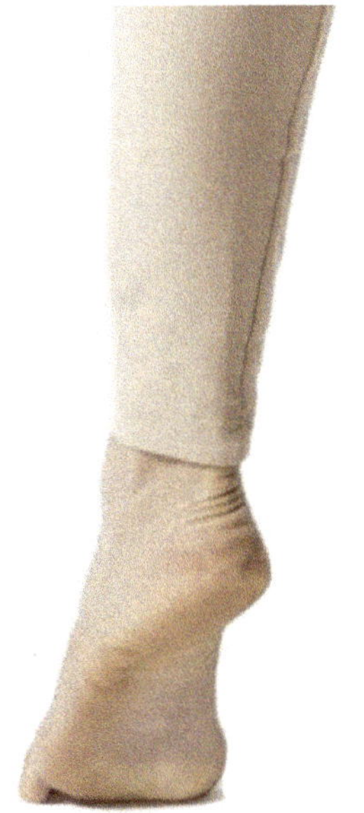
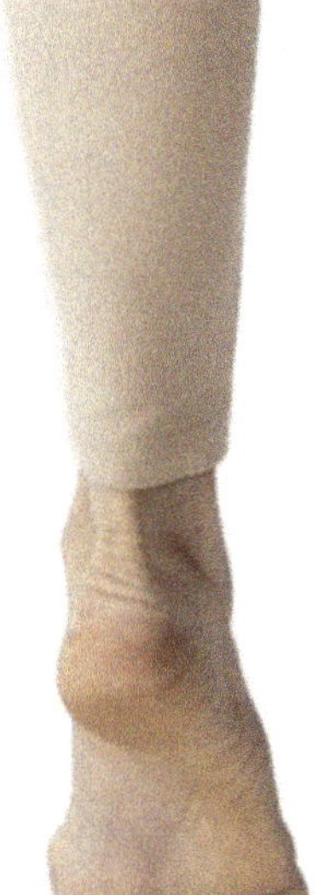
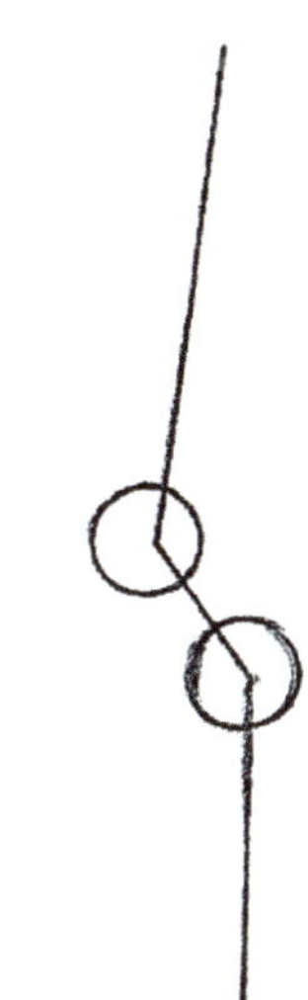
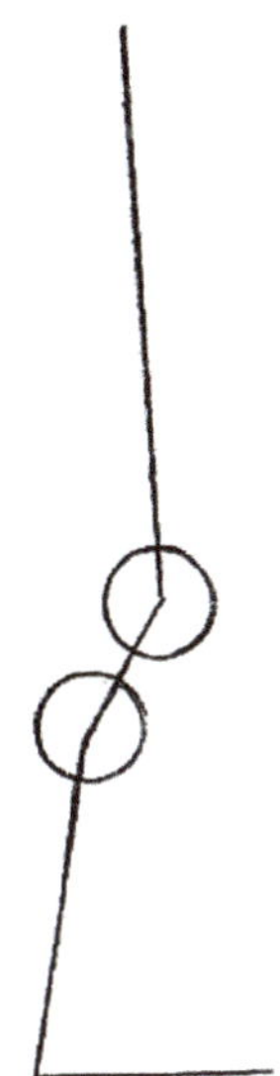

STEP 1

Draw the basic shape of the lower leg and foot. Circle the joint of the ankle.

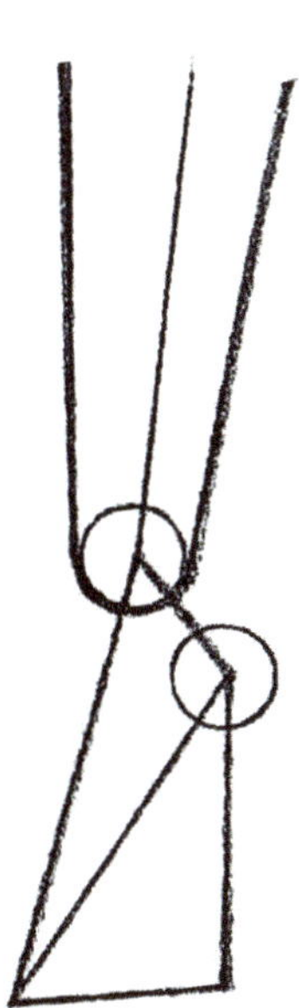
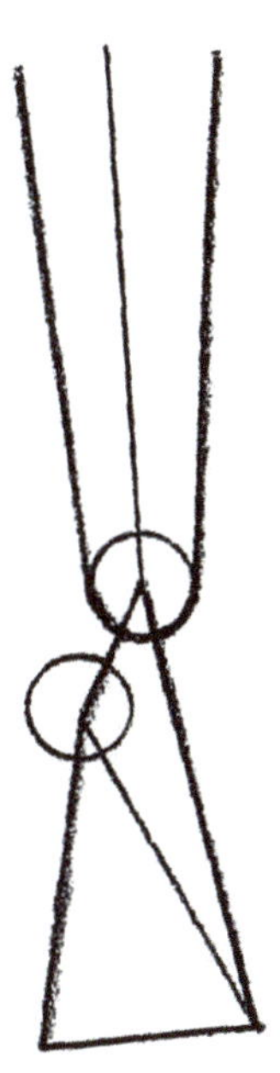

STEP 2

Draw in the shape of the legs and feet using geometric shapes.

PRACTICE YOUR WORK

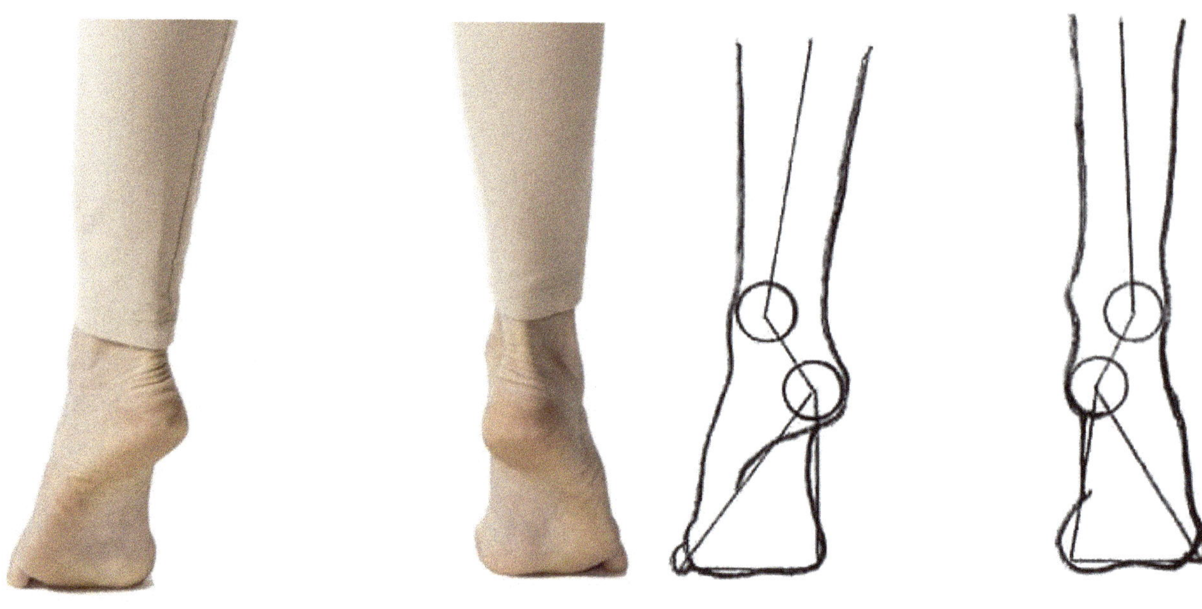

STEP 3

Draw the skin outline using the basic
geometric shapes as a guide.

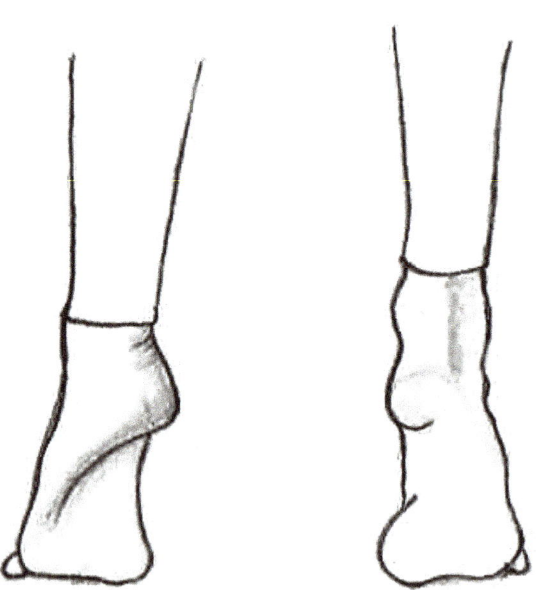

STEP 4

Draw in the details of the nails and skin.
Erase the geometric lines.

PRACTICE YOUR WORK

PRACTICE POSES

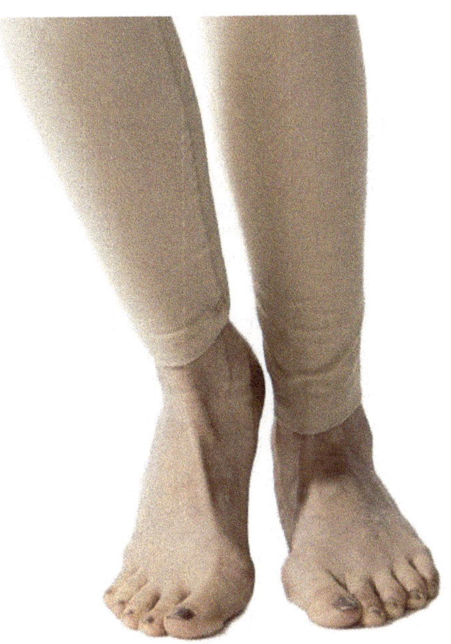

PRACTICE YOUR WORK

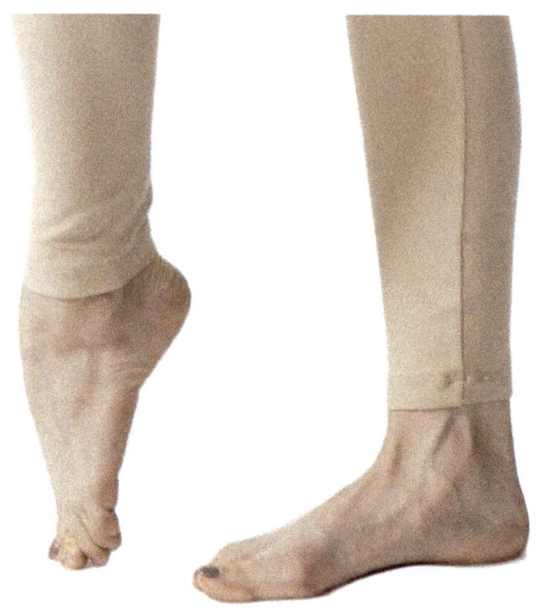

PRACTICE YOUR WORK

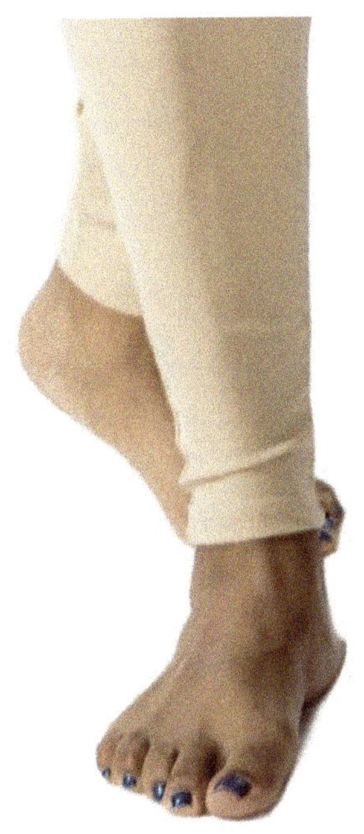

PRACTICE YOUR WORK

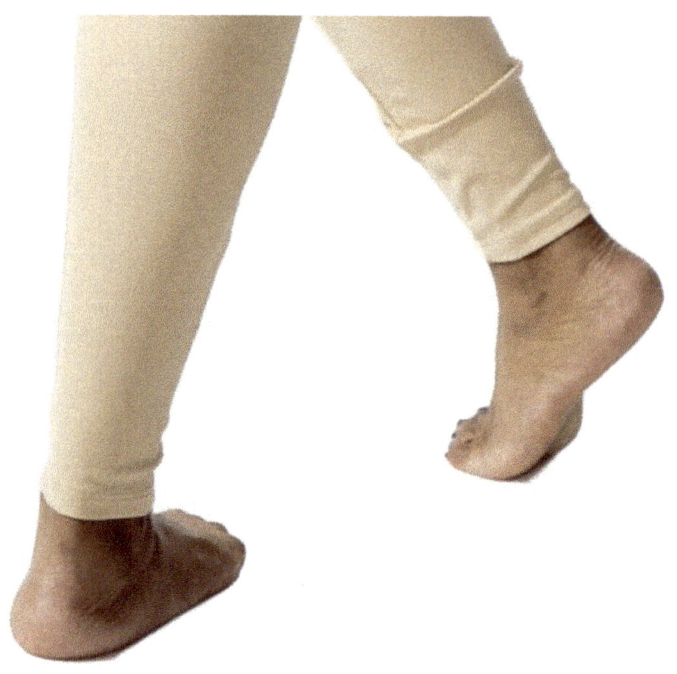

PRACTICE YOUR WORK

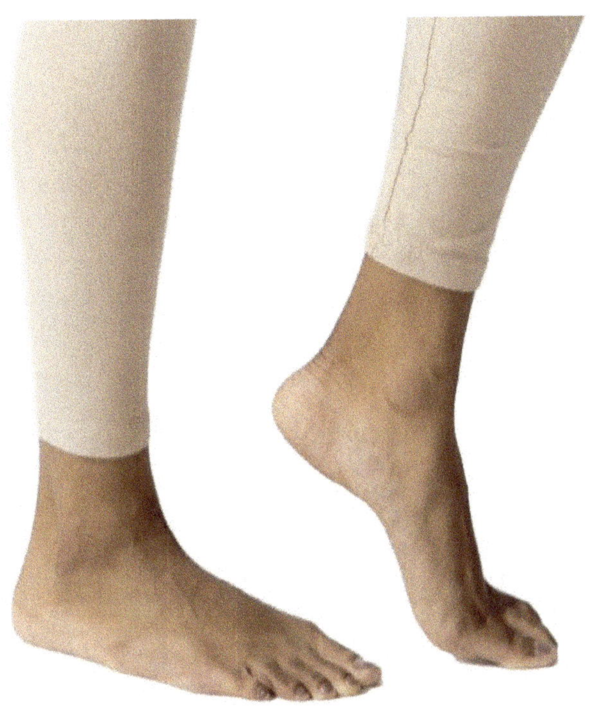

PRACTICE YOUR WORK

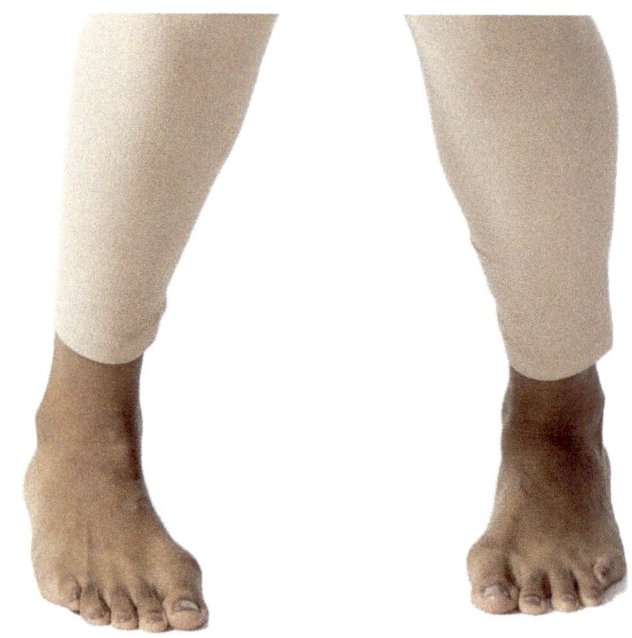

PRACTICE YOUR WORK

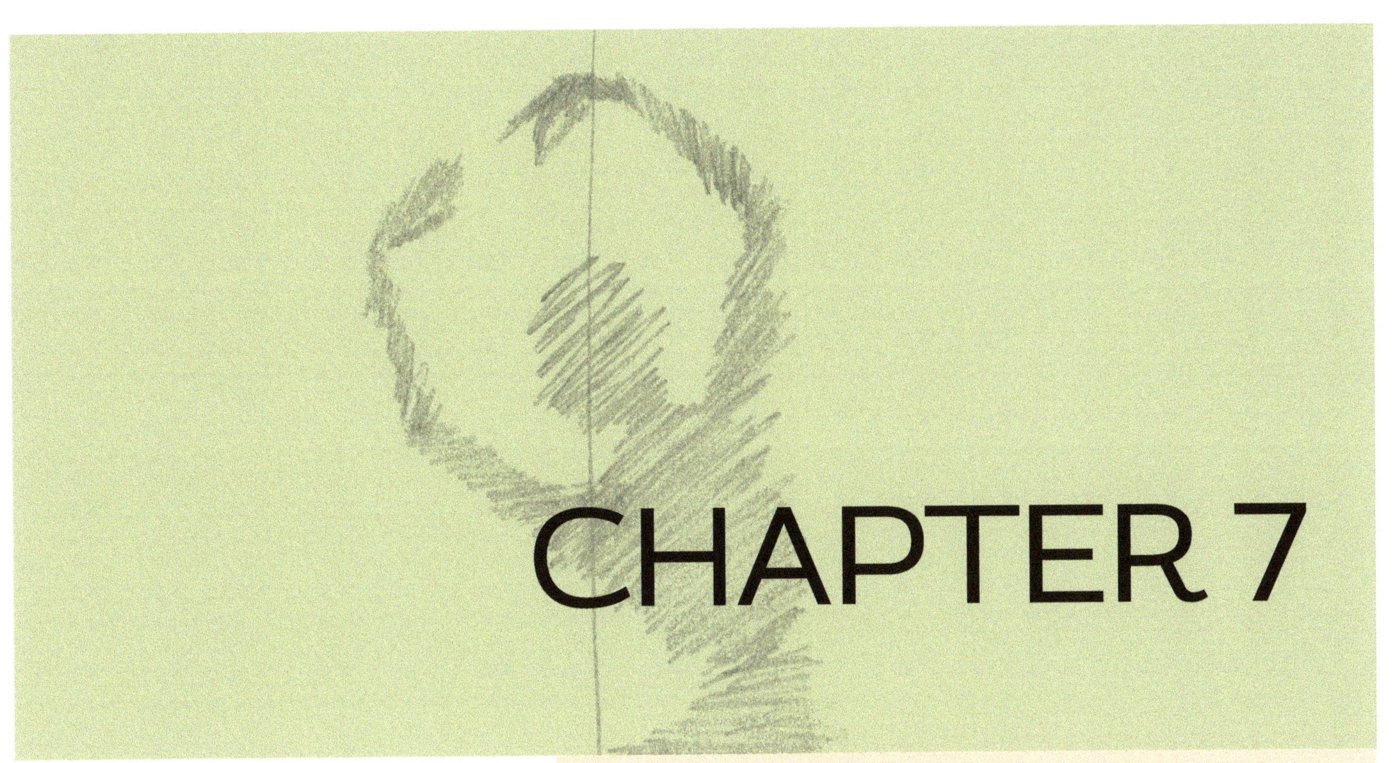

CHAPTER 7

Head Poses

FRONT HEAD VIEW

In this chapter, four views of the head are demonstrated, utilizing each of our model's unique looks and features. This first exercise illustrates the front view of the face. This demonstrates the basic proportions of drawing a face.

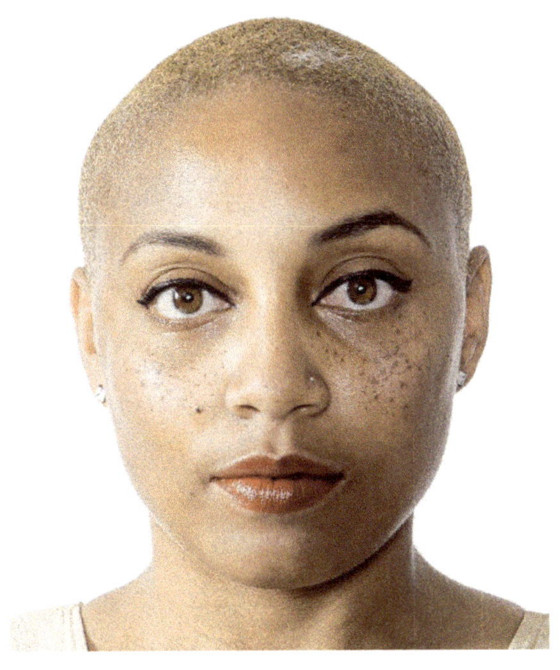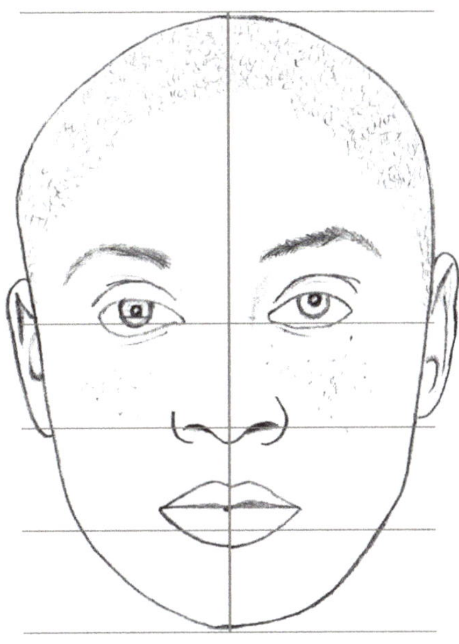

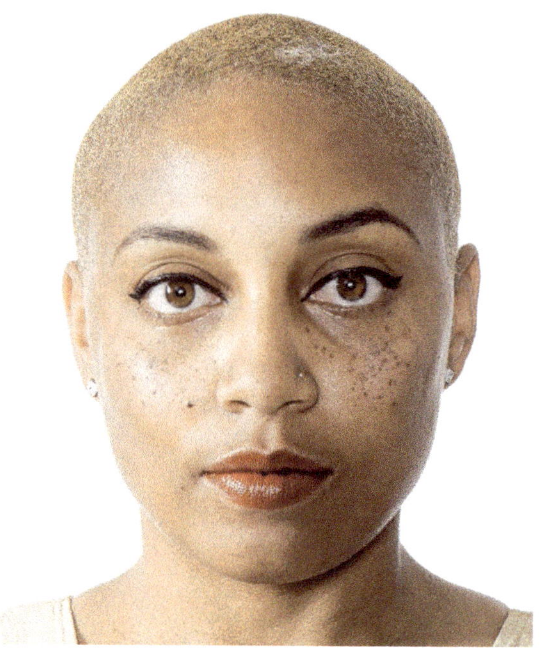

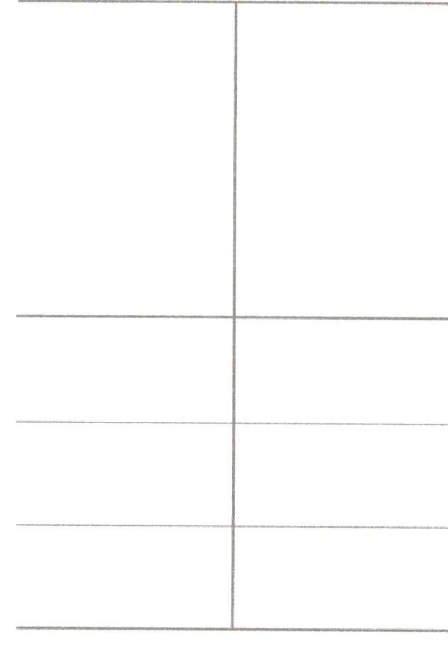

STEP 1
Draw a vertical line. Mark the
top, bottom and center with
perpendicular lines. Split the
lower portion into 3 equal spaces
with two additional lines.

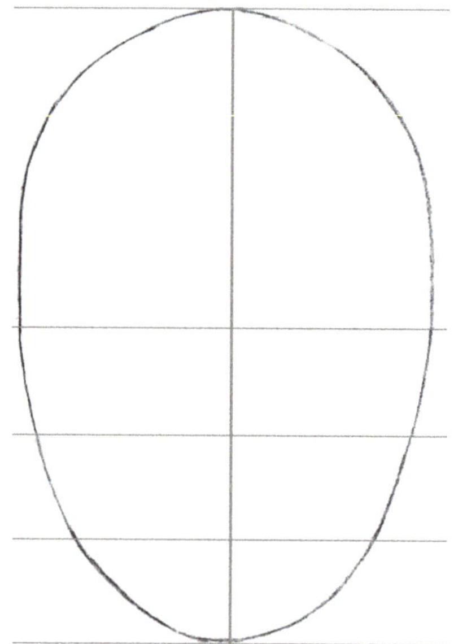

STEP 2
Draw an oval shape for the head
centered on the grid.

PRACTICE YOUR WORK

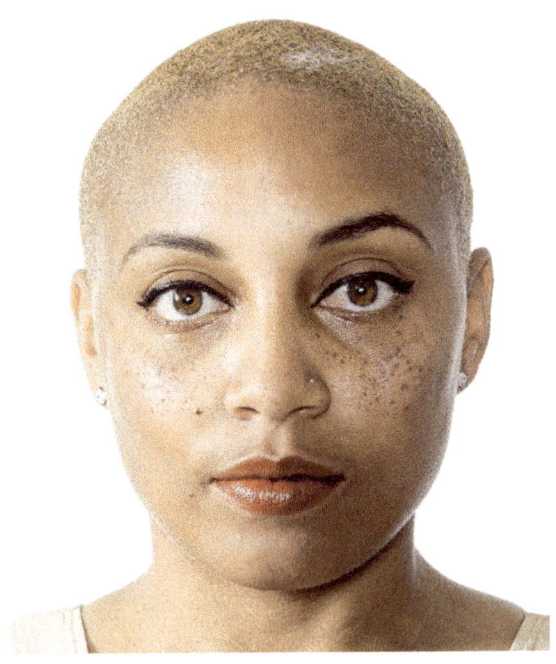

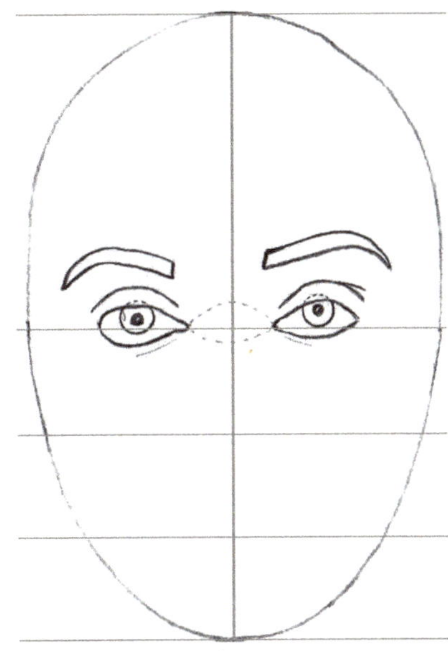

STEP 3

Draw in eyes on the center line with an eye space between each eye. Draw in the eyebrows and eyelids.

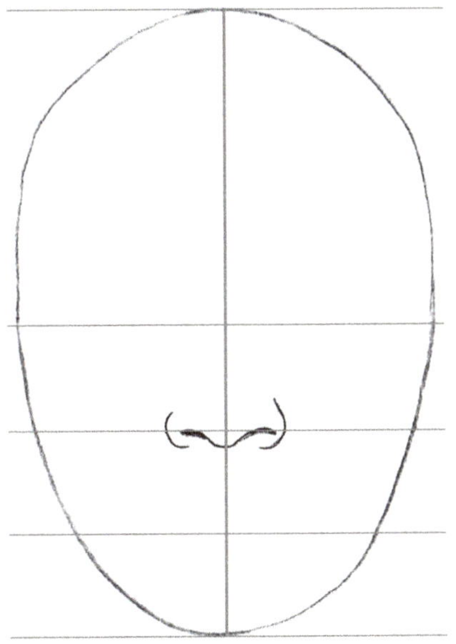

STEP 4

Draw the nose on the line below the eyes.

PRACTICE YOUR WORK

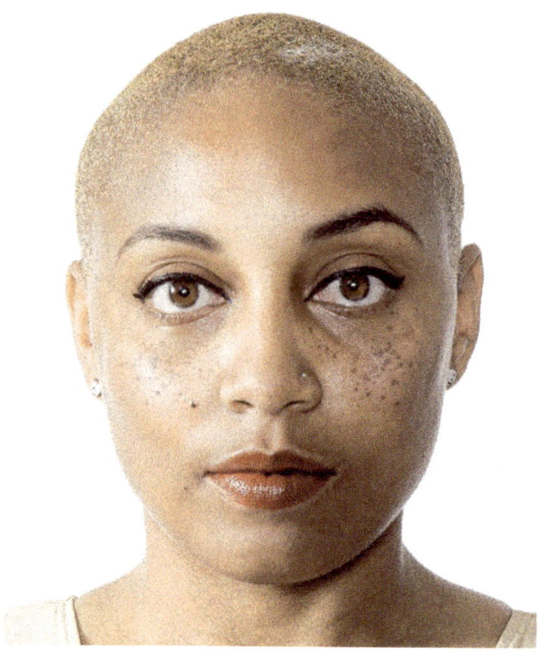

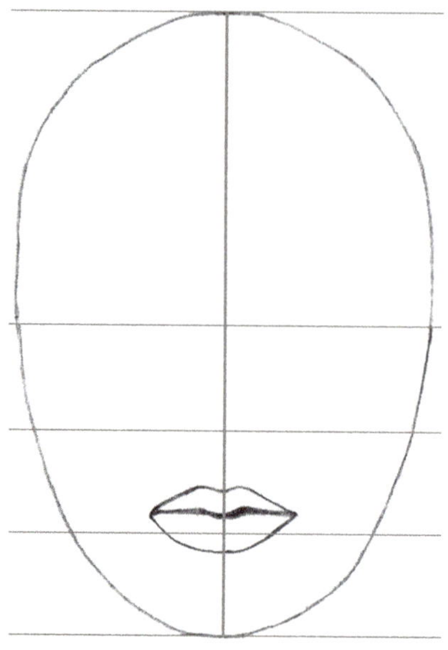

Step 5

Draw in the lips slightly above
the line below the nose.

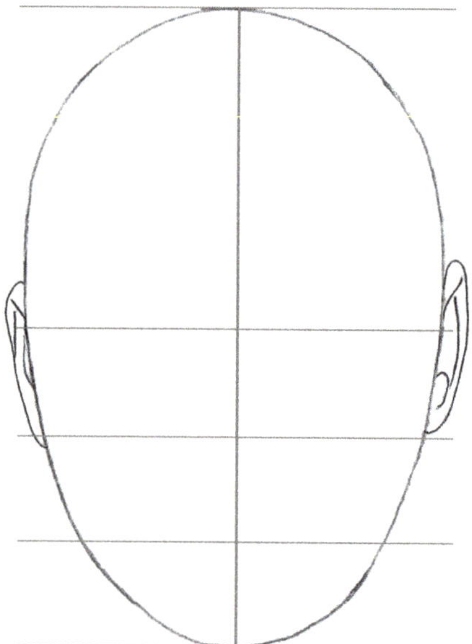

Step 6

Draw in the ears in the center.
*Note: The ears line up in height
to the eyelids.*

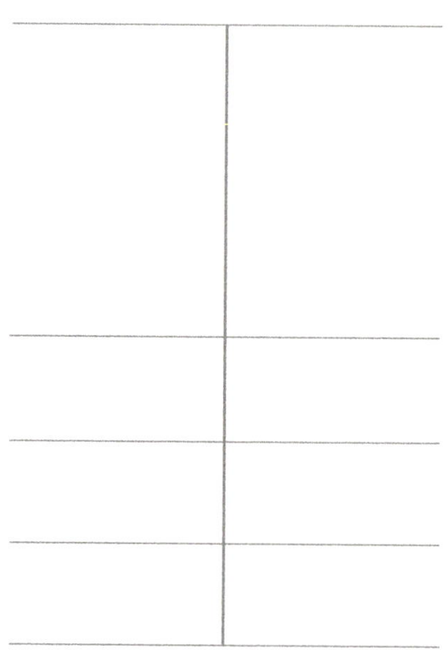

Practice Your Work

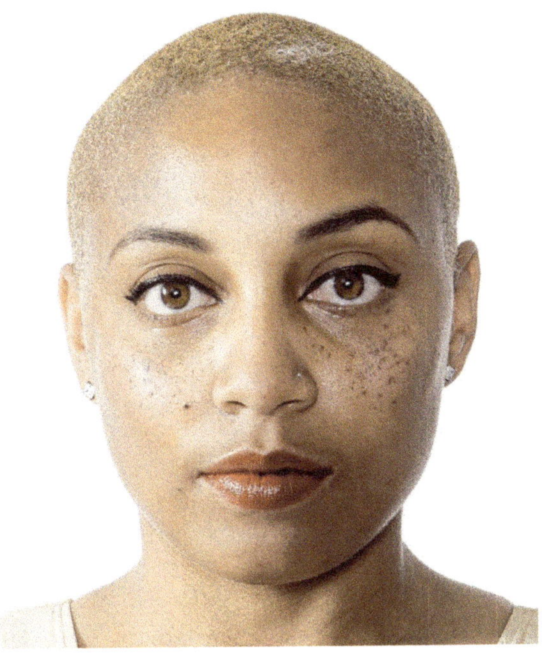

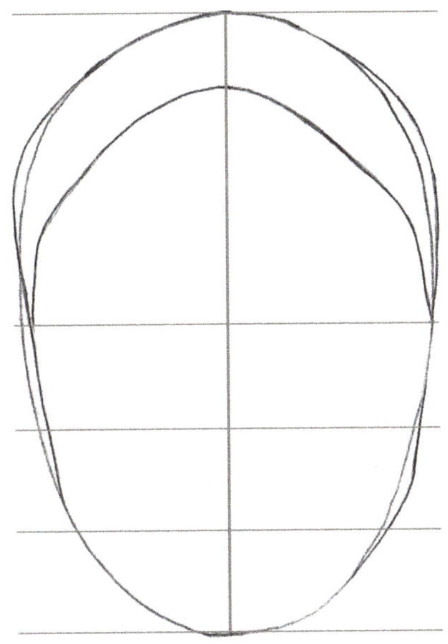

STEP 7

Draw in the hair line and structure
of the face.

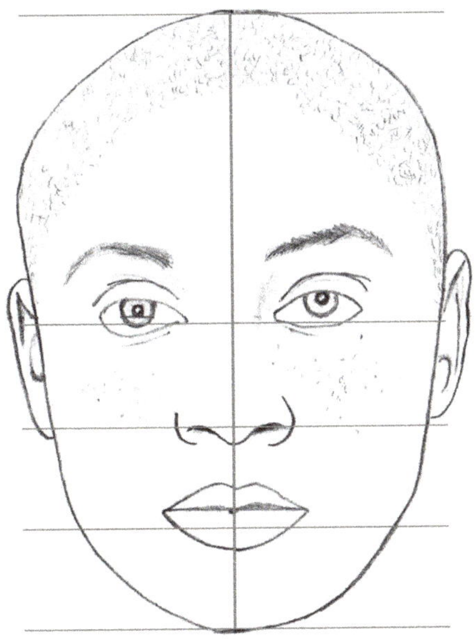

STEP 8

Draw in finishing details of shading,
hair, freckles and makeup.

PRACTICE YOUR WORK

PRACTICE YOUR WORK

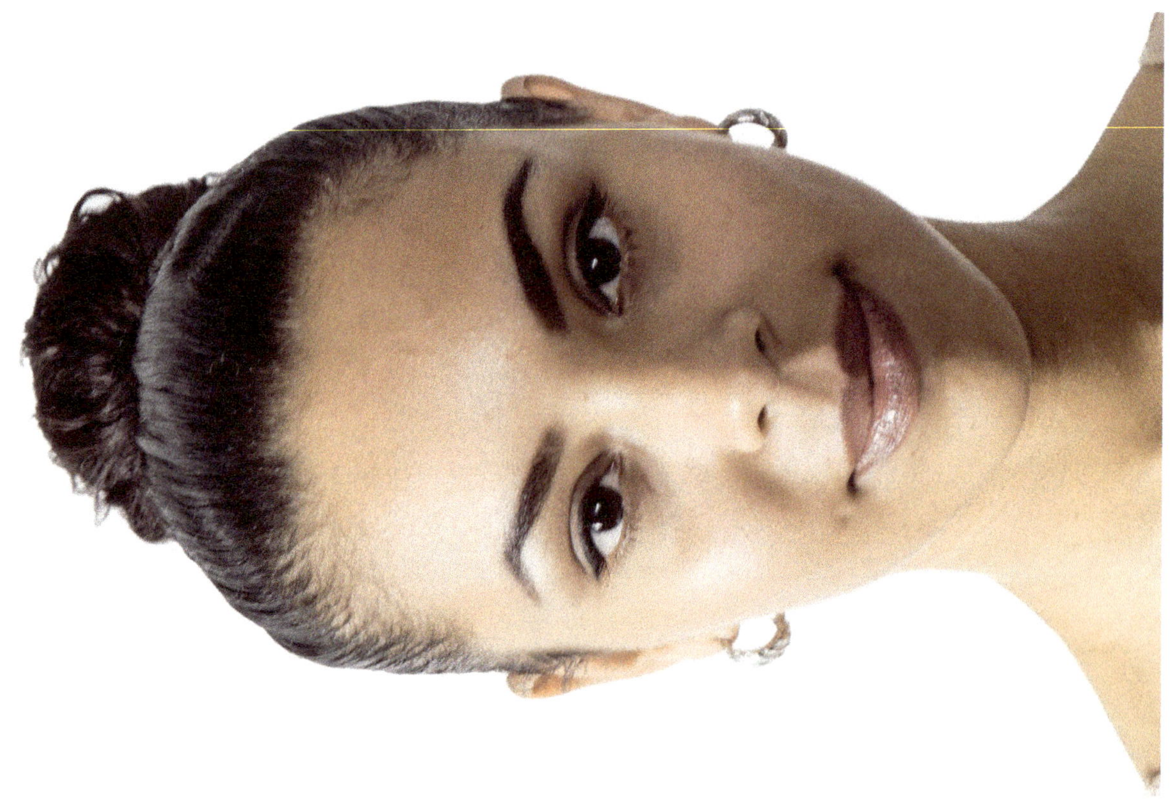

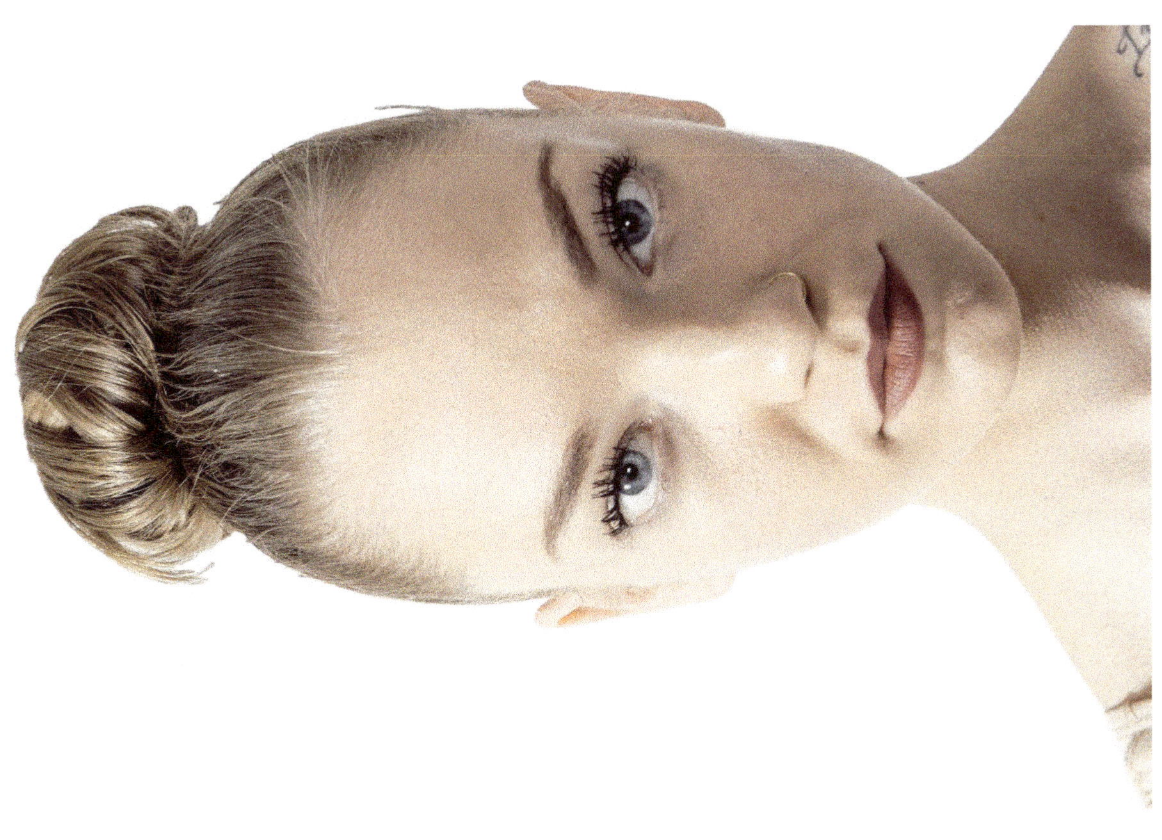

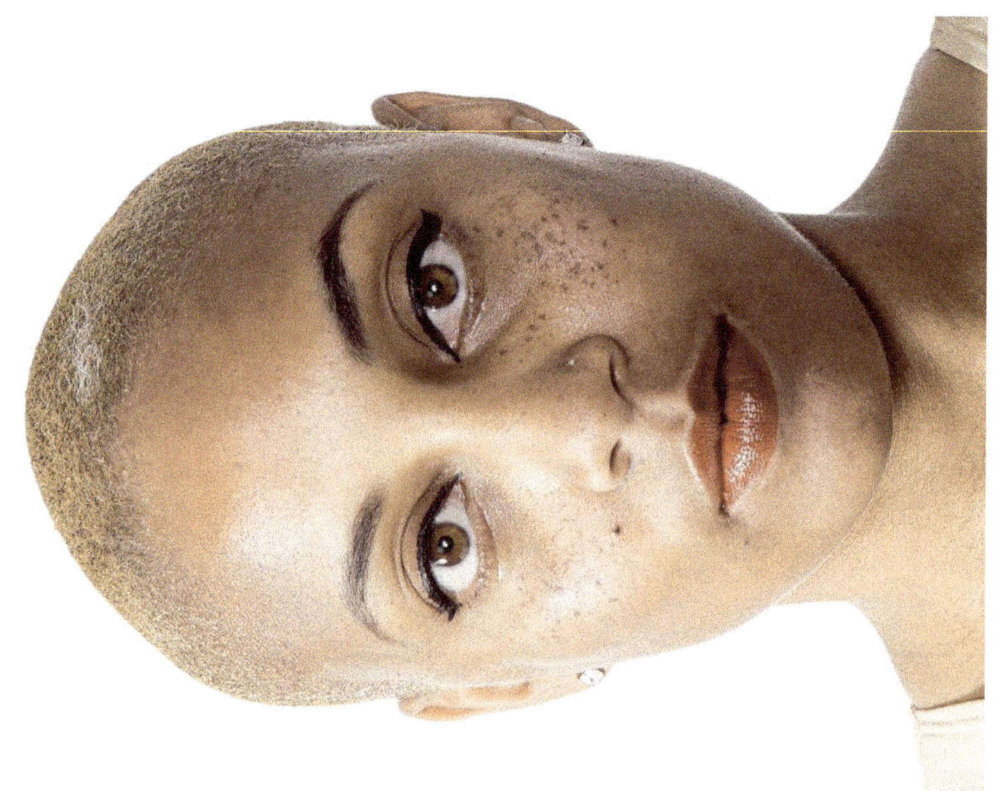

SIDE HEAD VIEW

The side view or profile of the model follows the same grid layout, but positioning and details are vastly different than the front view.

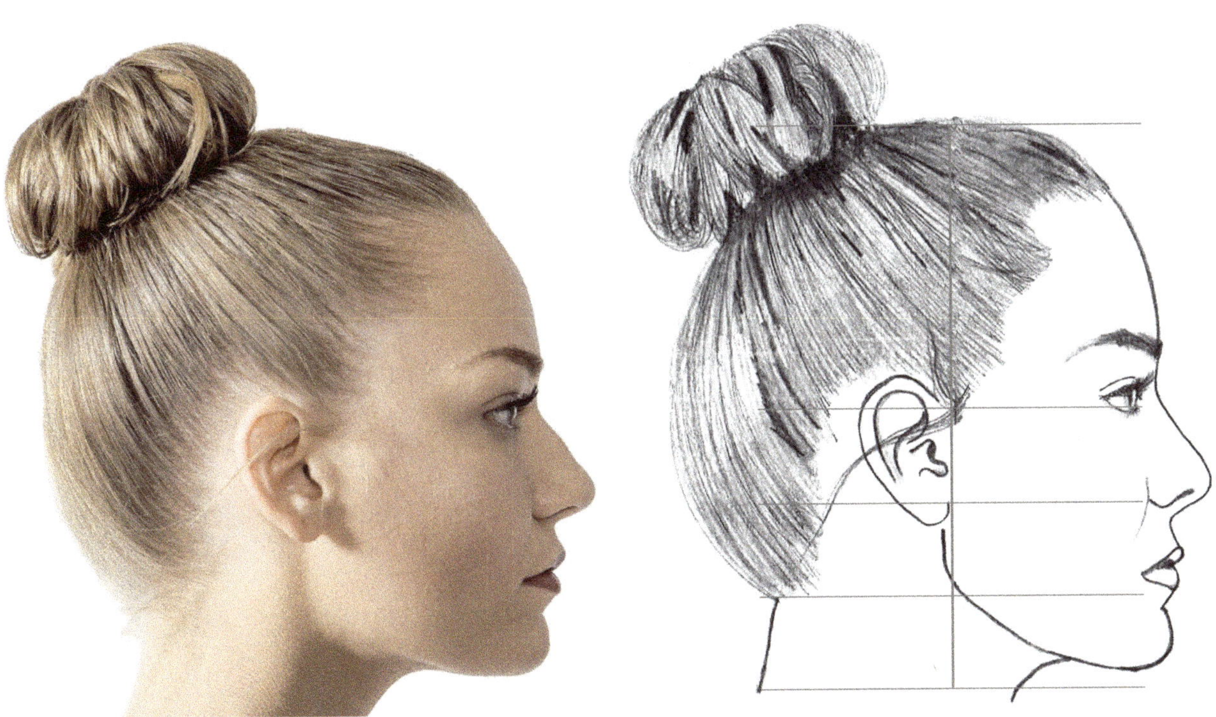

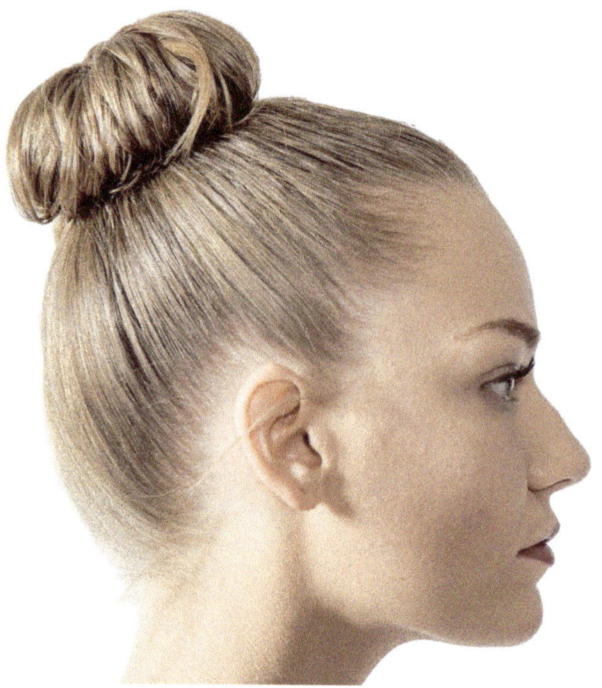

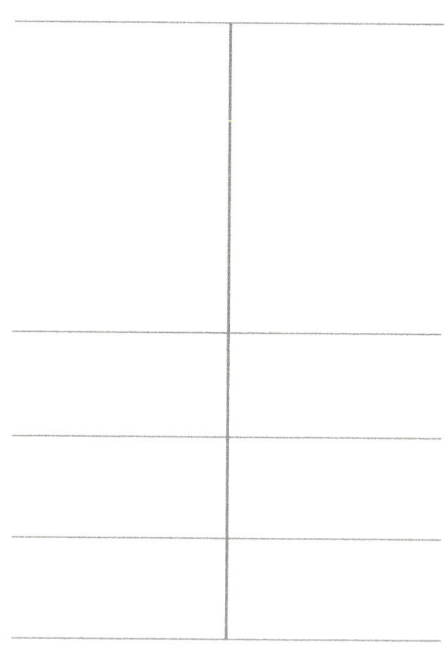

STEP 1
Draw the grid guideline for the
head features as done in the
previous exercise.

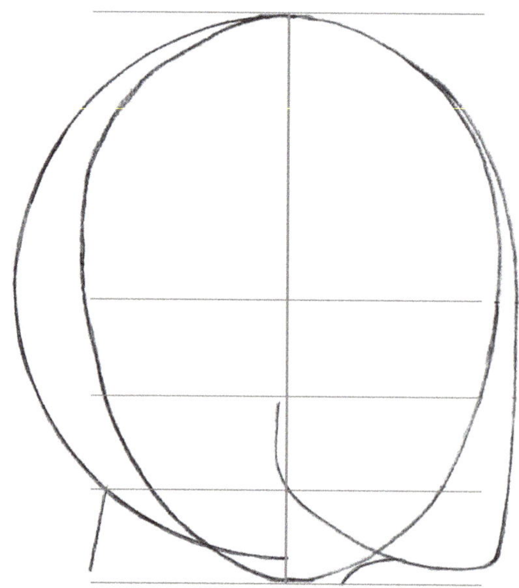

STEP 2
Draw a center oval shape as a
guide. Draw chin on the right side
and a half circle on left side for
back of the head.

PRACTICE YOUR WORK

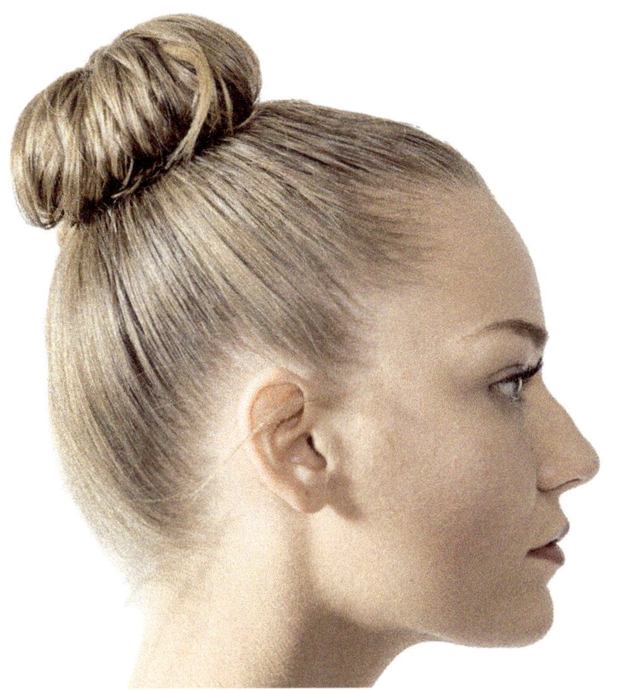

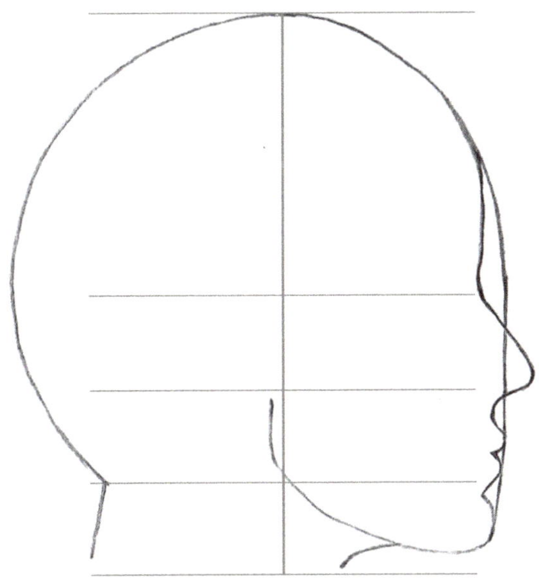

STEP 3

Draw the outline of the facial profile.

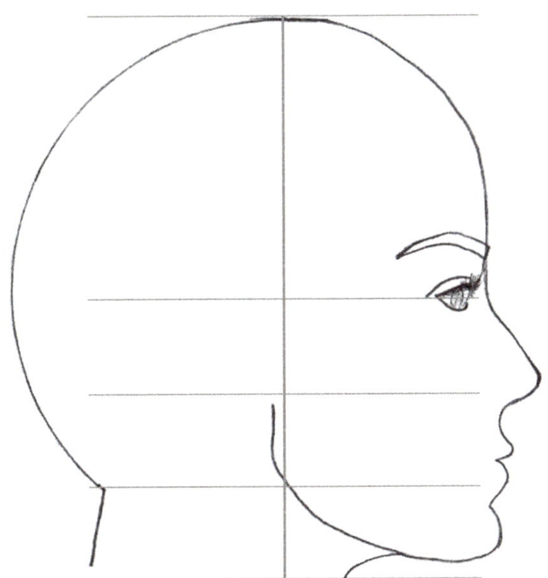

STEP 4

Draw in the eye at the center line. Draw in the eyebrow and eyelid.

PRACTICE YOUR WORK

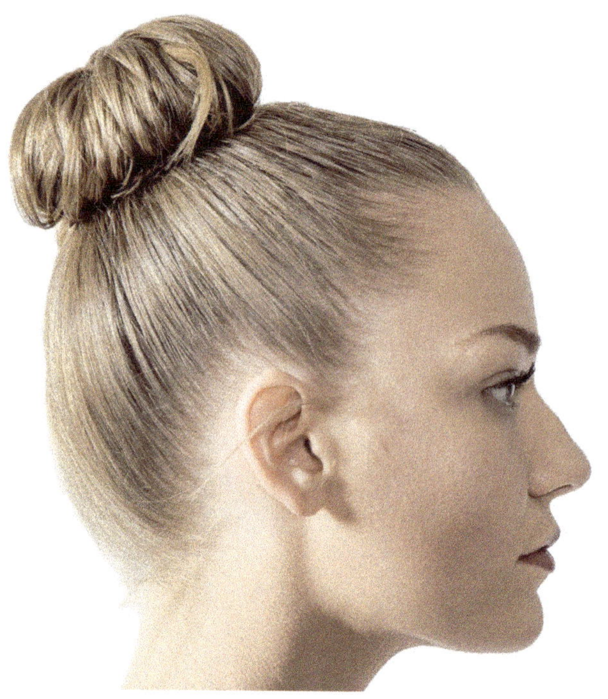

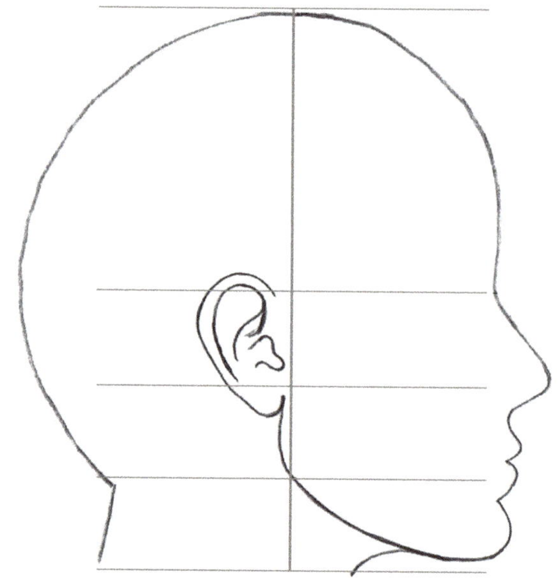

STEP 6

Draw in the detail of the ear
behind the vertical line.

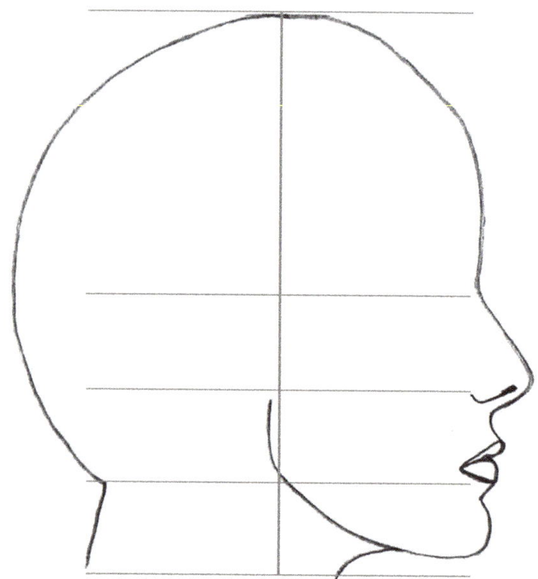

STEP 5

Draw in the nostril on the line
below the eyes. Draw the lips
slightly above the lower line.

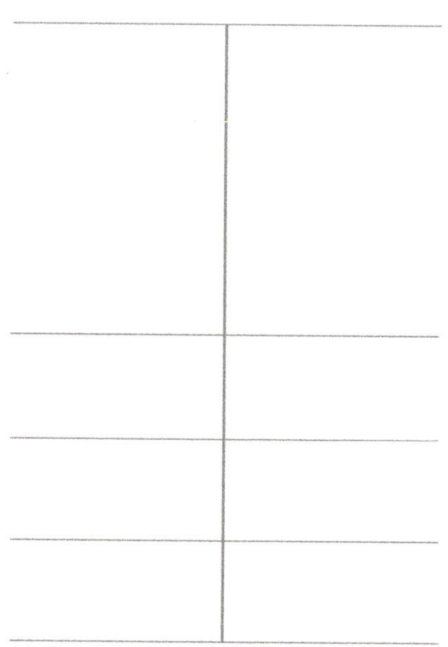

PRACTICE YOUR WORK

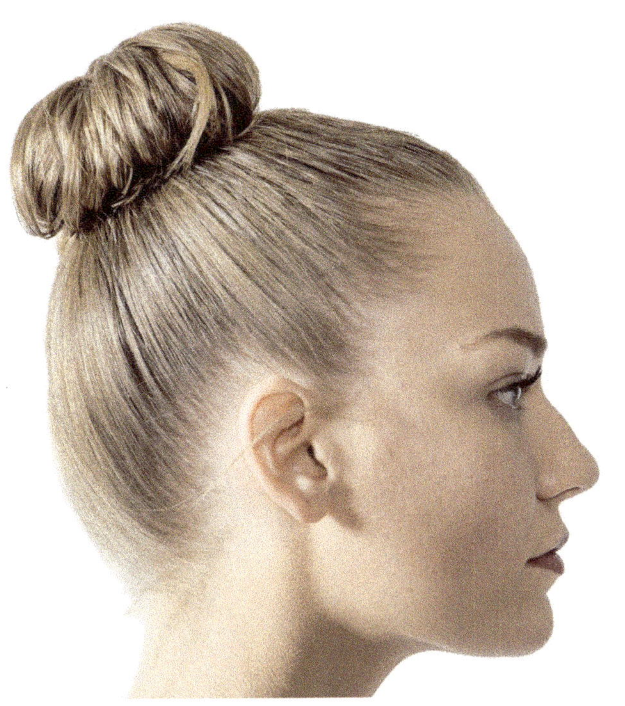

Step 7
Draw in the hair line and
structure of the face.

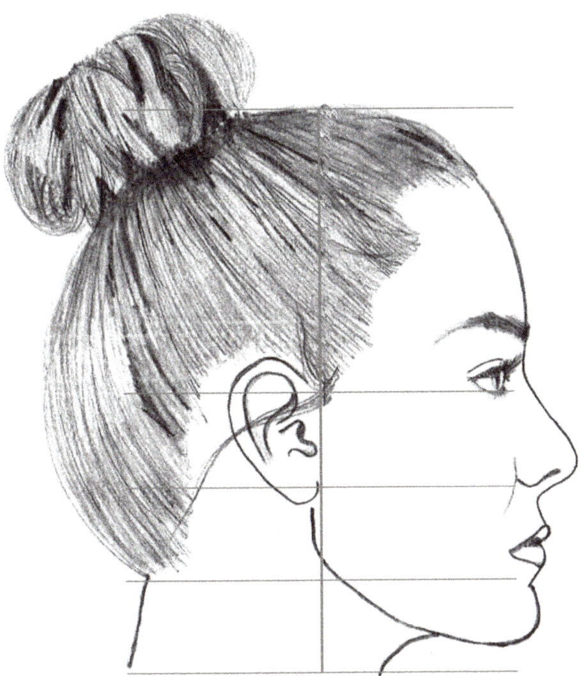

Step 8
Draw in finishing details of
shading, hair, freckles and
makeup.

Practice your work

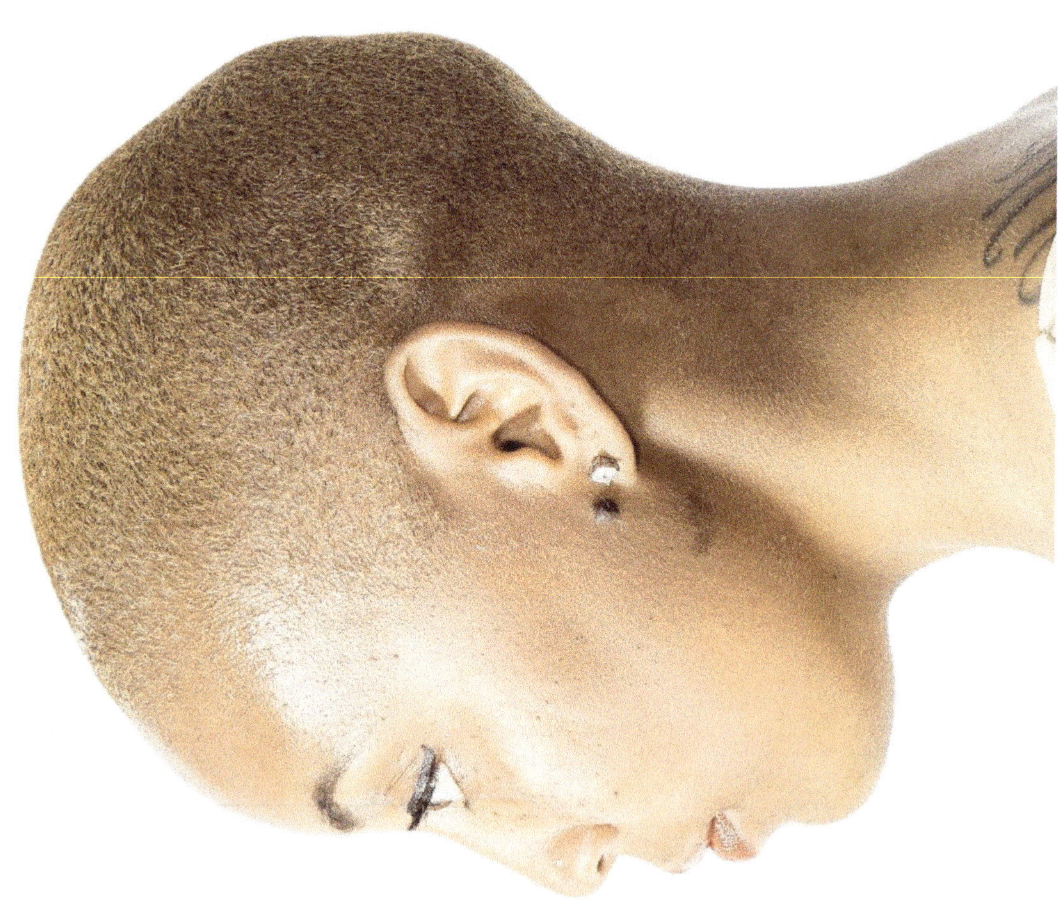

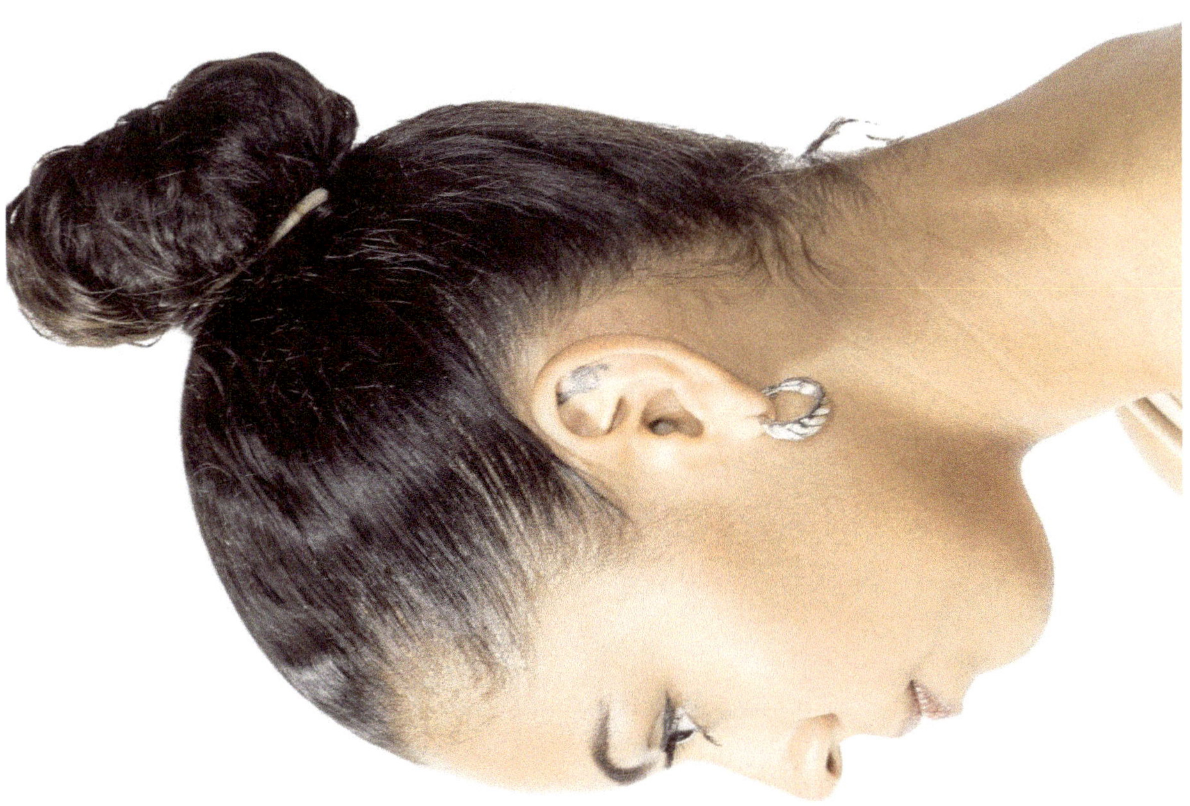

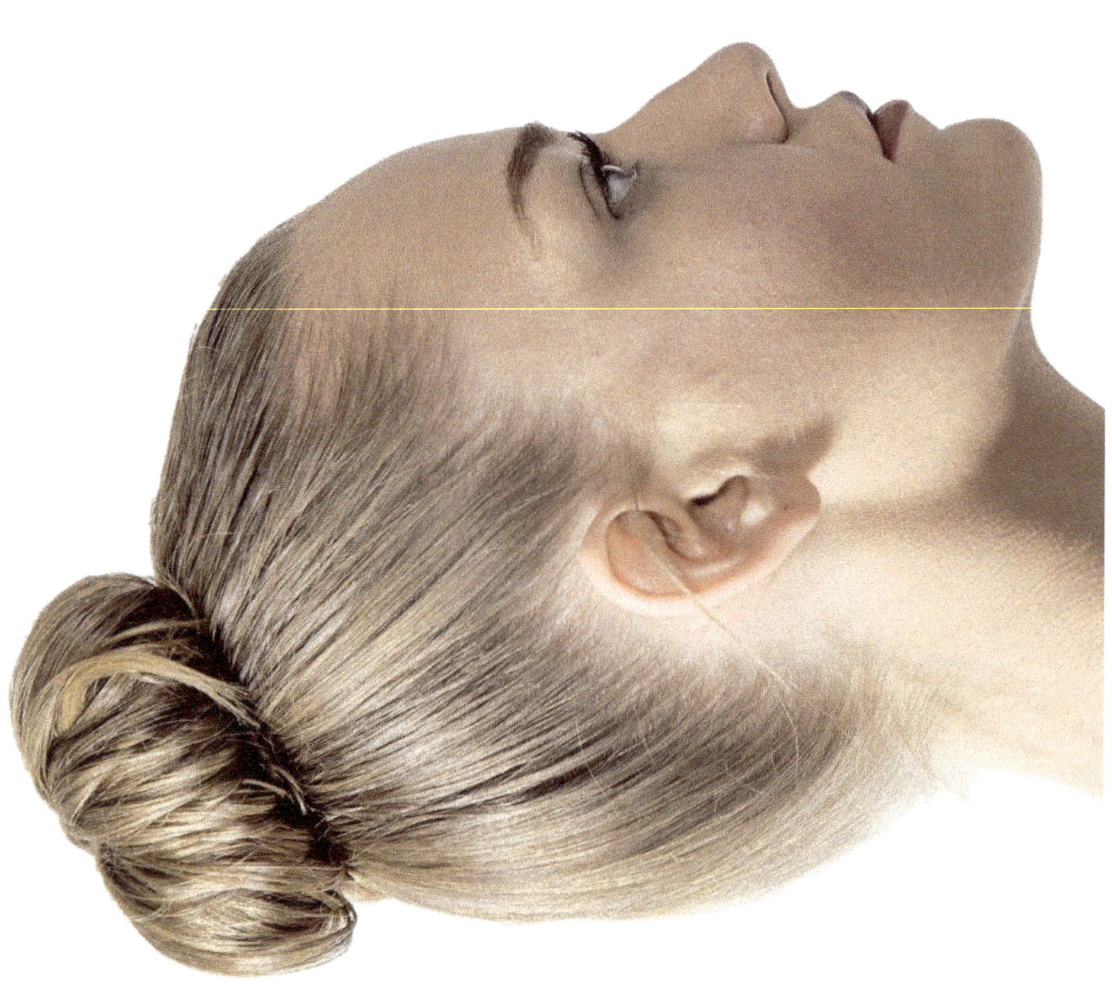

3/4 FRONT HEAD VIEW

The 3/4 view of the front utilizes both profile and frontal view details. This exercise cannot utilize the same general grid as the previous exercises, as the perspective has changed.

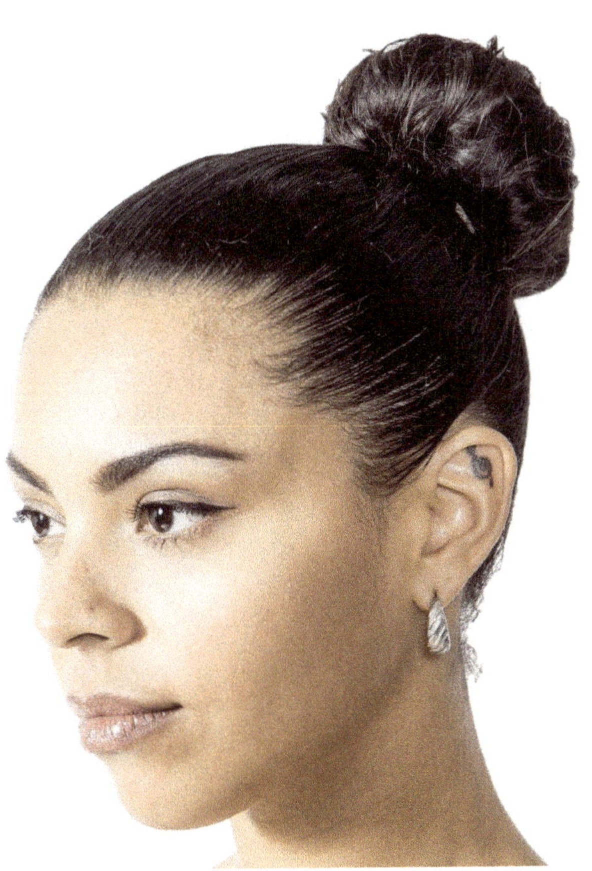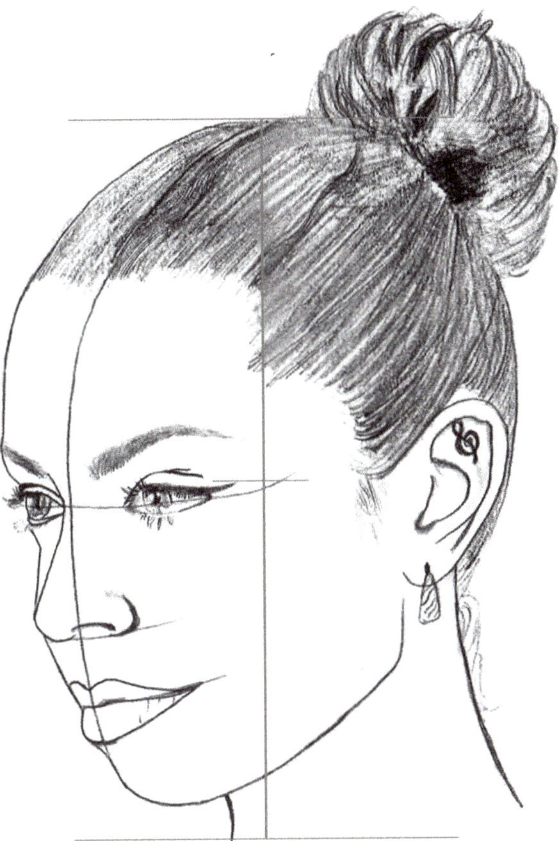

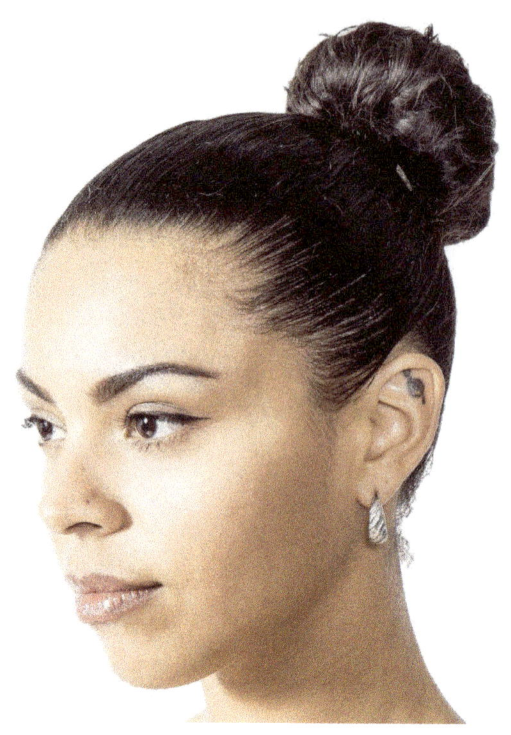

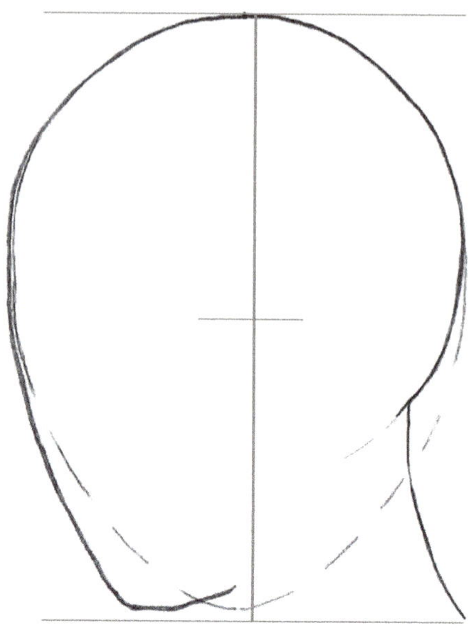

STEP 1

Draw in the top and bottom guidelines. Mark the center and draw in the oval shape for the head. Define the head shape of the chin and back of the head.

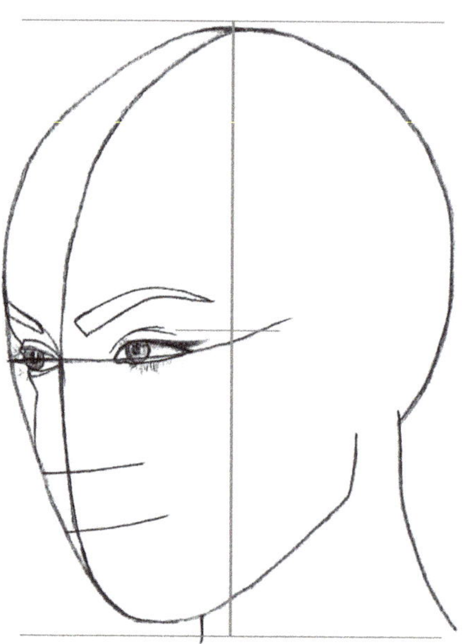

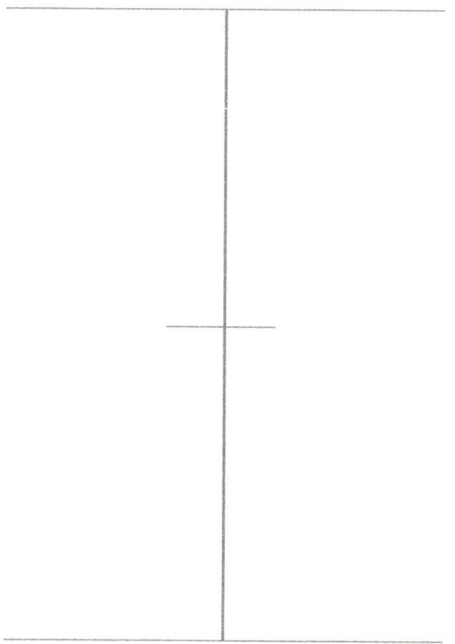

STEP 2

Draw in a guide to mark the center of the face and mark the lower division lines. Draw in the eyes at the center line including eyebrows and eyelids

PRACTICE YOUR WORK

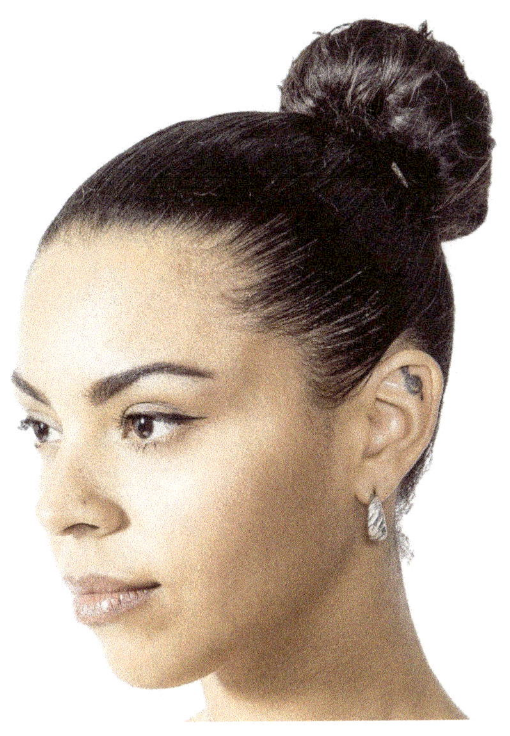

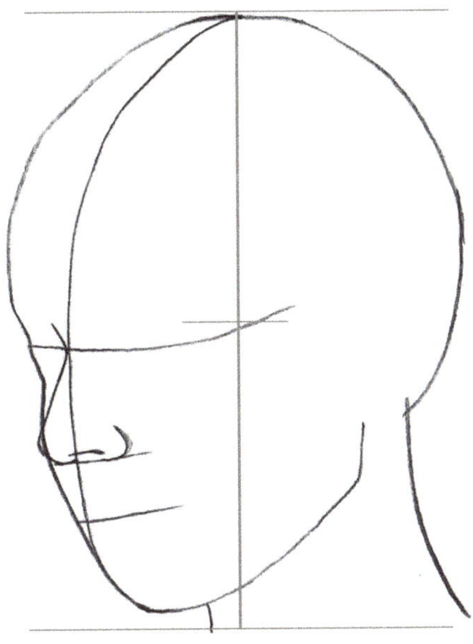

Step 4

Draw the nose, 1/3 below the eye line.

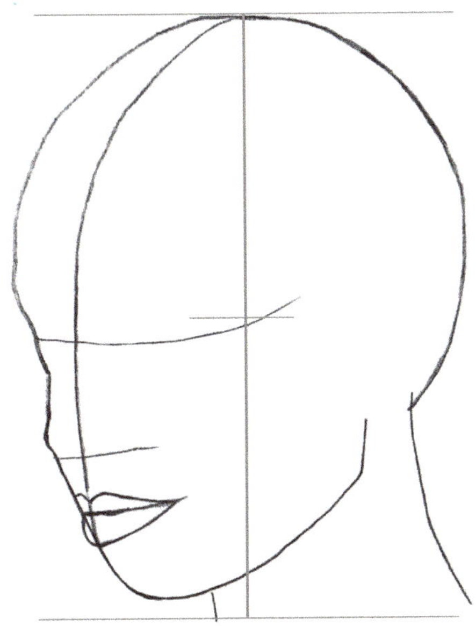

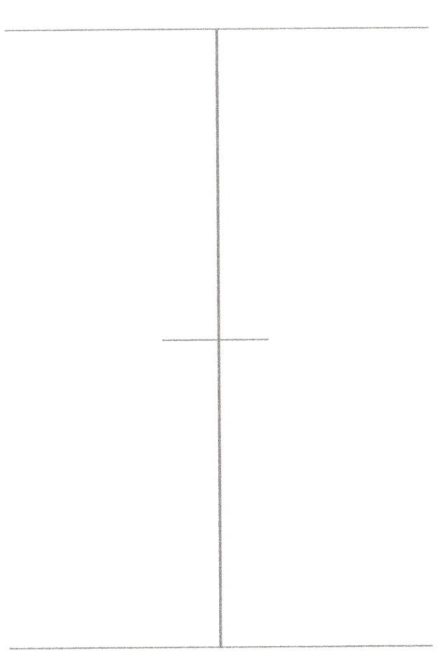

Practice your work

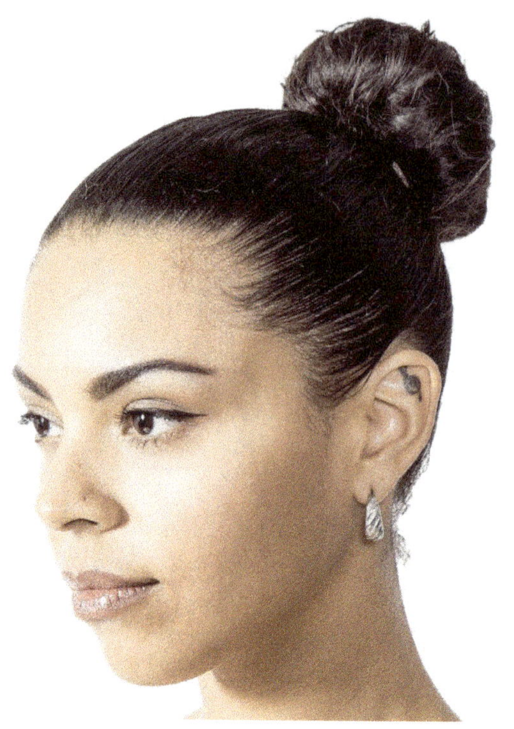

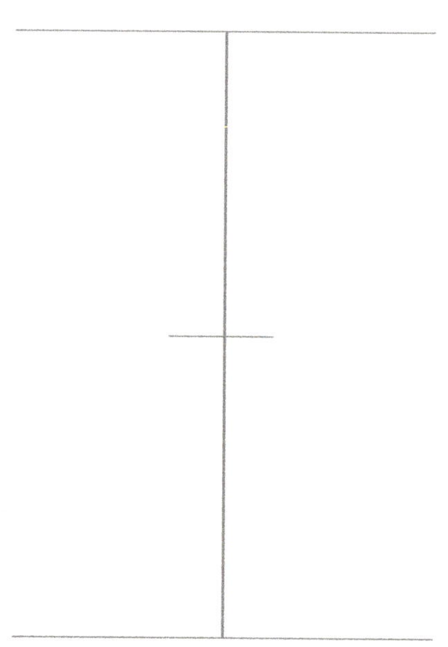

STEP 6

Draw in the ears and the outline
of the hairline.

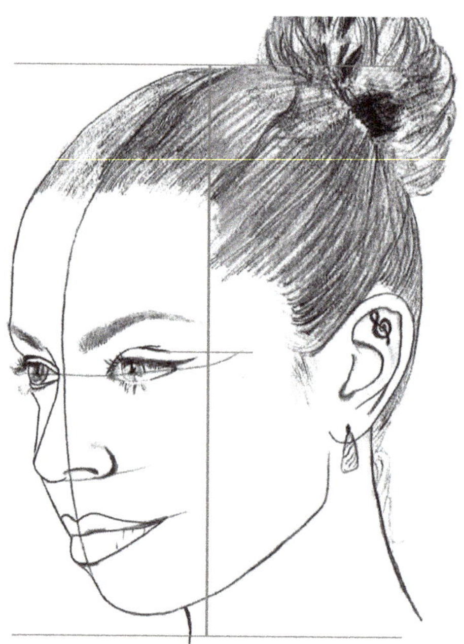

STEP 8

Draw in the finishing details of
the hair, earrings and jaw bone
definition

PRACTICE YOUR WORK

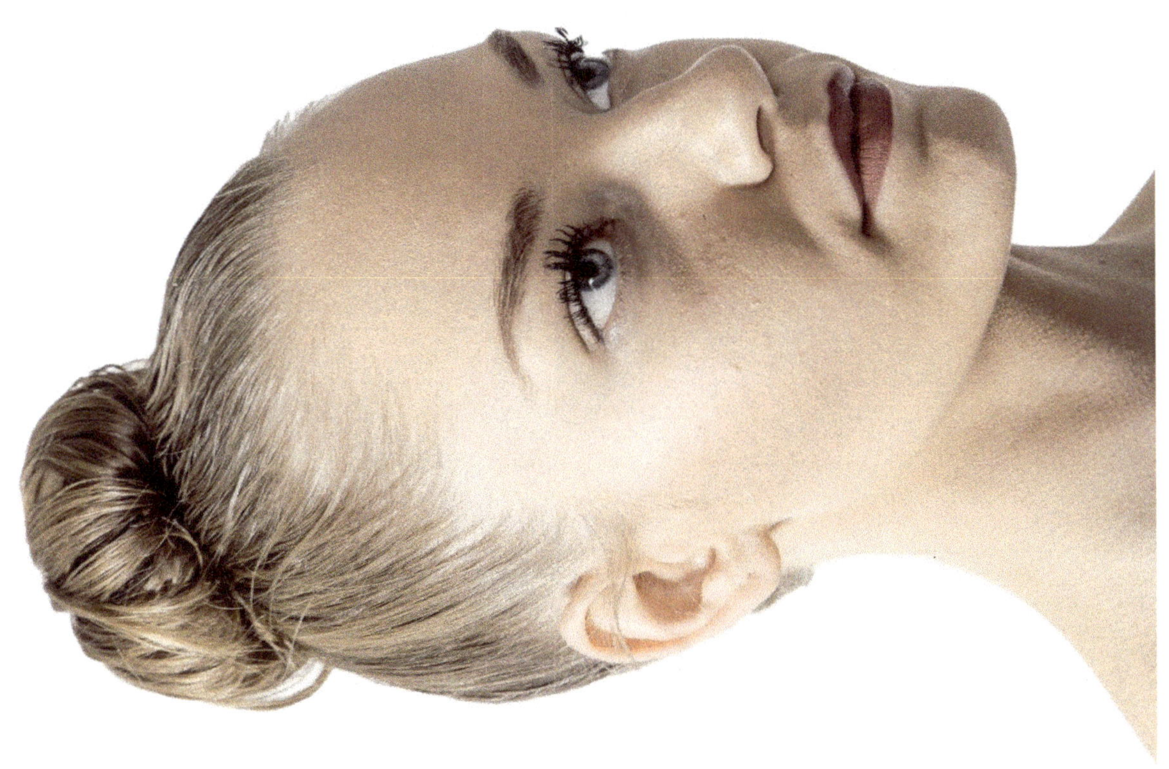

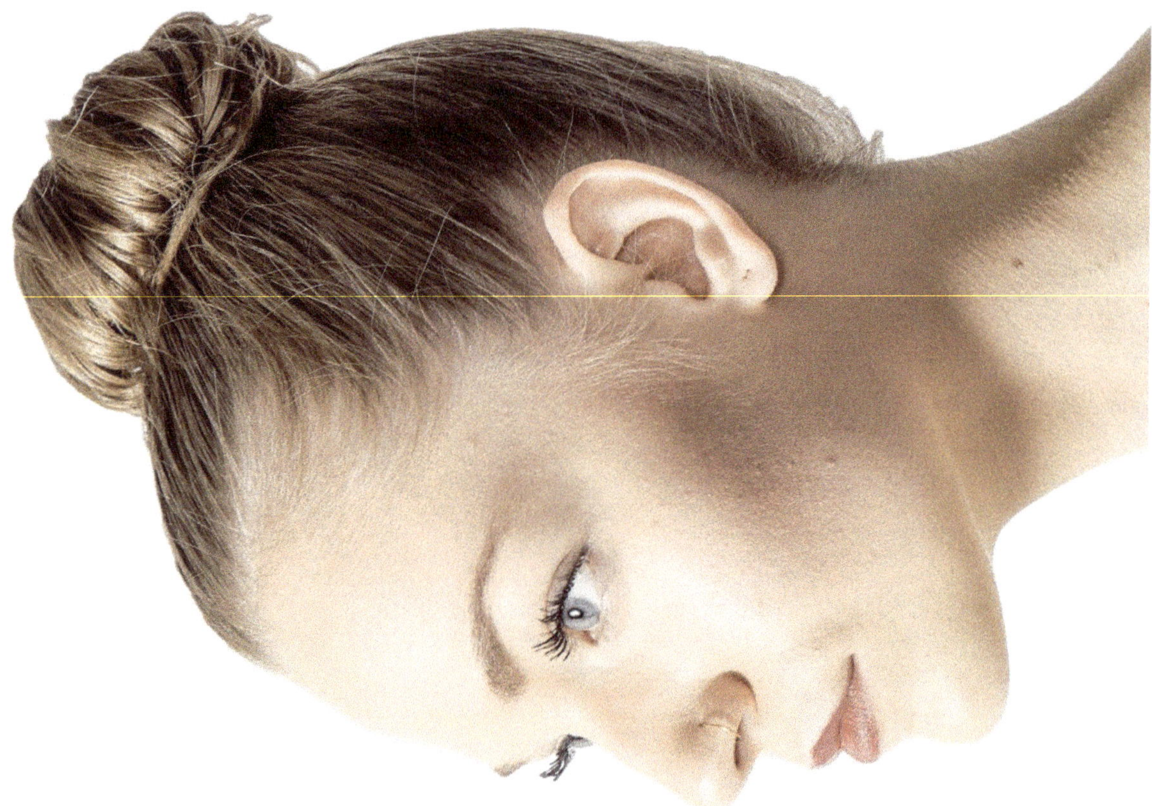

PRACTICE YOUR WORK

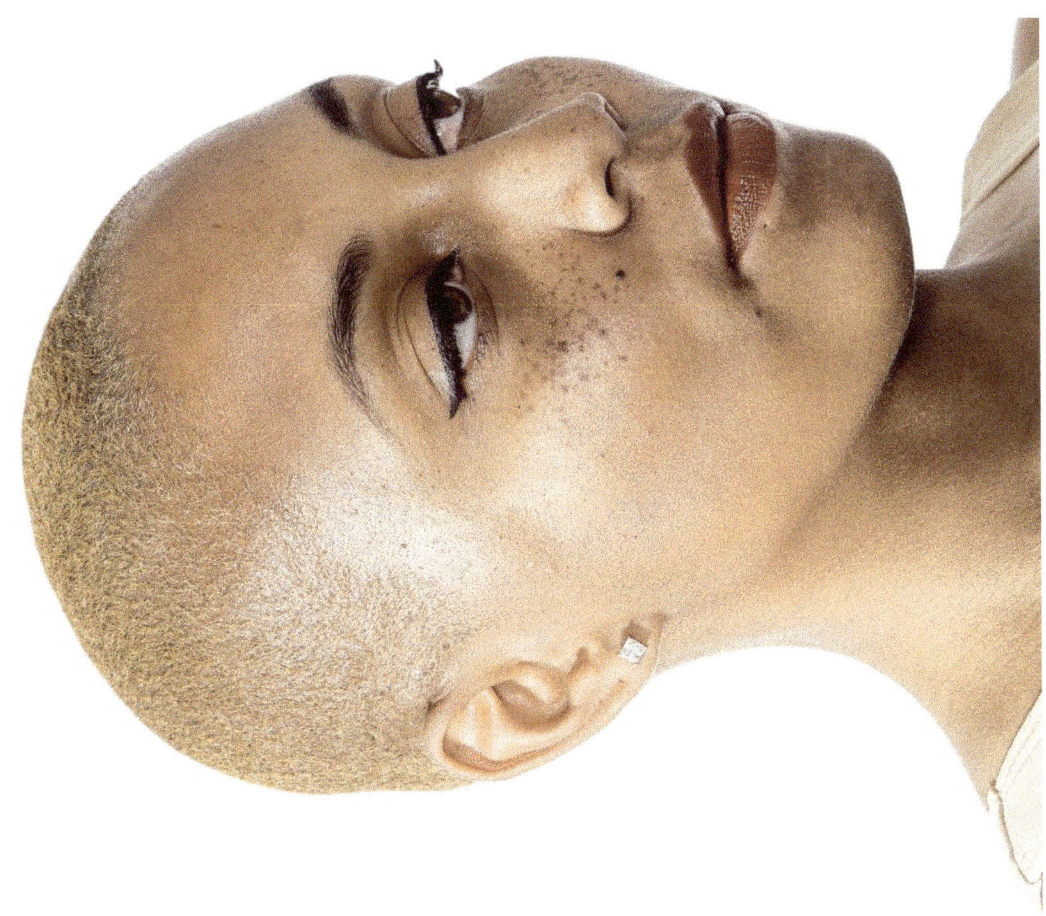

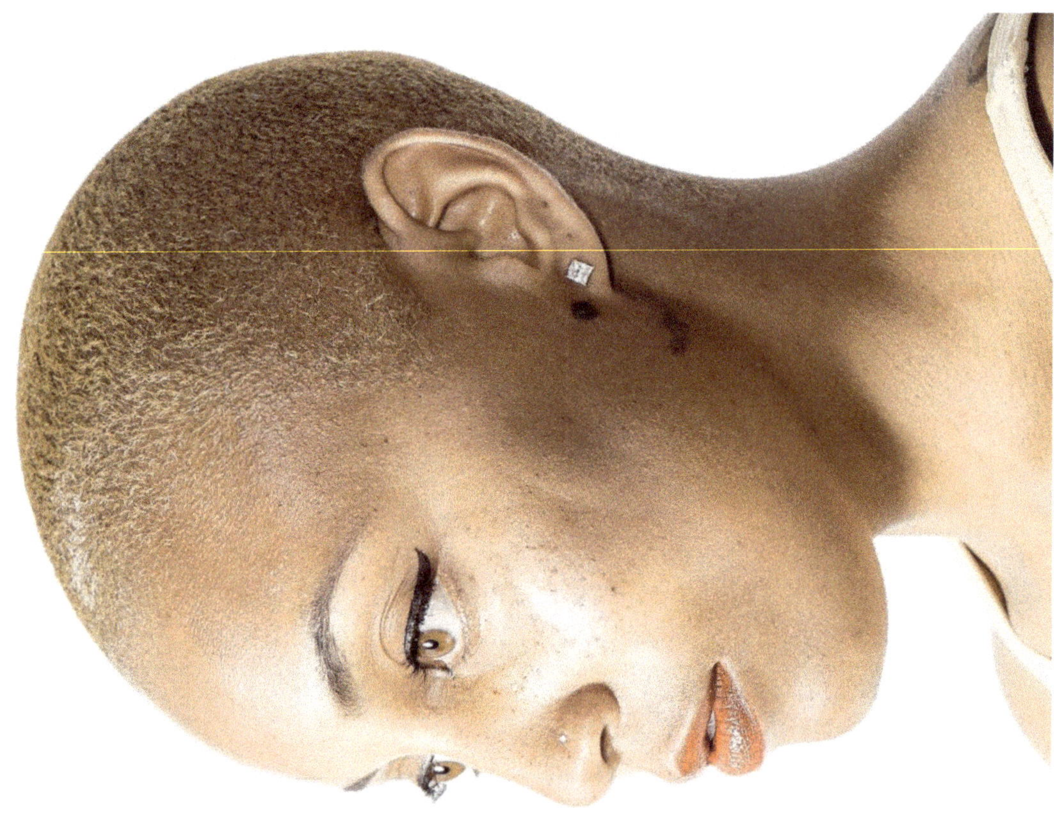

BACK HEAD VIEW

The back view is the simplest to illustrate. Use the same grid layout as the first two exercises in this chapter.

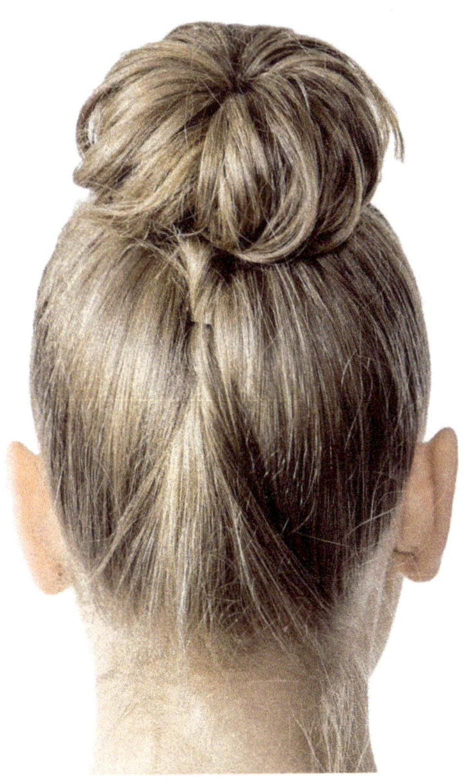
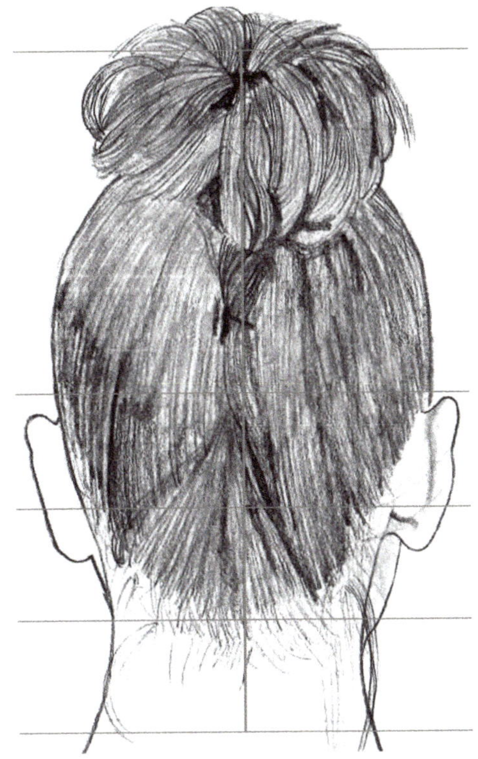

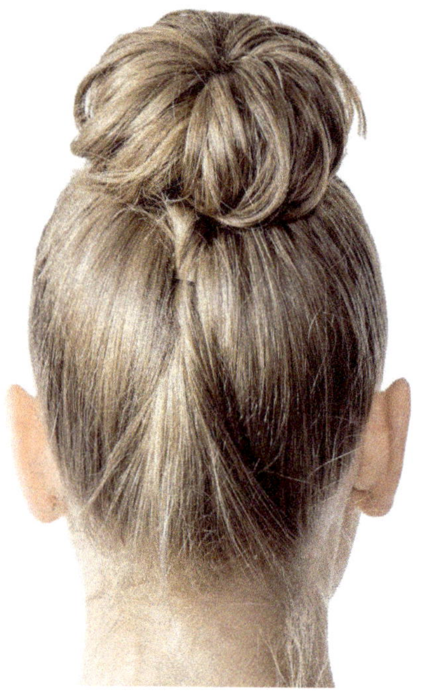

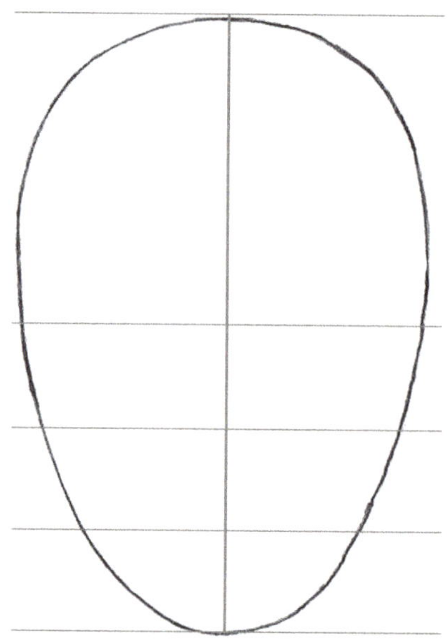

STEP 1

Draw in your guidelines. Draw in
the oval shape for the head.

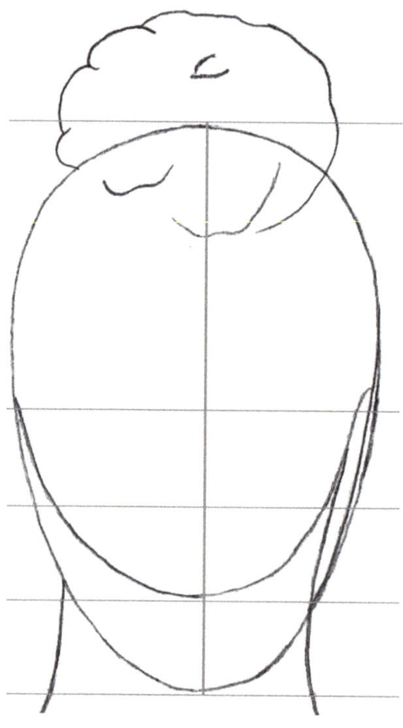

STEP 2

Draw in the hairline. Draw in the
side of the face that is seen.

PRACTICE YOUR WORK

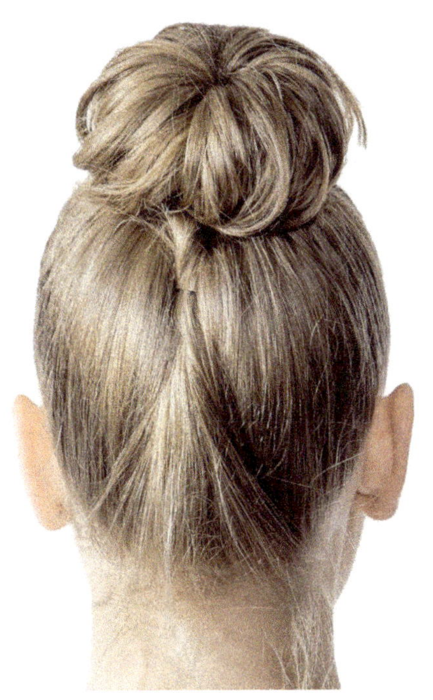

Step 3

Draw in the model's ears.

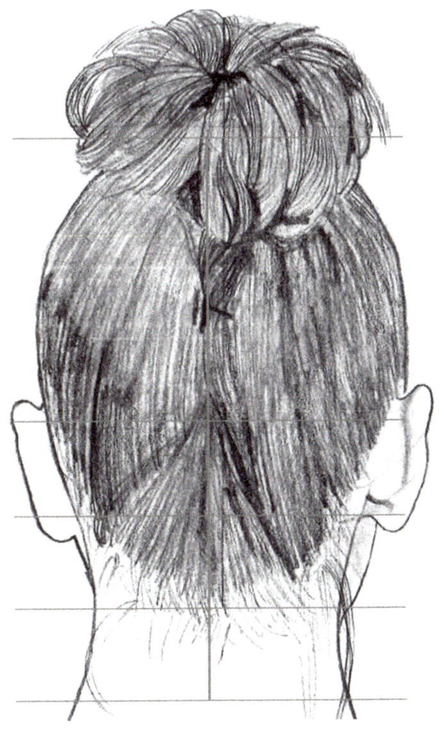

Step 4

Draw in the finishing details of
shadows, hair, and skin.

Practice your work

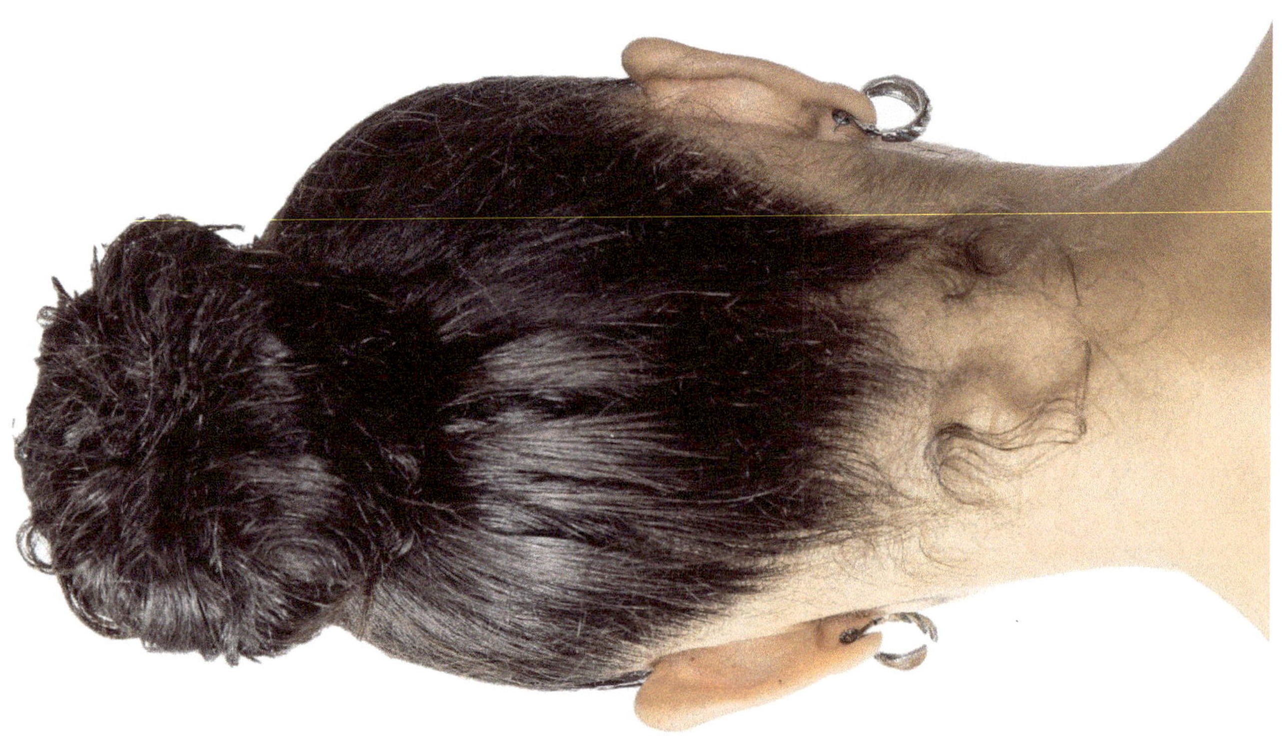

Practice your work

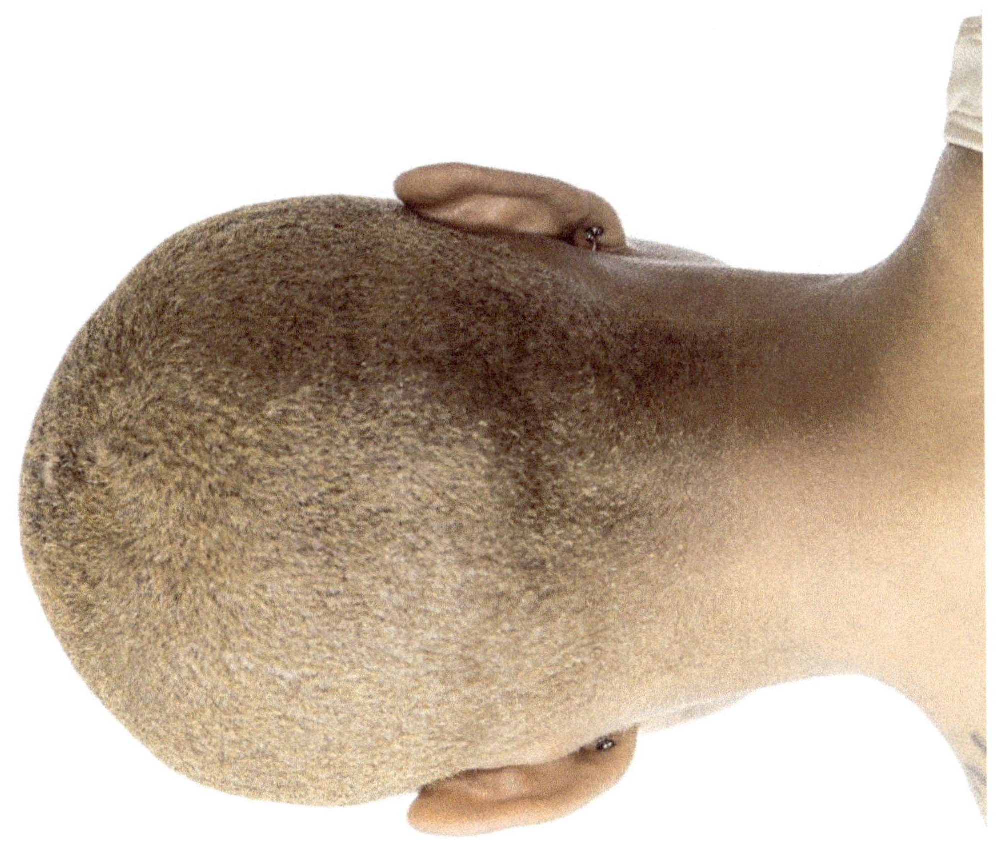

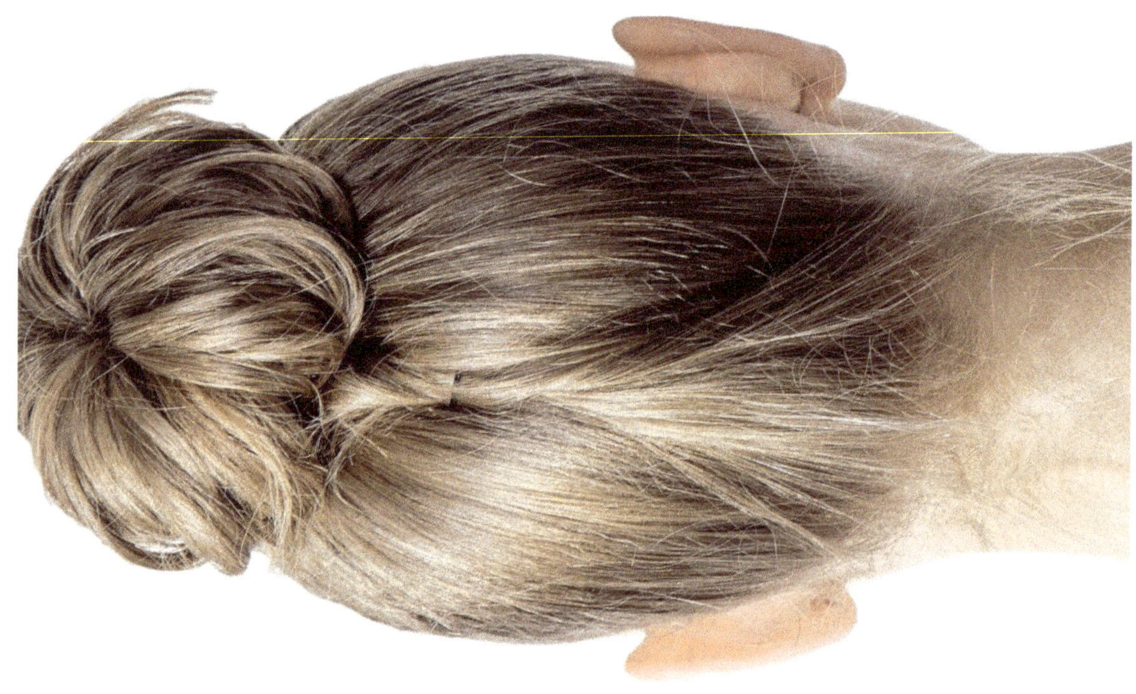

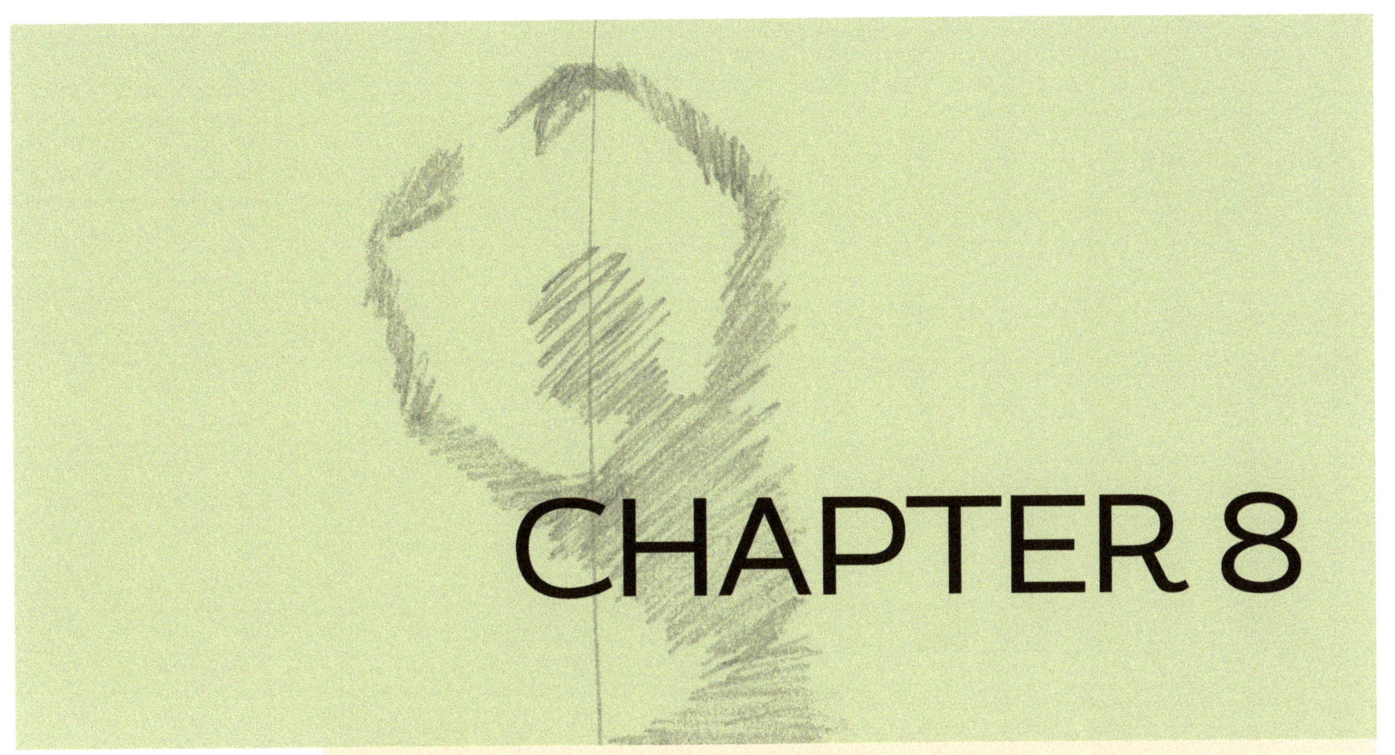

CHAPTER 8

Shading Techniques

HATCHING

Shading brings life and adds dimension to an illustration. This chapter discusses three methods. The first method demonstrated is hatching. Hatching is a shading technique that is a continuous movement of lines that follow the direction of the body. This creates depth.

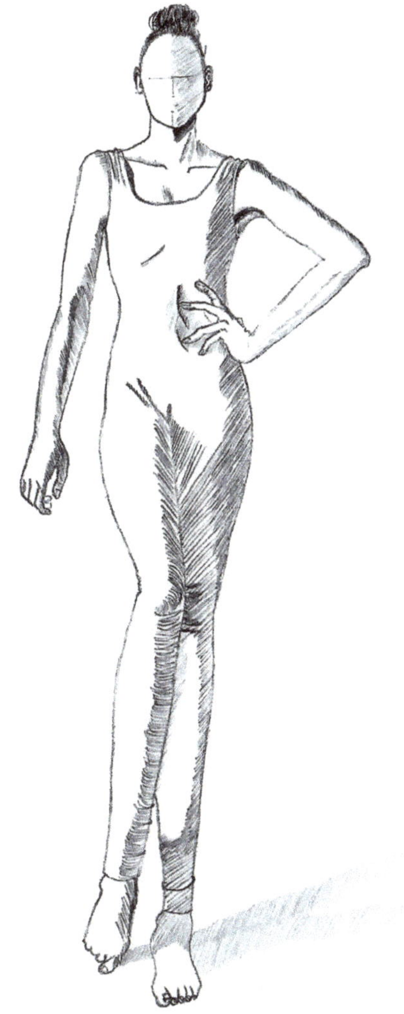

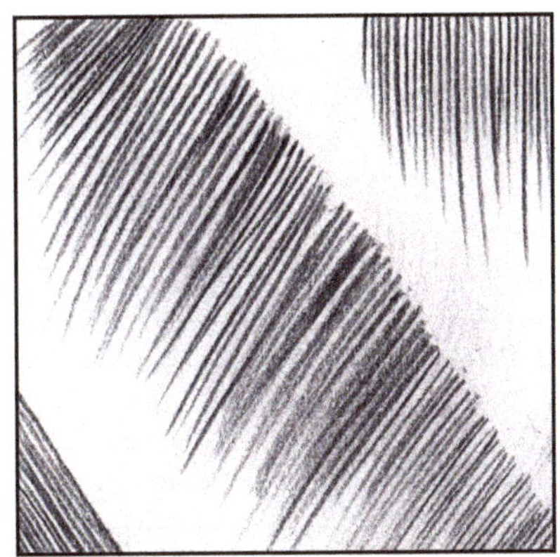

Try for yourself

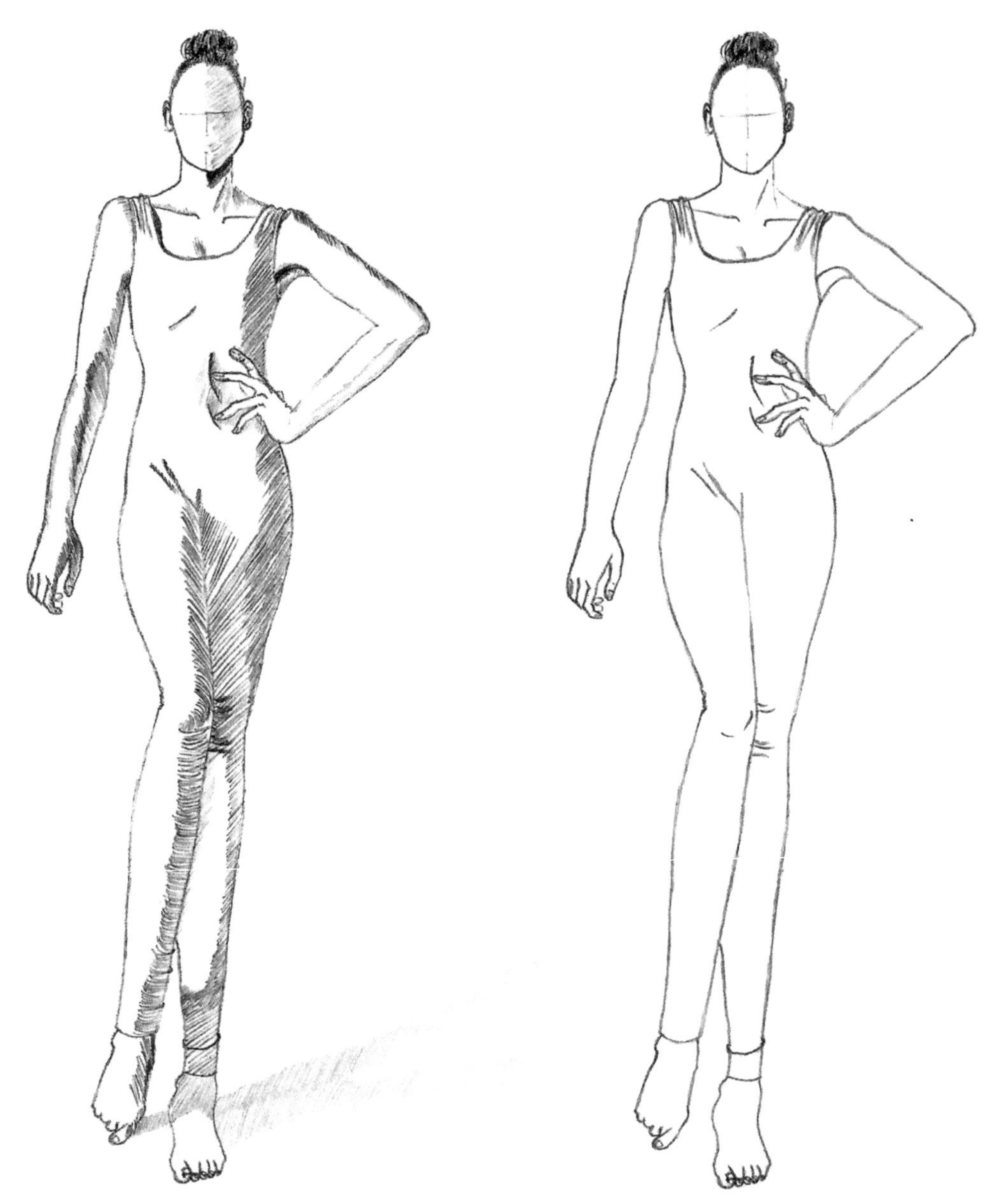

PRACTICE YOUR WORK

CROSS HATCHING

The second method, shown below, is cross hatching. Cross hatching is similar to hatching, but utilizes a second set of hatching markes in the opposite directin to create criss-cross shapes.

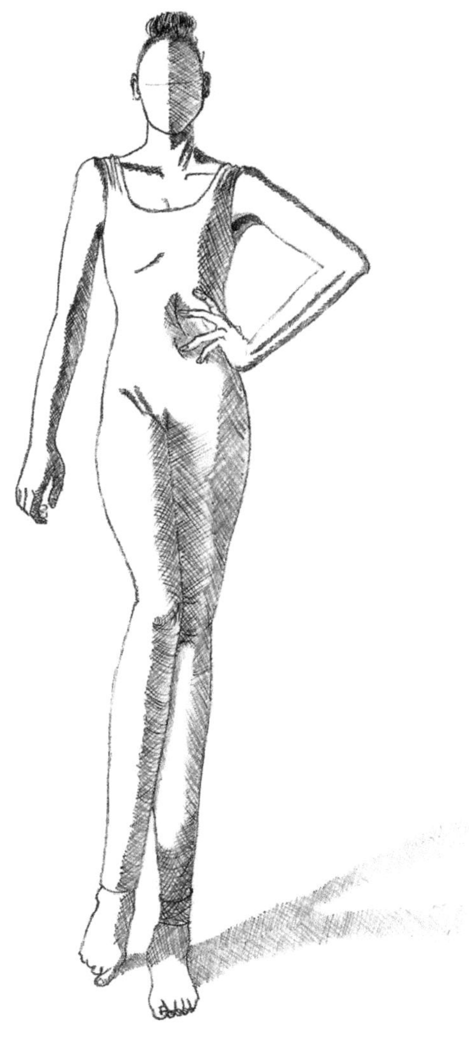

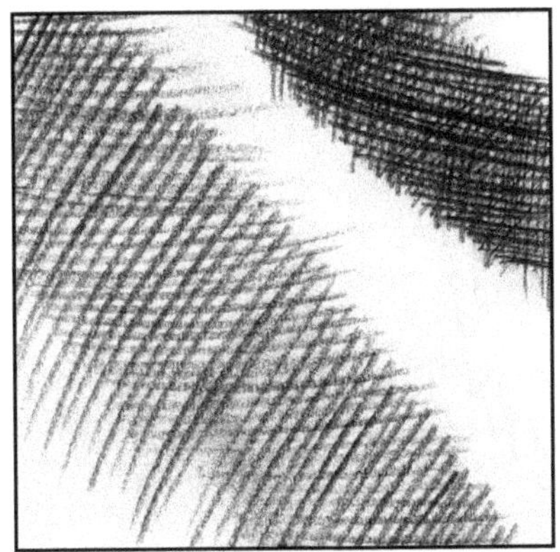

Try for yourself

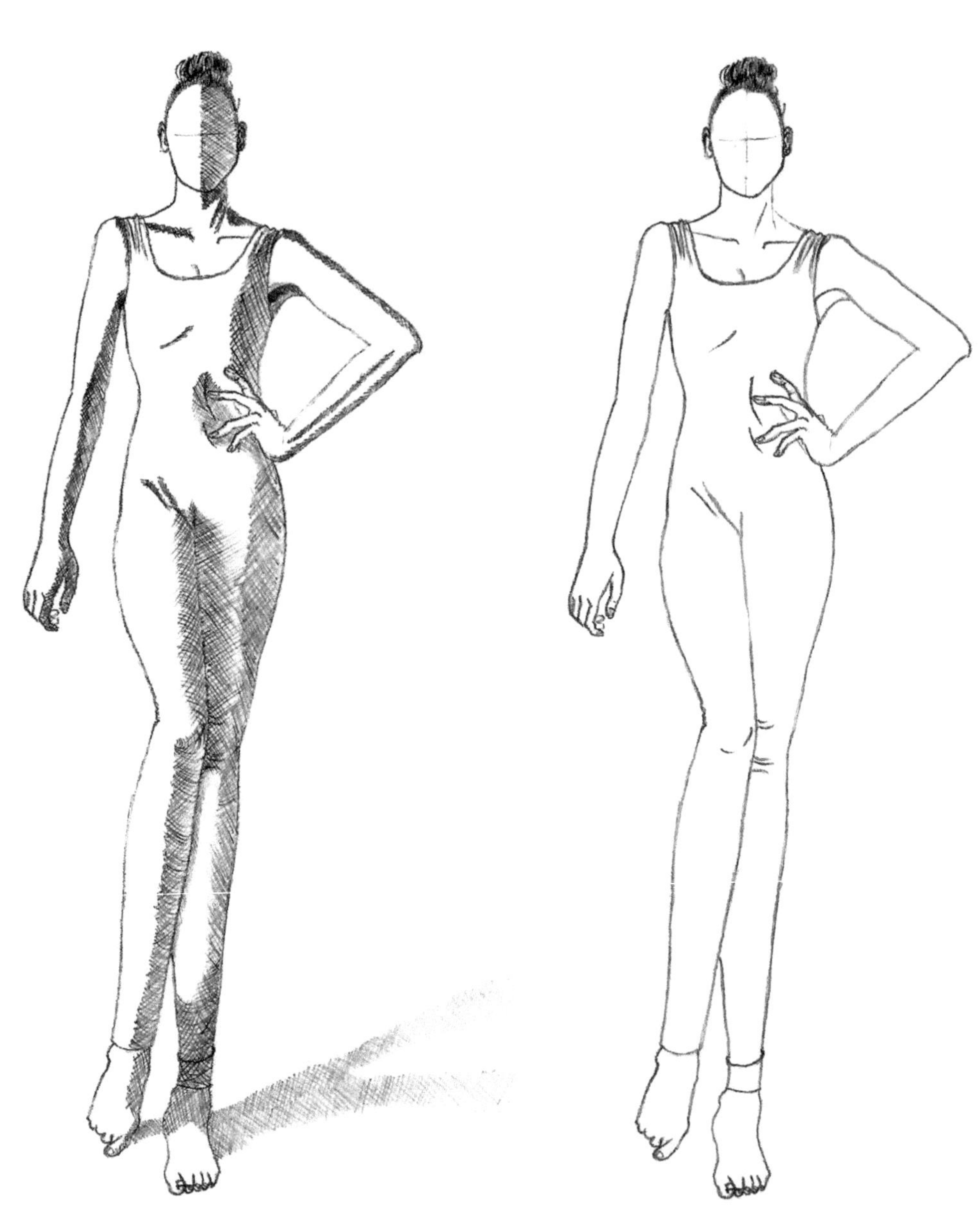

Practice your work

SMUDGING

The third shading technique is smudging. This shading technique utilizes the properties of a soft lead pencil. Smudging is a way to add depth by the level of pencil intensity. The markings used to smudge can be hatch marks or as simple as using the side of your pencil lead to shade, then smudge the pencil markings with your finger.

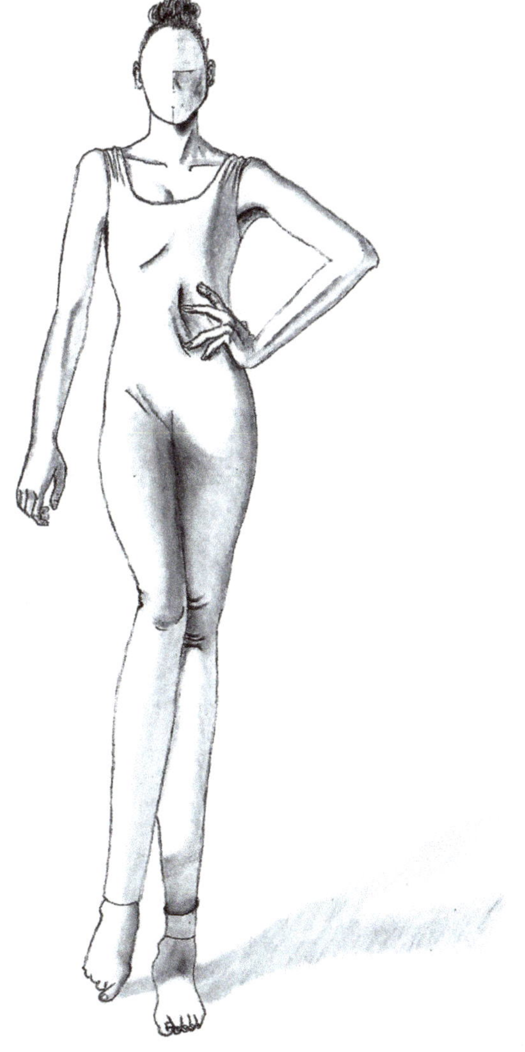

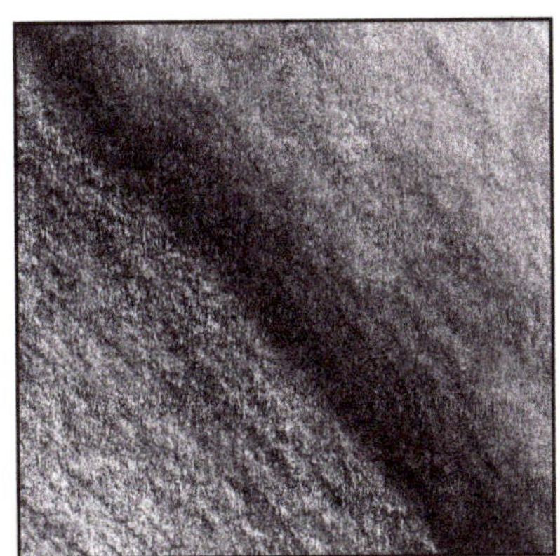

Try for yourself

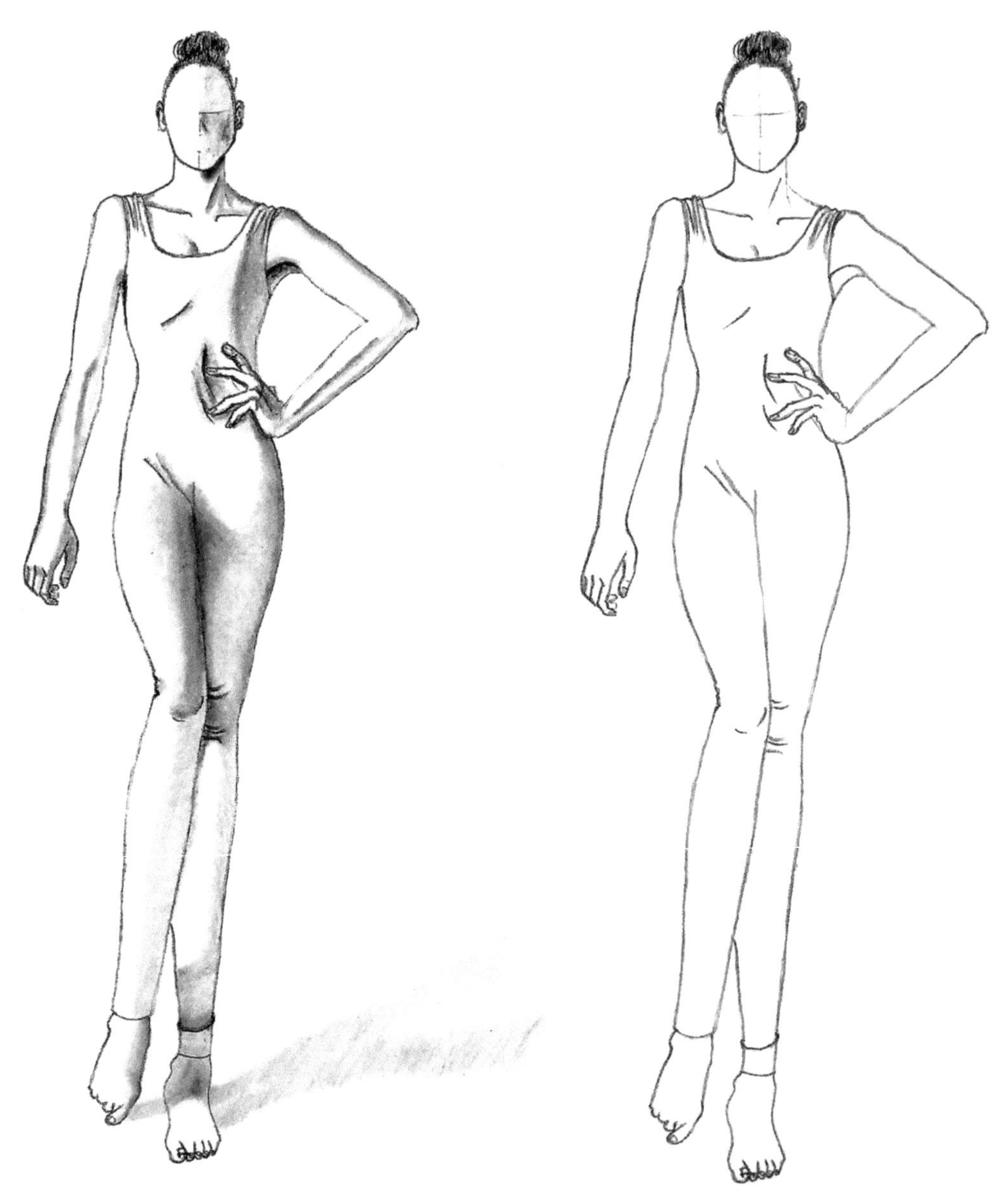

PRACTICE YOUR WORK

DIRECTIONAL SHADING

For properly shading, one must know what direction the light is originating from. On the following pages, practice the previously demonstrated methods, or try a method that has not been discussed in this book Various light sources are depicted with a sun for direction of the light source.

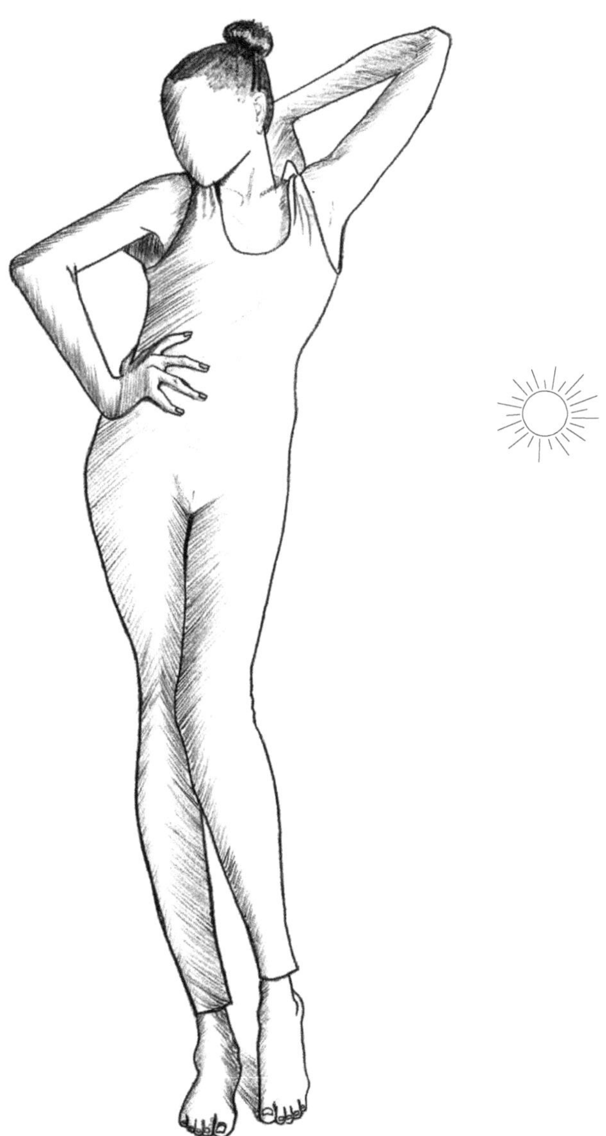

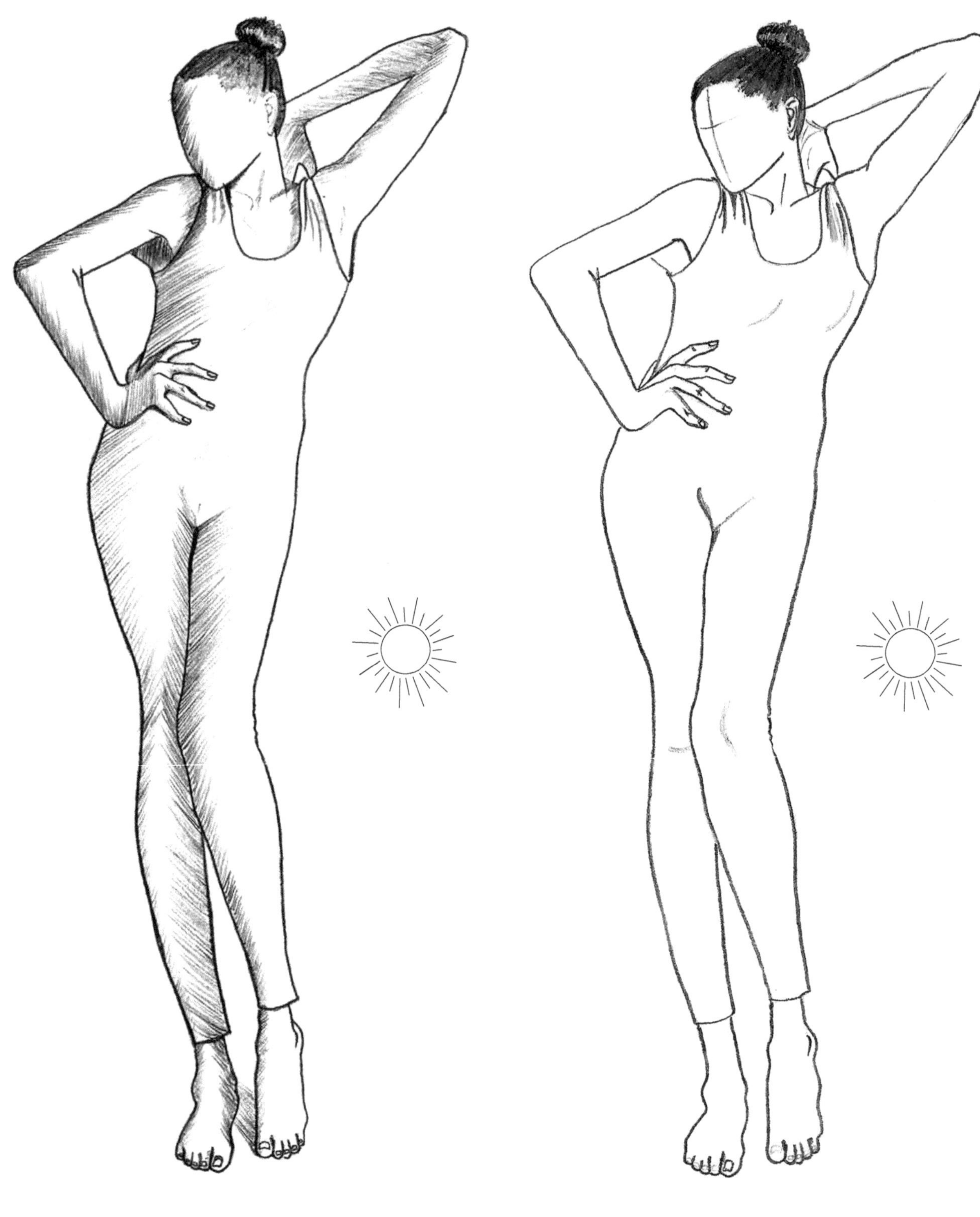

Practice Hatching
Directional Shading

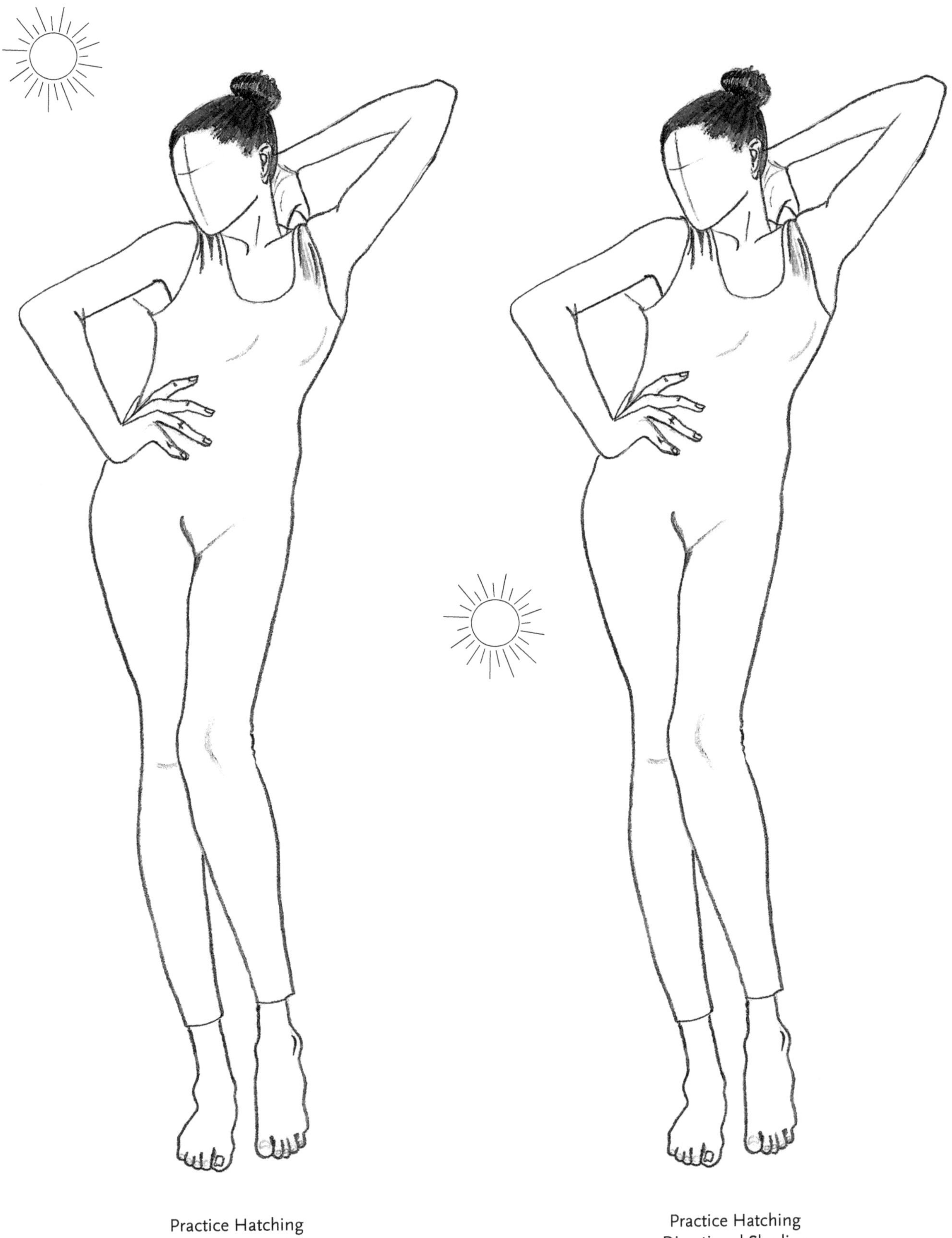

Practice Hatching
Directional Shading

Practice Hatching
Directional Shading

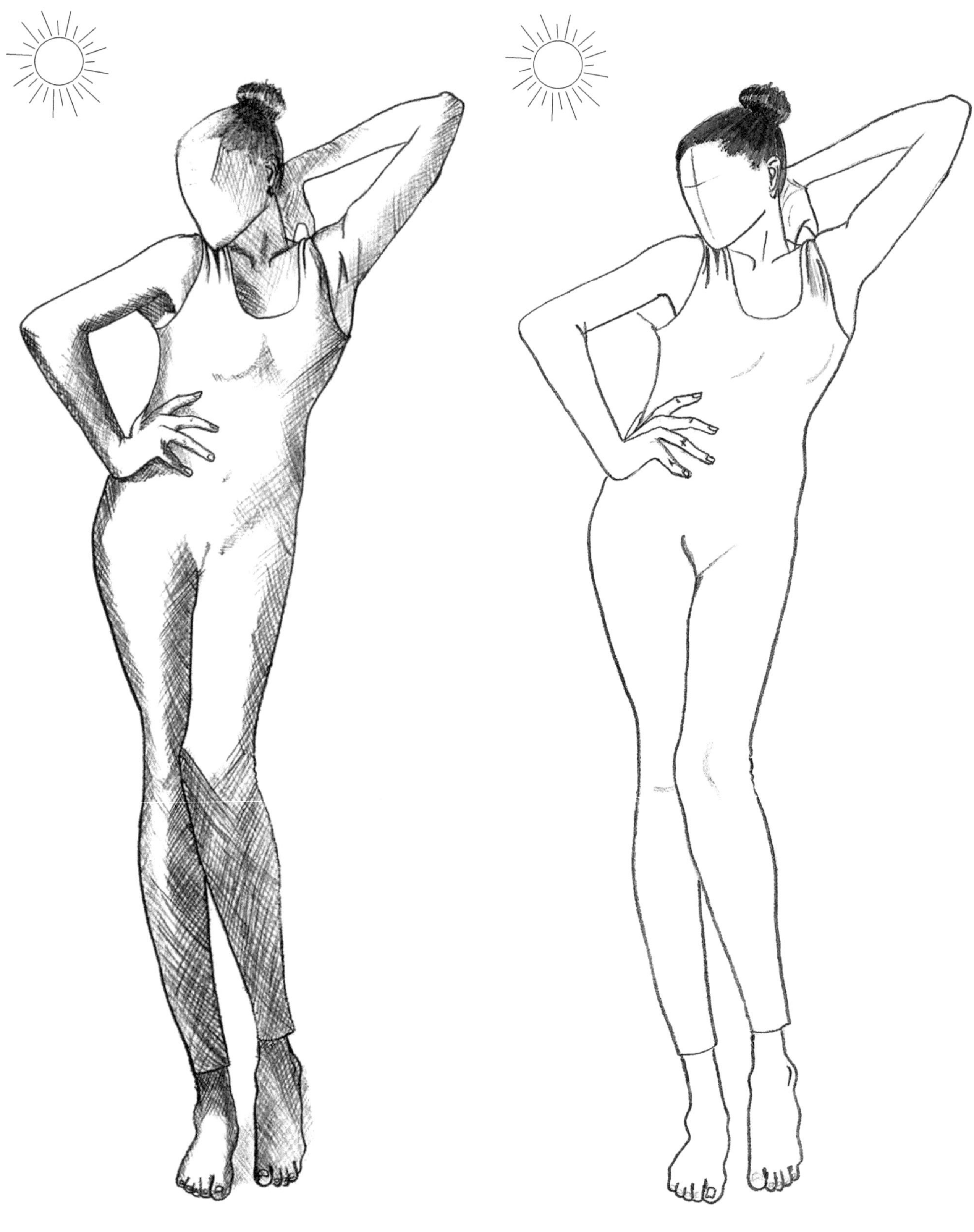

Practice Cross Hatching
Directional Shading

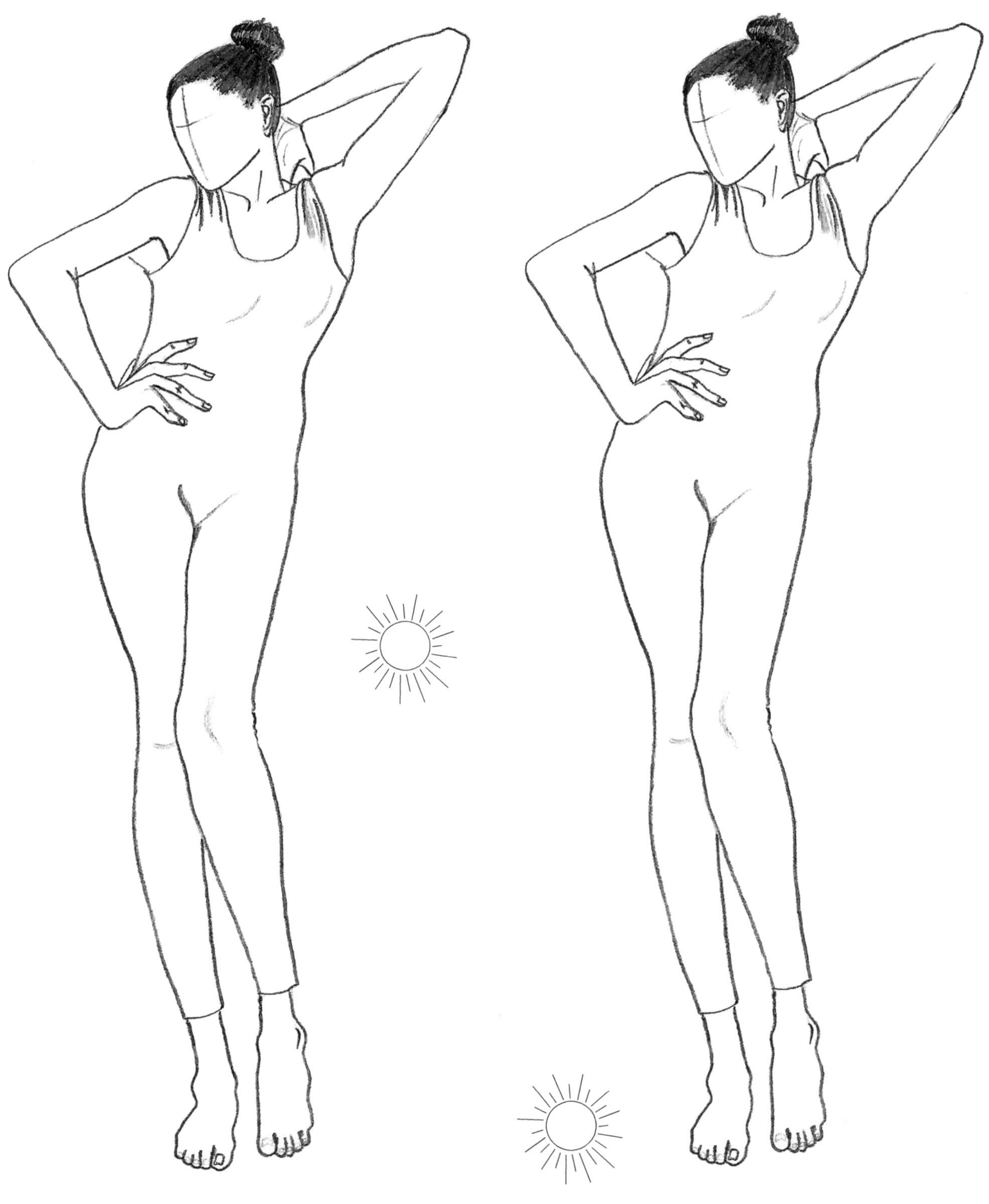

Practice Cross Hatching
Directional Shading

Practice Cross Hatching
Directional Shading

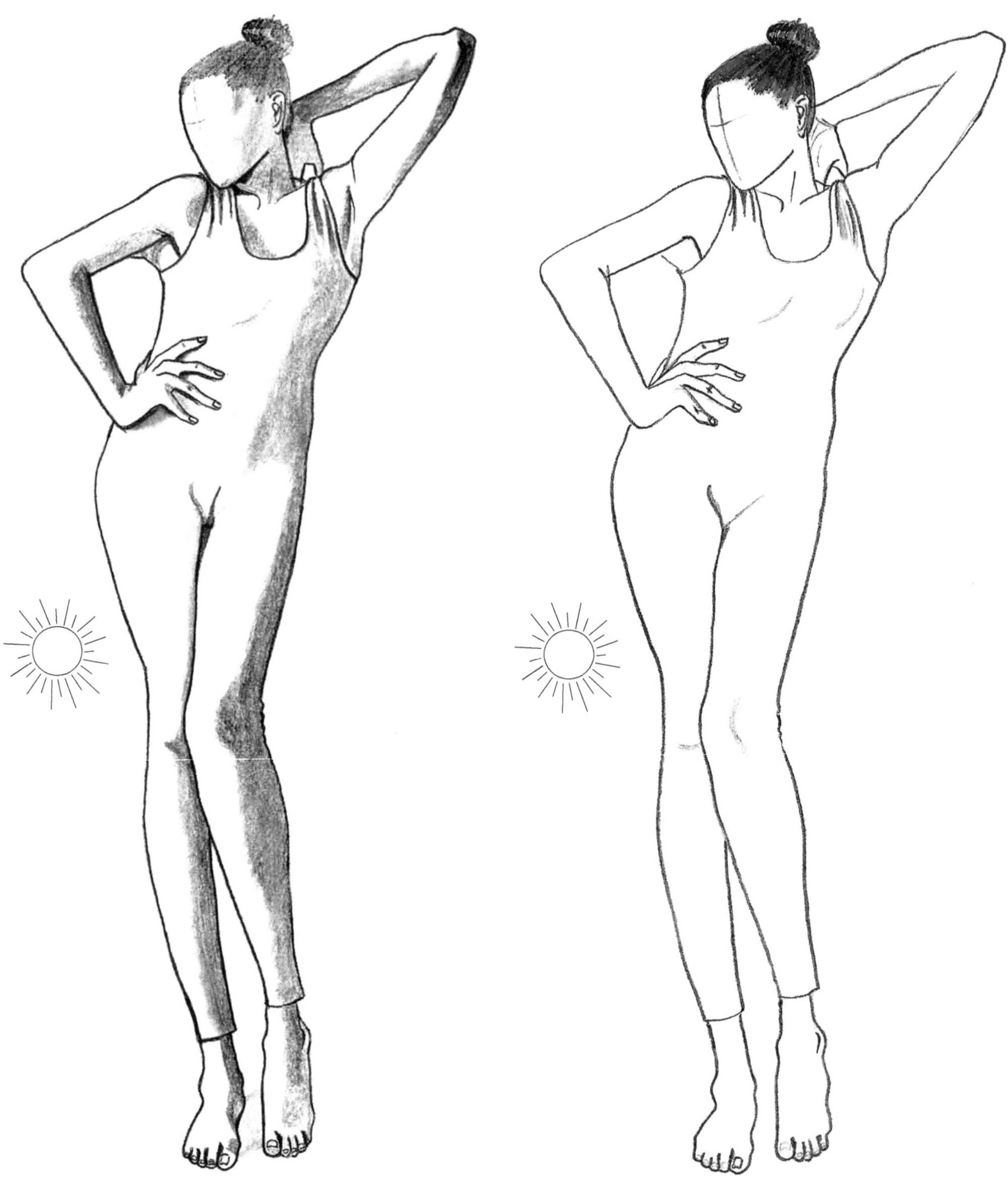

Practice Smudging
Directional Shading

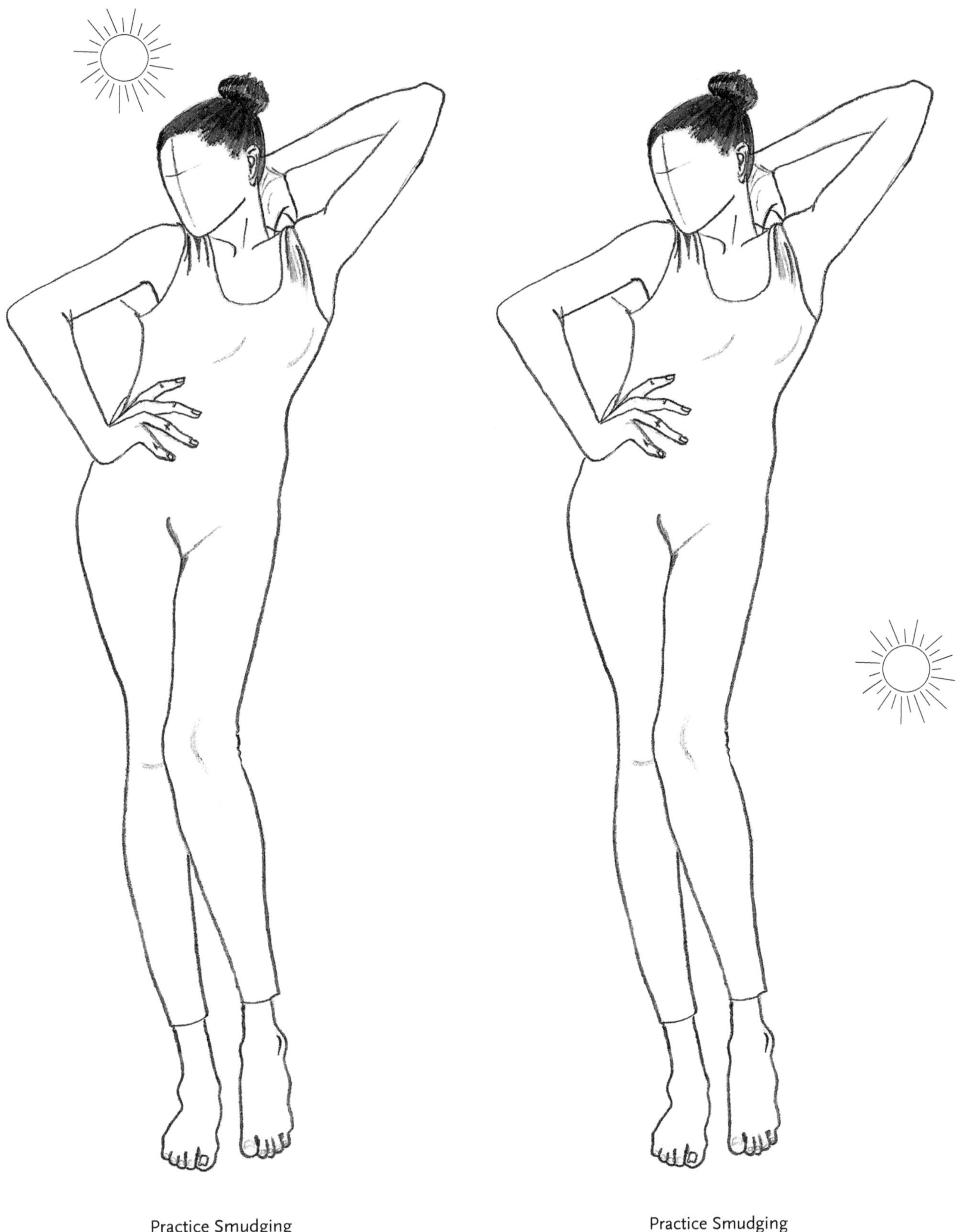

Practice Smudging
Directional Shading

Practice Smudging
Directional Shading

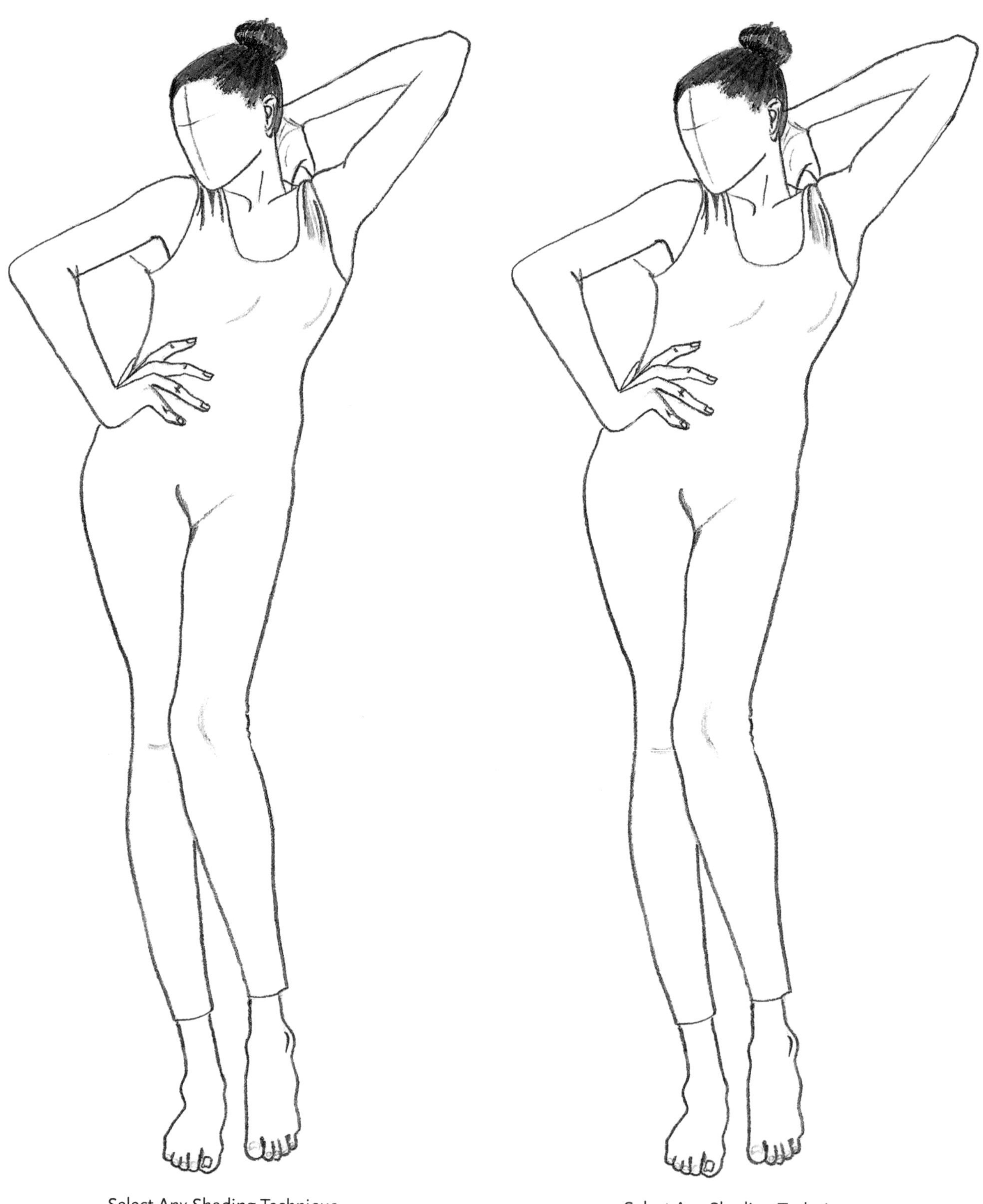
Select Any Shading Technique
Select Any Light Source
Select Any Shading Technique
Select Any Light Source

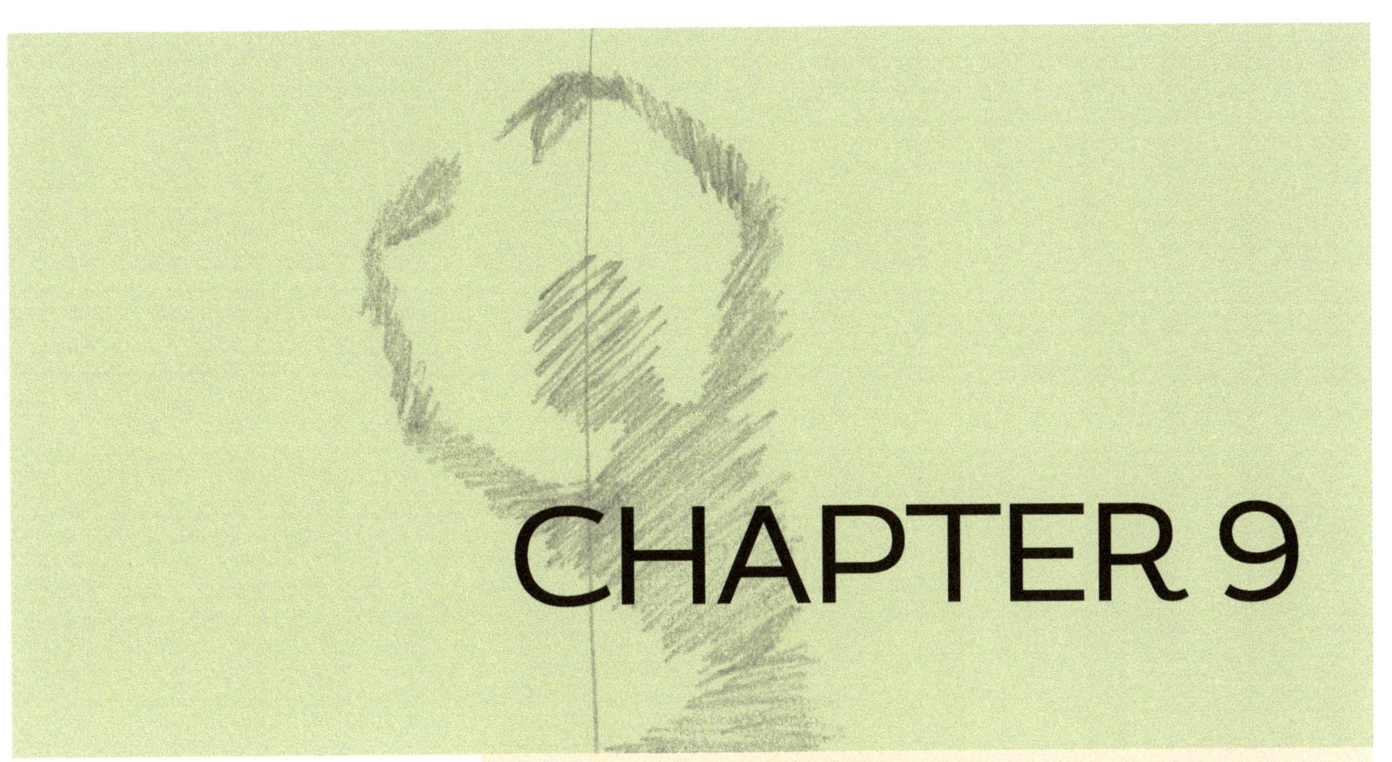

CHAPTER 9

Clothing & Poses

JEANS, BLOUSE & KITTEN HEALS

The following pages present the same outfit with different models, poses and light sources. Practice skills demonstrated throughout this book.

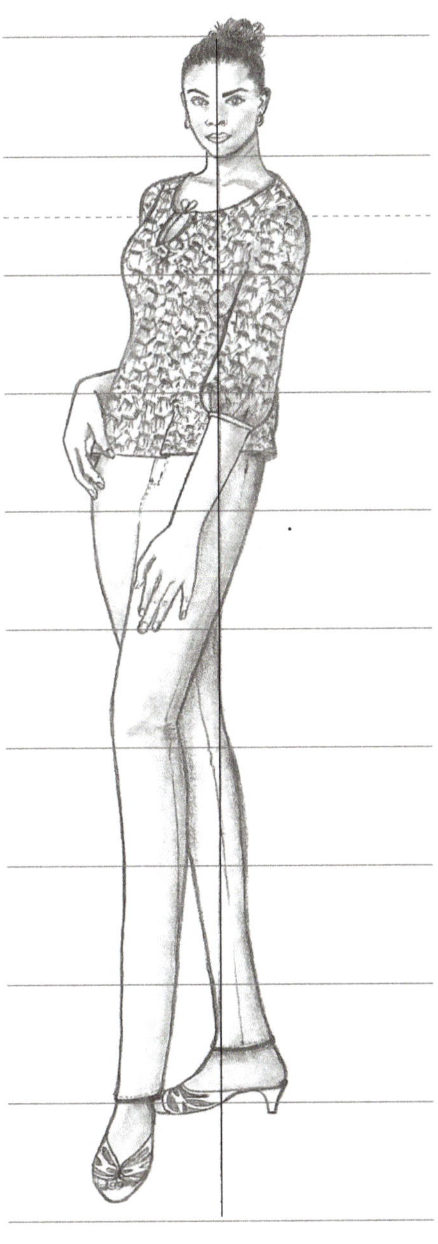

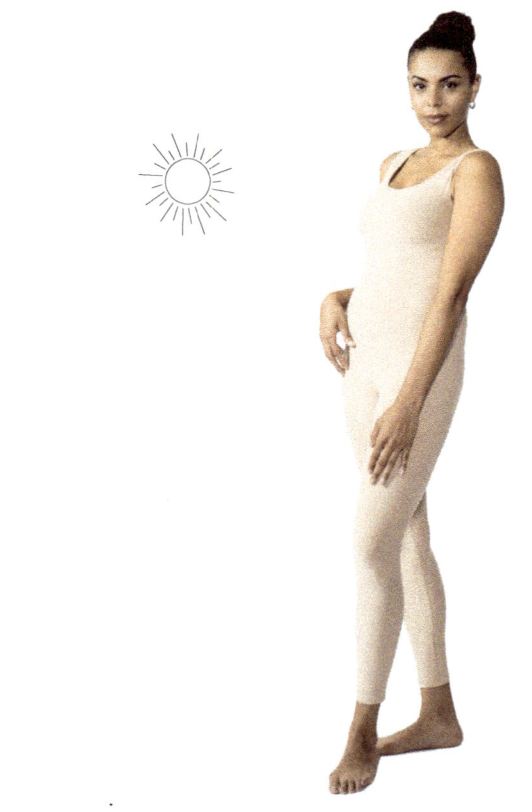

OUTFIT

A simple jean, bloussant top and kitten heals.

POSE

A simple pose with a light source.

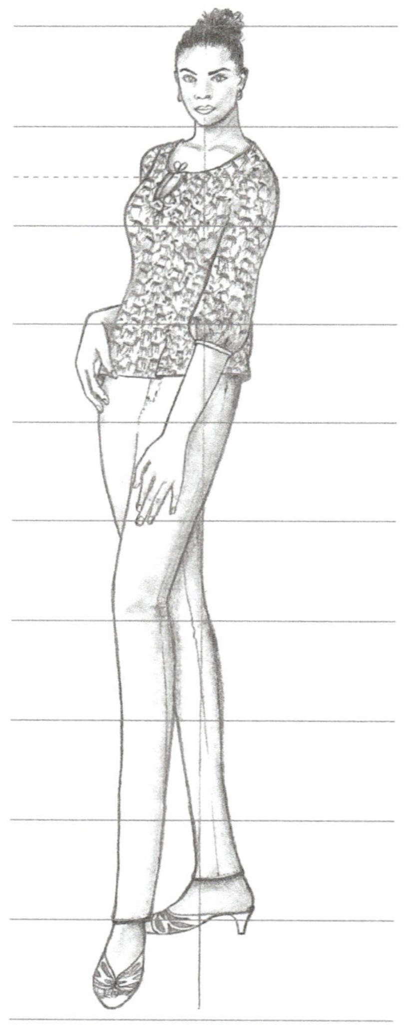

OUTFIT & POSE

This example incorporates the outfit, pose and light source.

OUTFIT

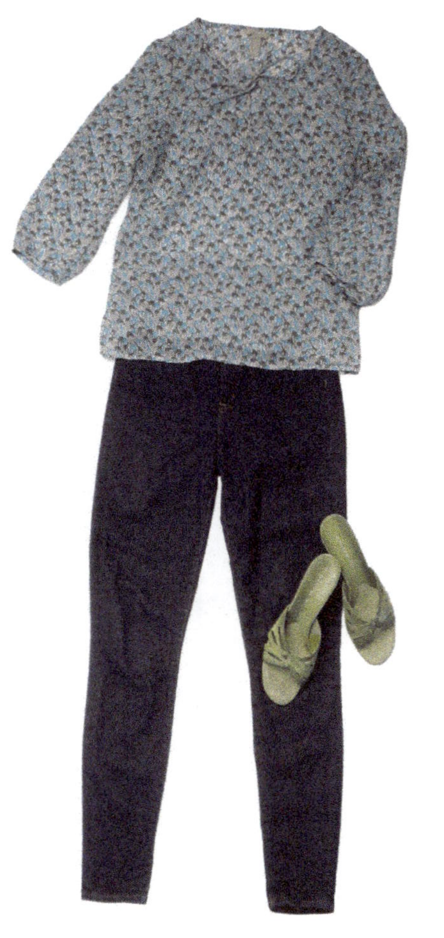

A simple jean, bloussant top and kitten heals.

POSE

A simple pose with a light source.

OUTFIT & POSE

Follow the steps in previous sections for drawing the figure and shading. Add the outfit to the pose.

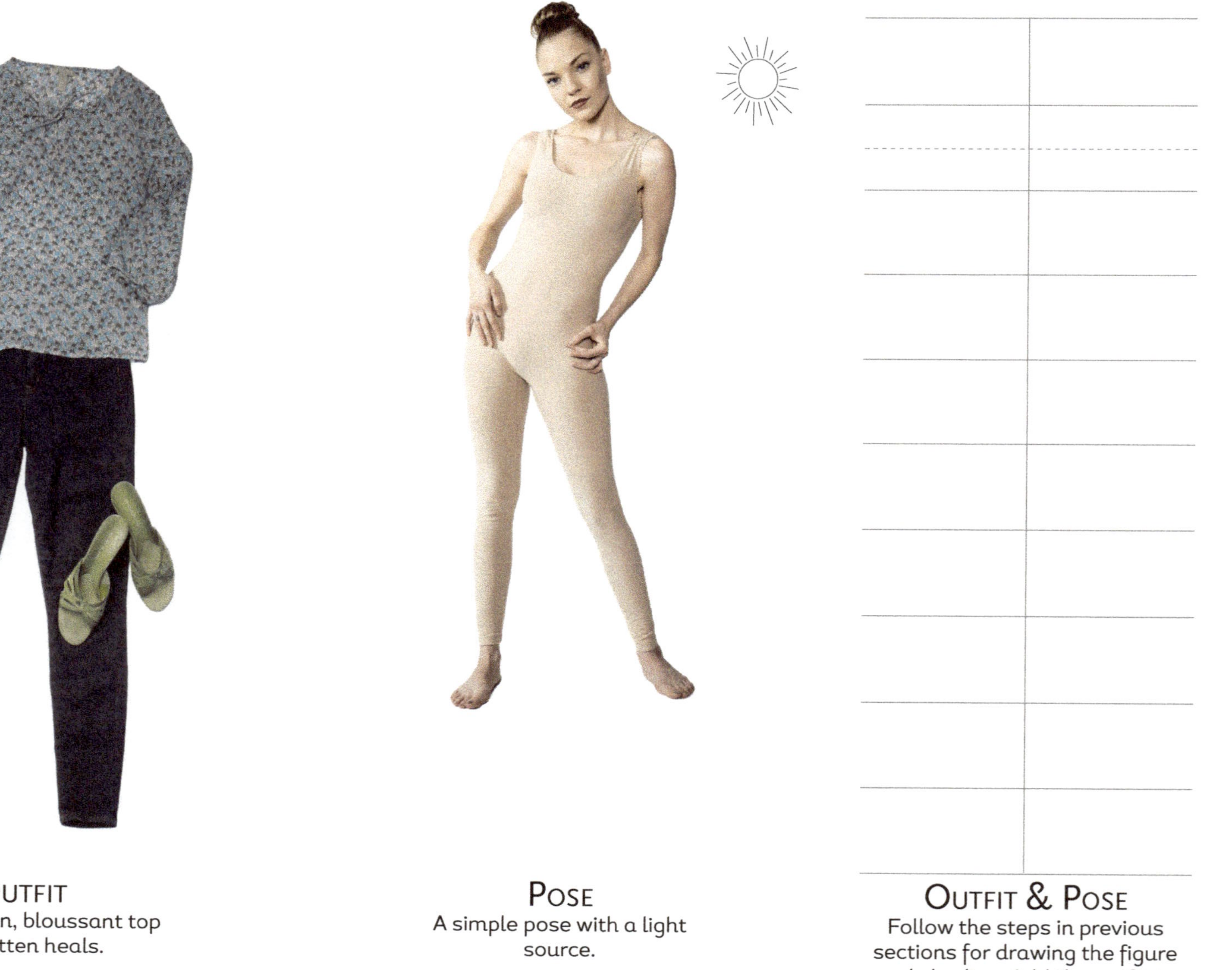

OUTFIT

A simple jean, bloussant top and kitten heals.

POSE

A simple pose with a light source.

OUTFIT & POSE

Follow the steps in previous sections for drawing the figure and shading. Add the outfit to the pose.

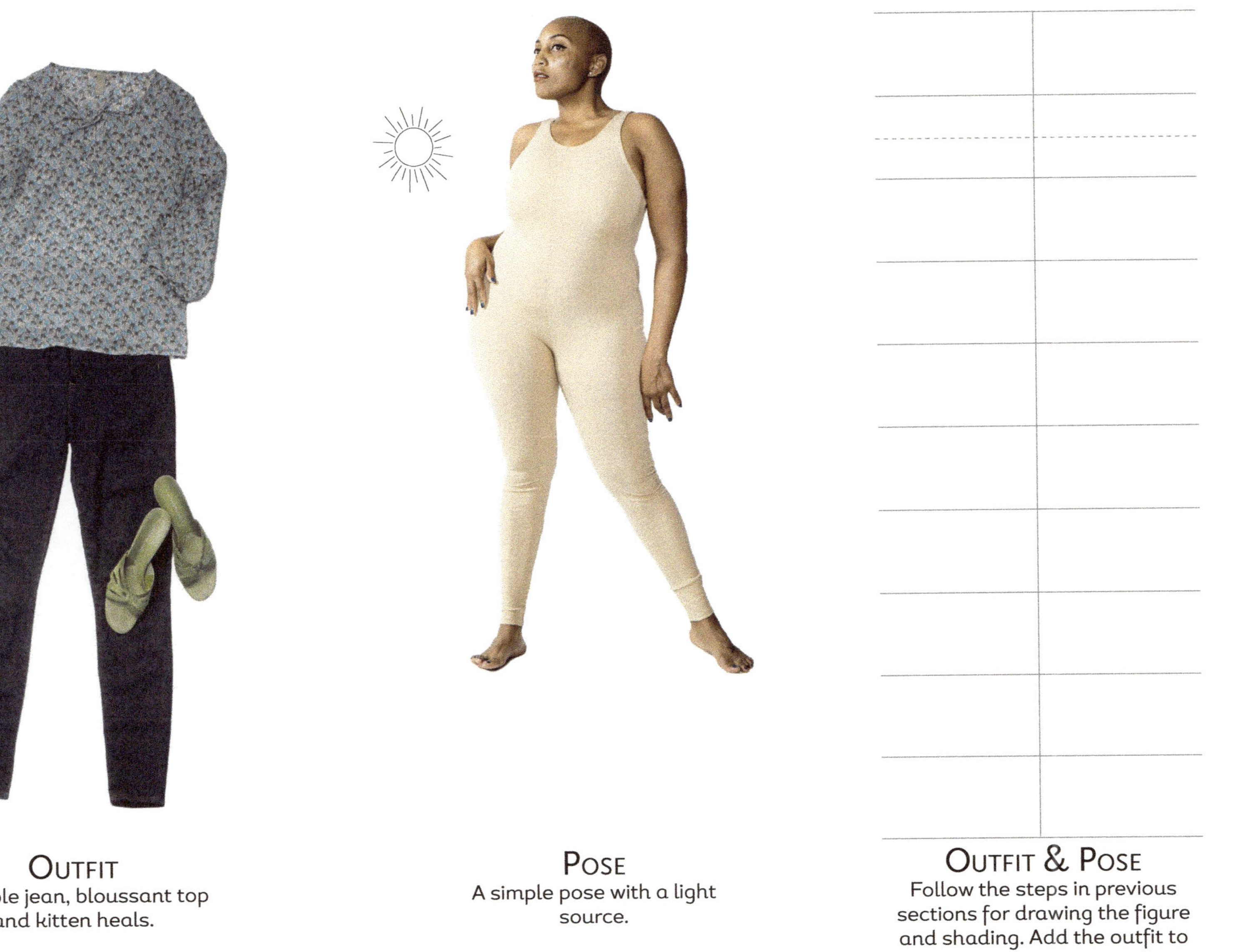

OUTFIT

A simple jean, bloussant top and kitten heals.

POSE

A simple pose with a light source.

OUTFIT & POSE

Follow the steps in previous sections for drawing the figure and shading. Add the outfit to the pose.

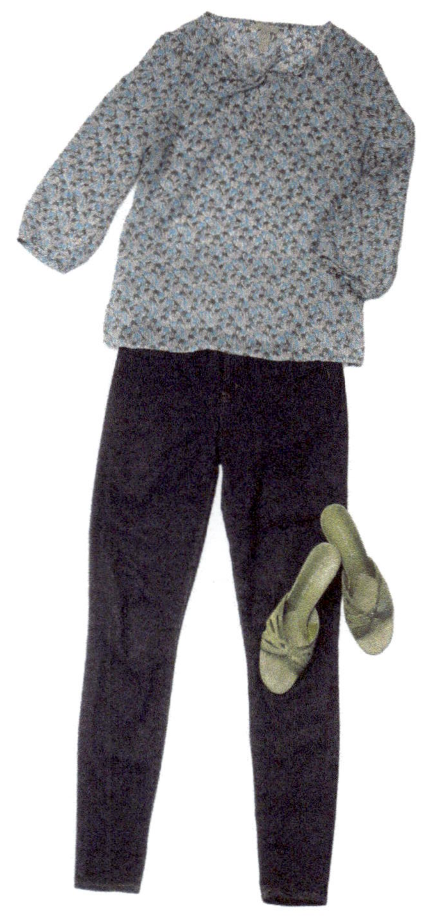

OUTFIT

A simple jean, bloussant top and kitten heals.

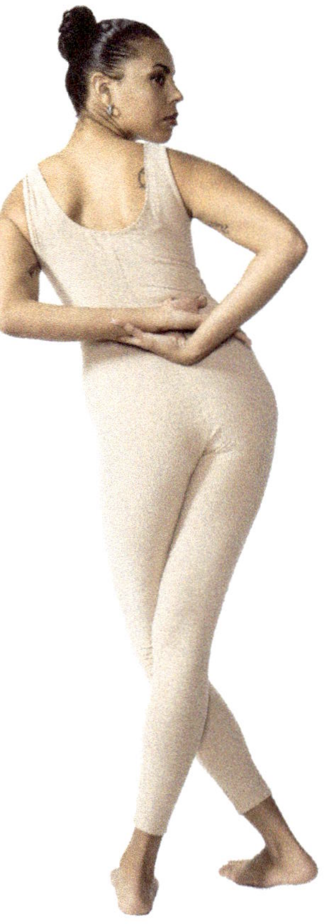

POSE

A simple pose with a light source.

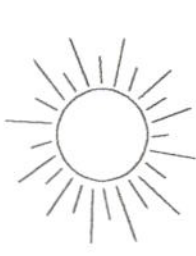

OUTFIT & POSE

Follow the steps in previous sections for drawing the figure and shading. Add the outfit to the pose.

A-LINE DRESS & STRAPPY SANDALS

The following pages present the same outfit with different models, poses and light sources. Practice skills demonstrated throughout this book.

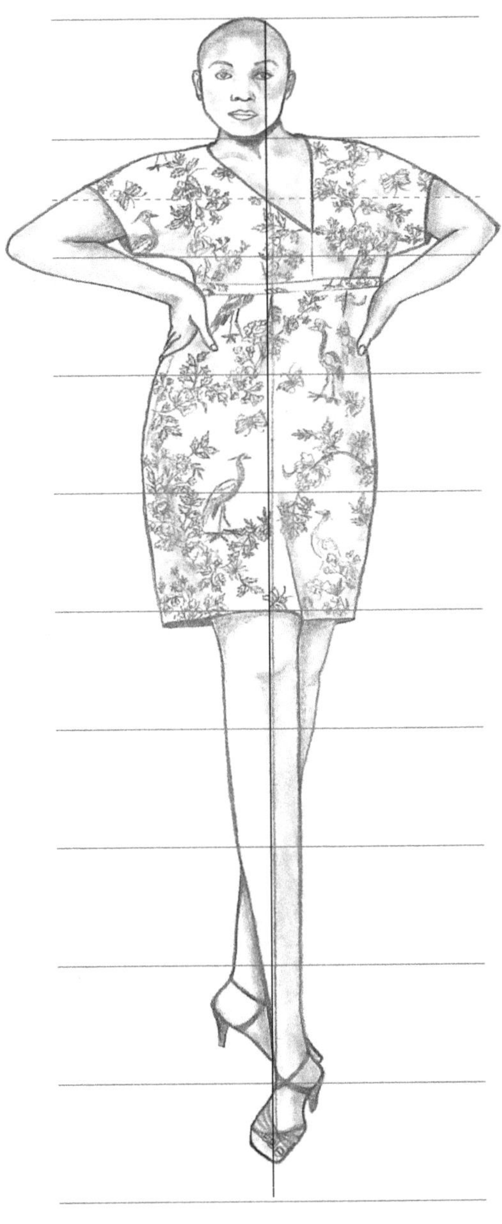

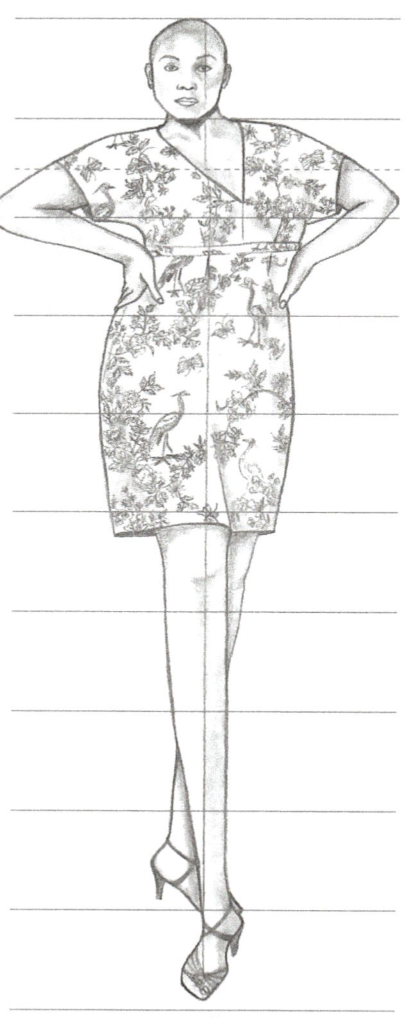

OUTFIT

A high-waisted, dolman sleeved, a-line dress and strappy sandals.

POSE

A simple pose with a light source.

OUTFIT & POSE

This example incorporates the outfit, pose and light source.

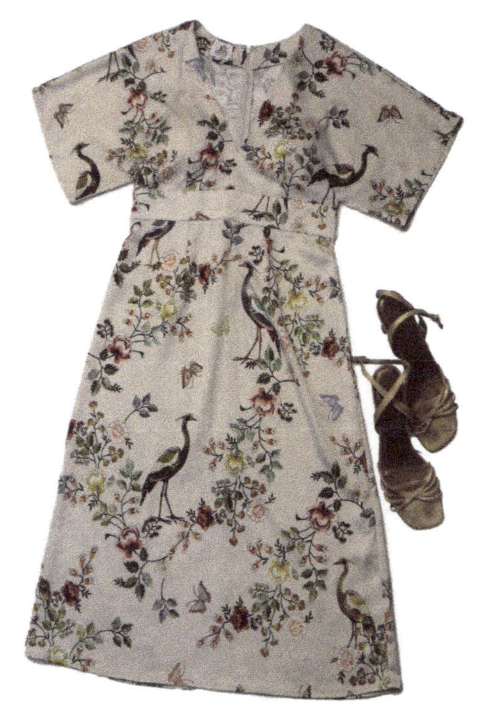

OUTFIT

A high-waisted, dolman sleeved, a-line dress and strappy sandals.

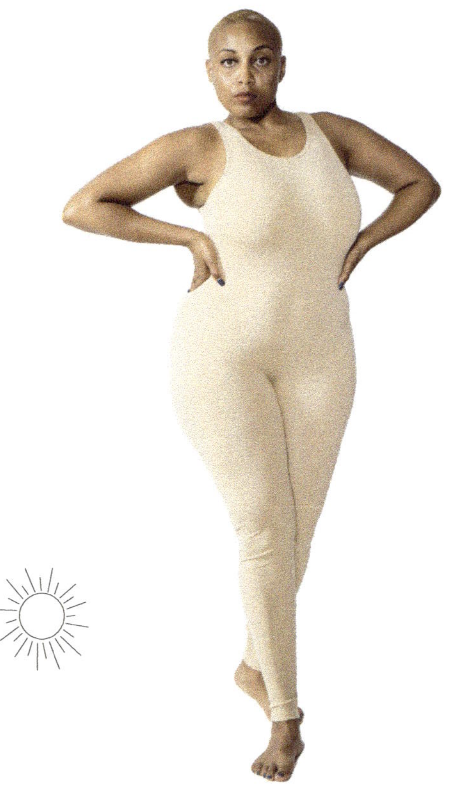

POSE

A simple pose with a light source.

OUTFIT & POSE

Follow the steps in previous sections for drawing the figure and shading. Add the outfit to the pose.

Outfit & Pose

This example incorporates the outfit, pose and light source.

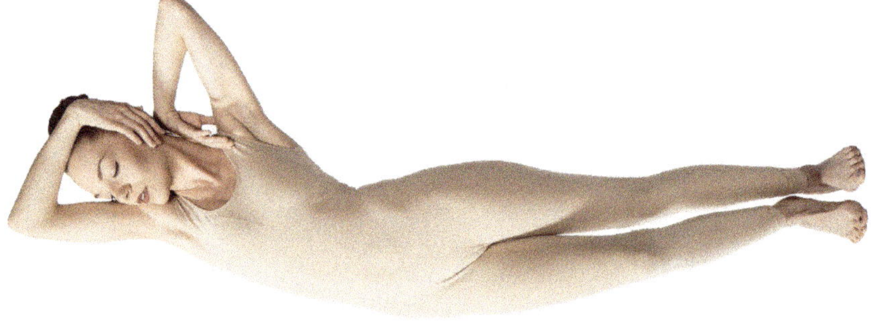

Pose

A simple pose with a light source.

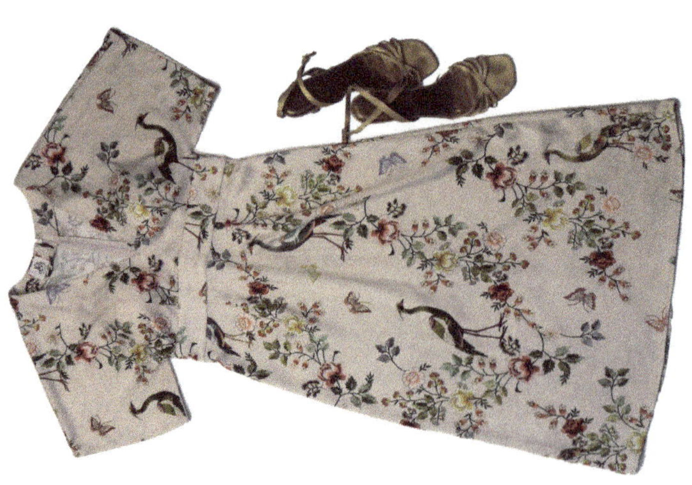

Outfit

A high-waisted, dolman sleeved, a-line dress and strappy sandals.

OUTFIT
A high-waisted, dolman sleeved, a-line dress and strappy sandals.

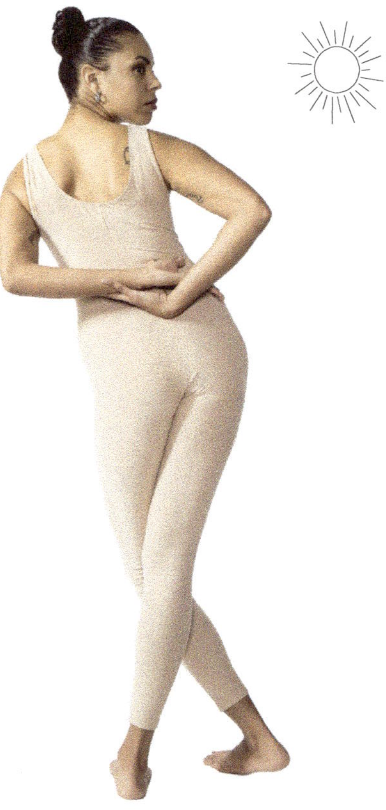

POSE
A simple pose with a light source.

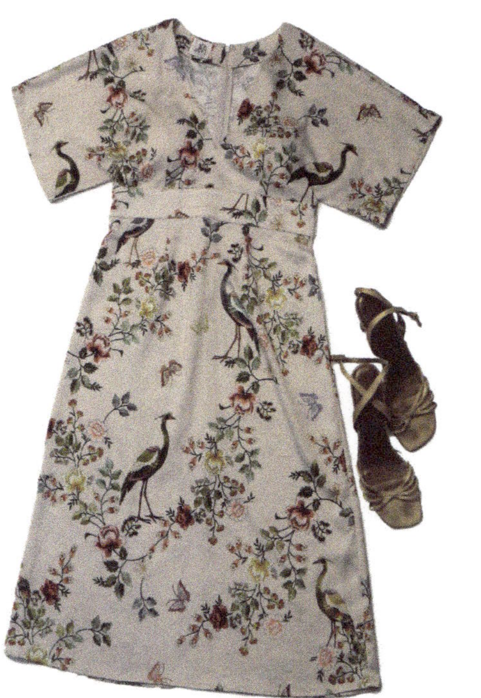

OUTFIT & POSE
Follow the steps in previous sections for drawing the figure and shading. Add the outfit to the pose.

OUTFIT & POSE

This example incorporates the outfit, pose and light source.

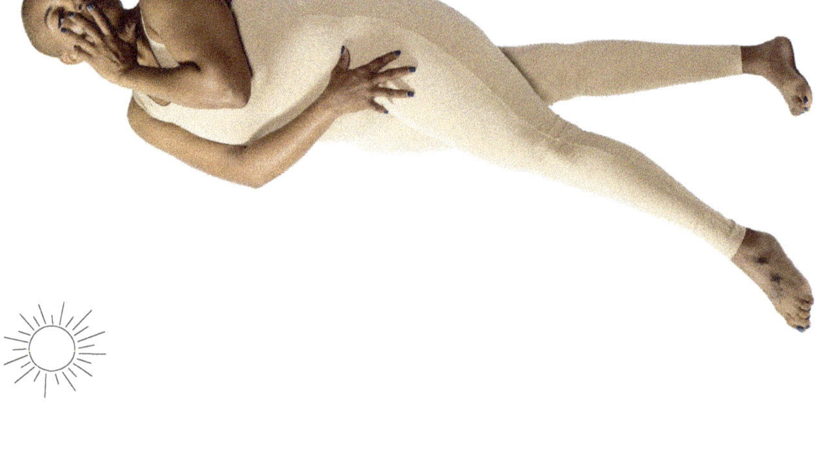

POSE

A simple pose with a light source.

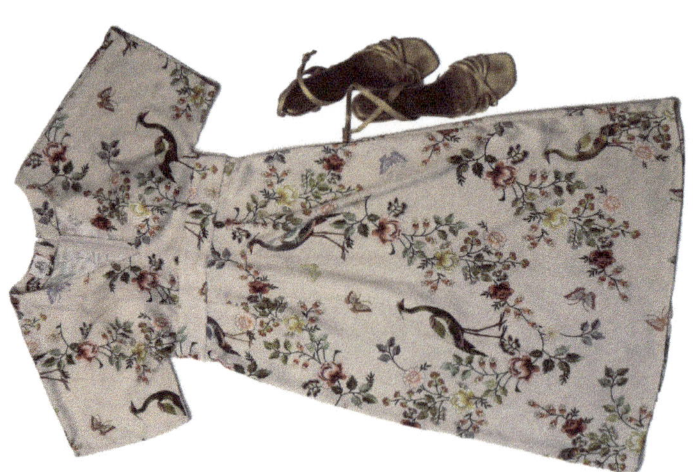

OUTFIT

A high-waisted, dolman sleeved, a-line dress and strappy sandals.

BATHING SUIT

The following pages present the same outfit with different models, poses and light sources. Practice skills demonstrated throughout this book.

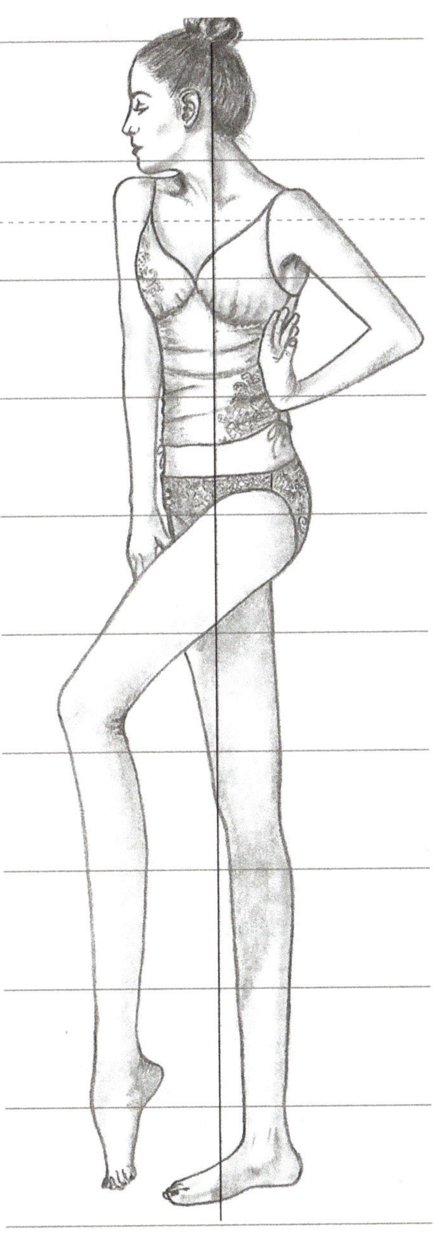

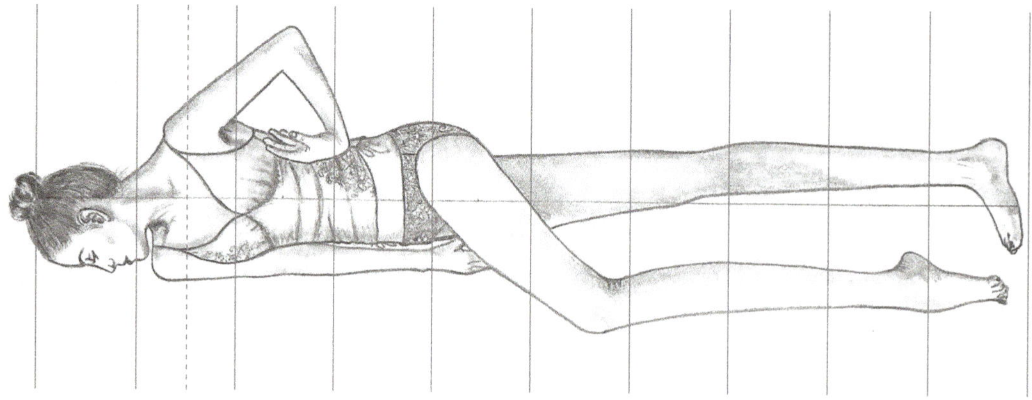

OUTFIT & POSE

This example incorporates the outfit, pose and light source.

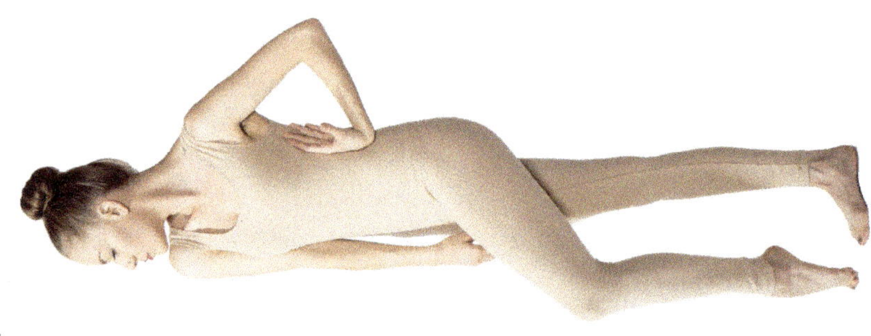

POSE

A simple pose with a light source.

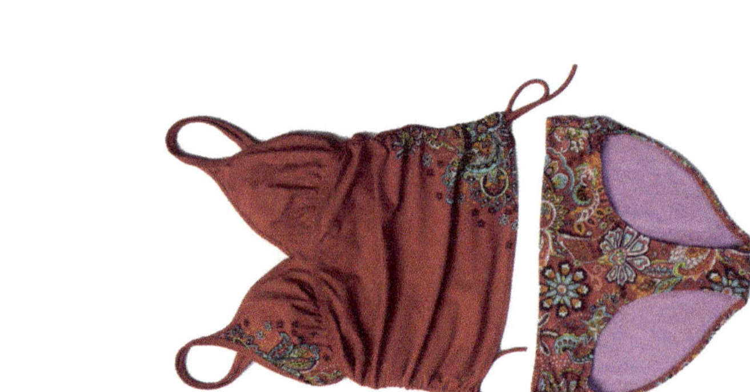

OUTFIT

Two piece bathing suit with side ruching and ties.

OUTFIT

Two piece bathing suit with side ruching and ties.

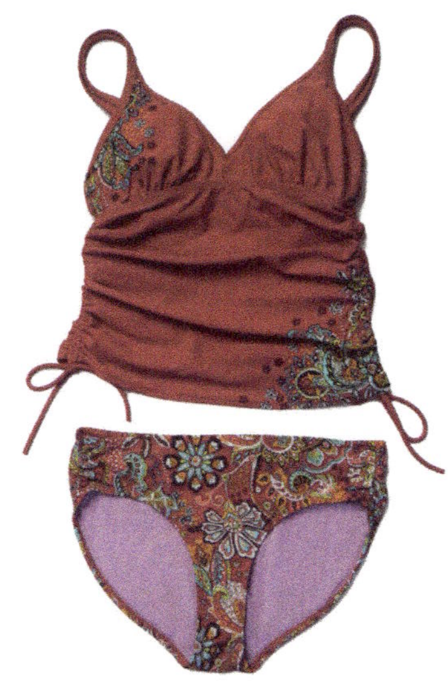

POSE

A simple pose with a light source.

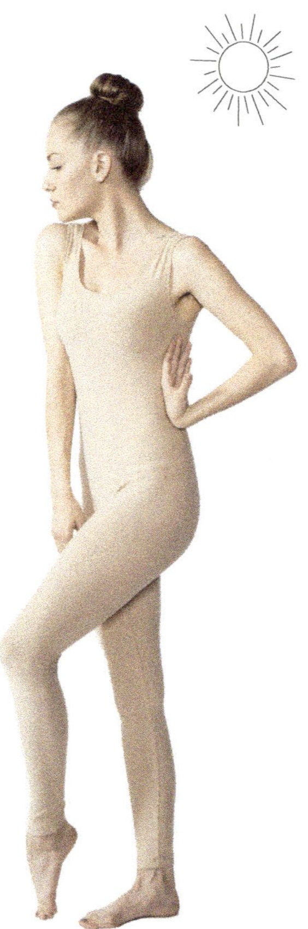

OUTFIT & POSE

Follow the steps in previous sections for drawing the figure and shading. Add the outfit to the pose.

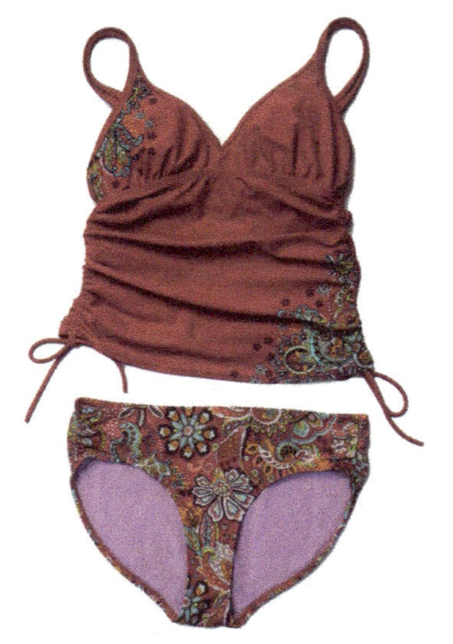

OUTFIT
Two piece bathing suit with side ruching and ties.

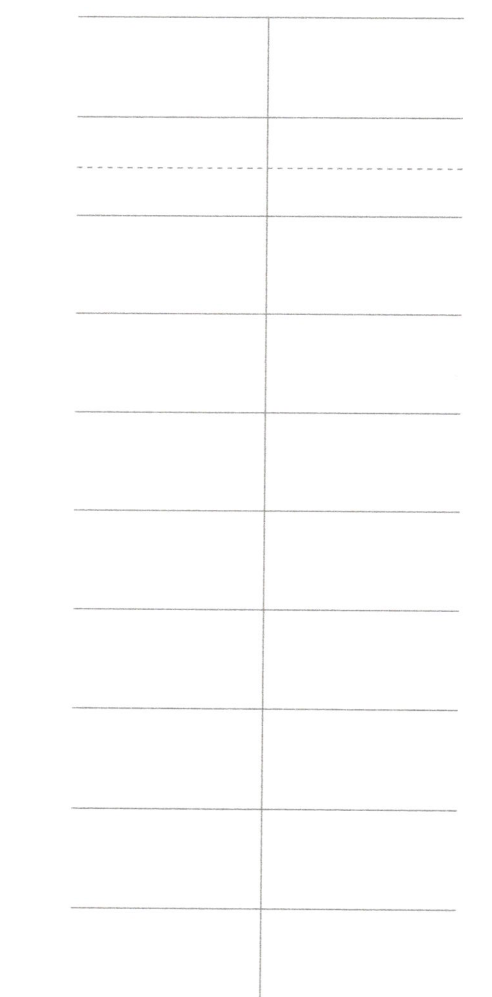

POSE
A simple pose with a light source.

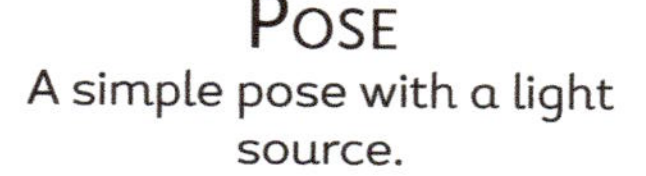

OUTFIT & POSE
This example incorporates the outfit, pose and light source.

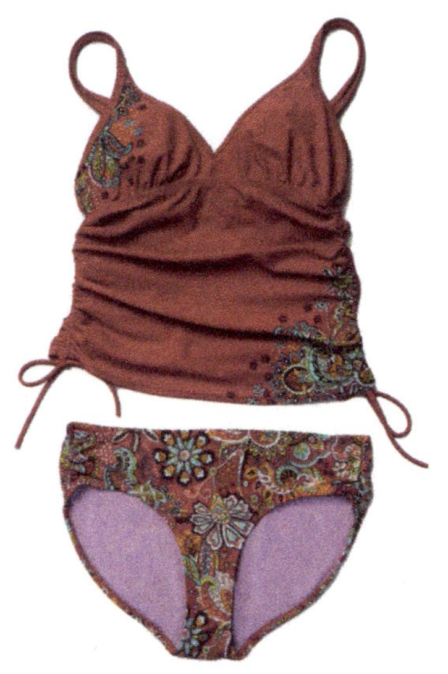

Outfit

Two piece bathing suit
with side ruching and ties.

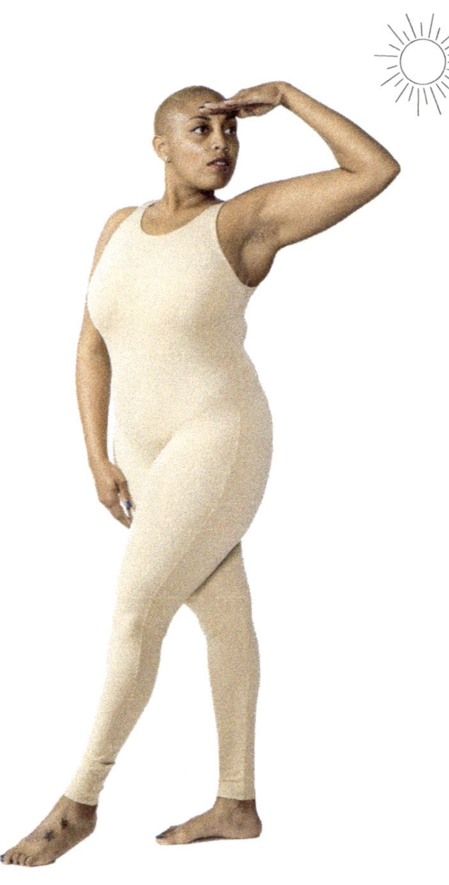

Pose

A simple pose with a light
source.

Outfit & Pose

Follow the steps in previous
sections for drawing the figure
and shading. Add the outfit to
the pose.

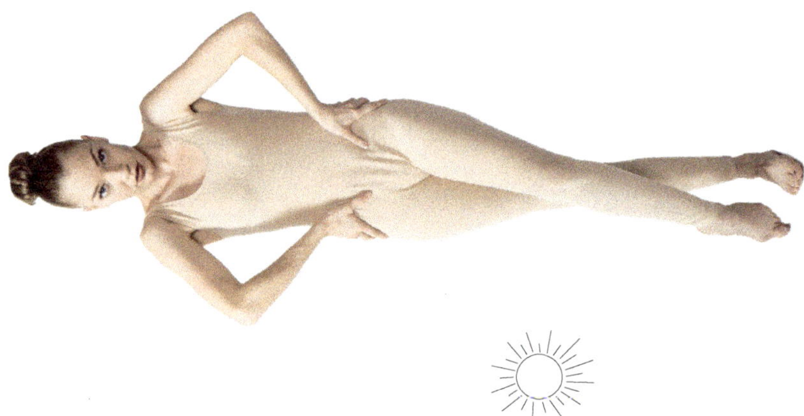

POSE

A simple pose with a light source.

OUTFIT & POSE

This example incorporates the outfit, pose and light source.

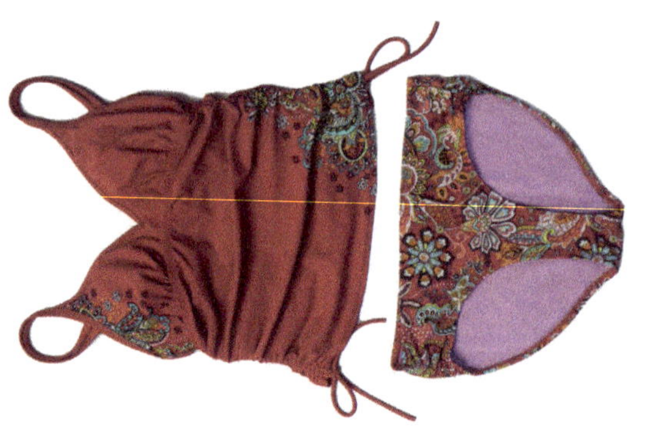

OUTFIT

Two piece bathing suit with side ruching and ties.

EVENING GOWN

The following pages present the same outfit with different models, poses and light sources. Practice skills demonstrated throughout this book.

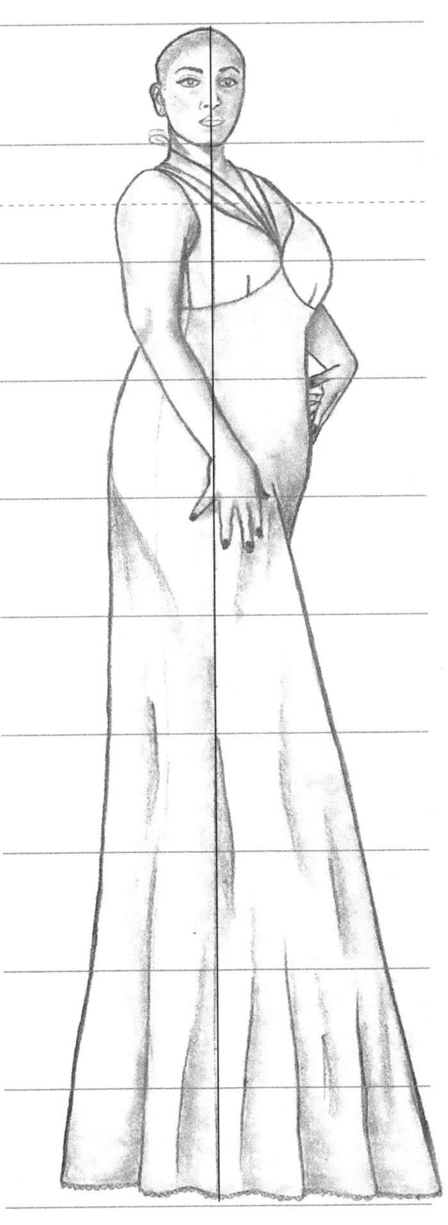

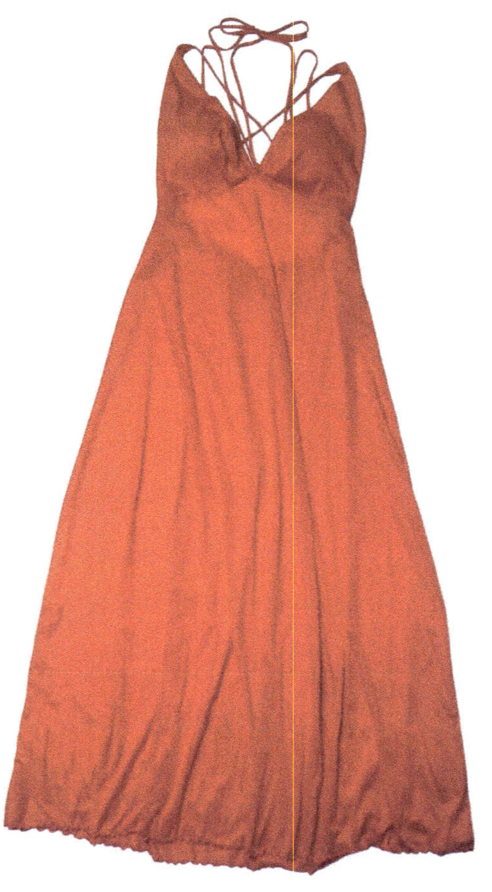

OUTFIT
Strappy evening gown with full skirt.

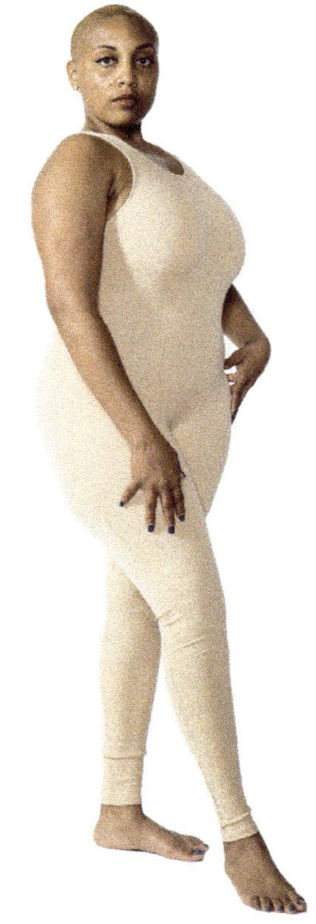

POSE
A simple pose with a light source.

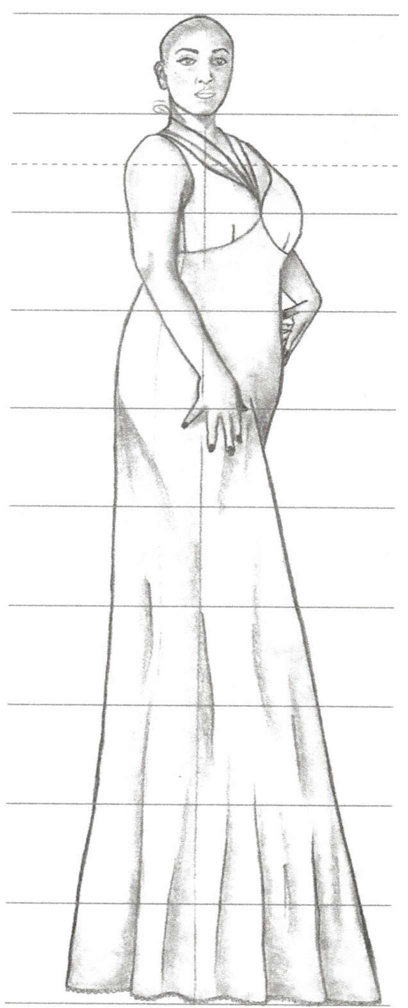

OUTFIT & POSE
This example incorporates the outfit, pose and light source.

Outfit

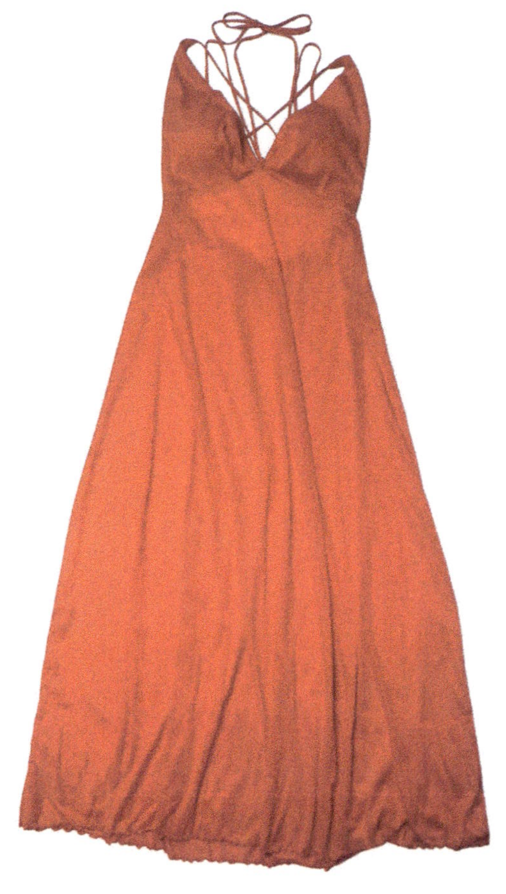

Strappy evening gown with full skirt.

Pose

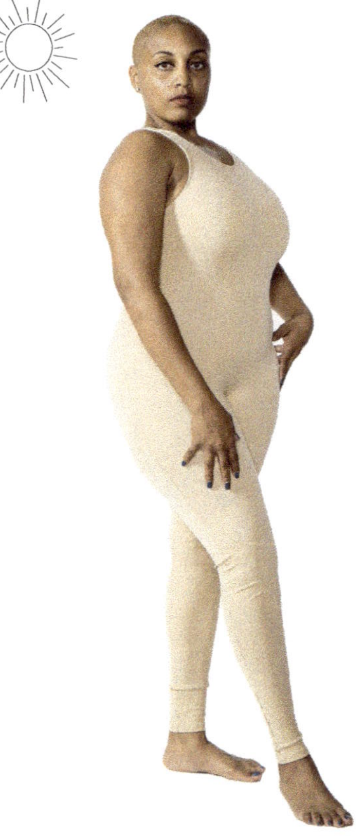

A simple pose with a light source.

Outfit & Pose

Follow the steps in previous sections for drawing the figure and shading. Add the outfit to the pose.

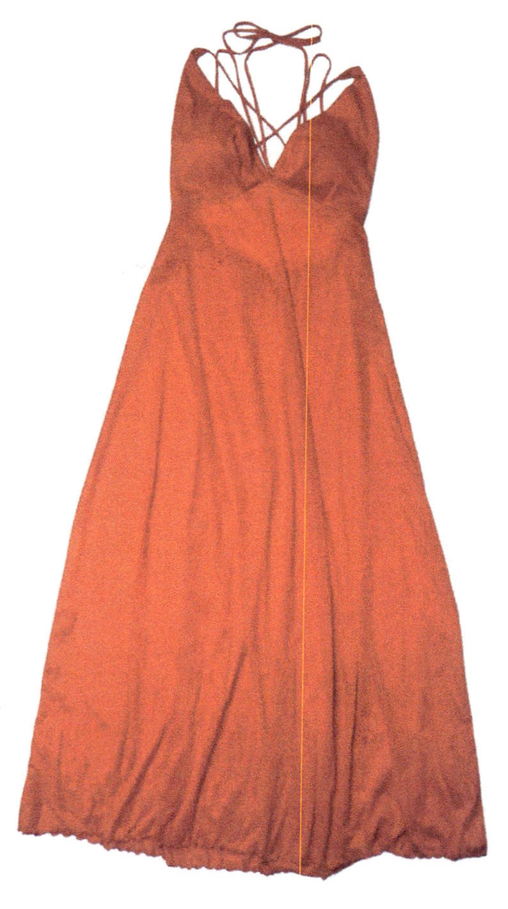

OUTFIT

Strappy evening gown
with full skirt.

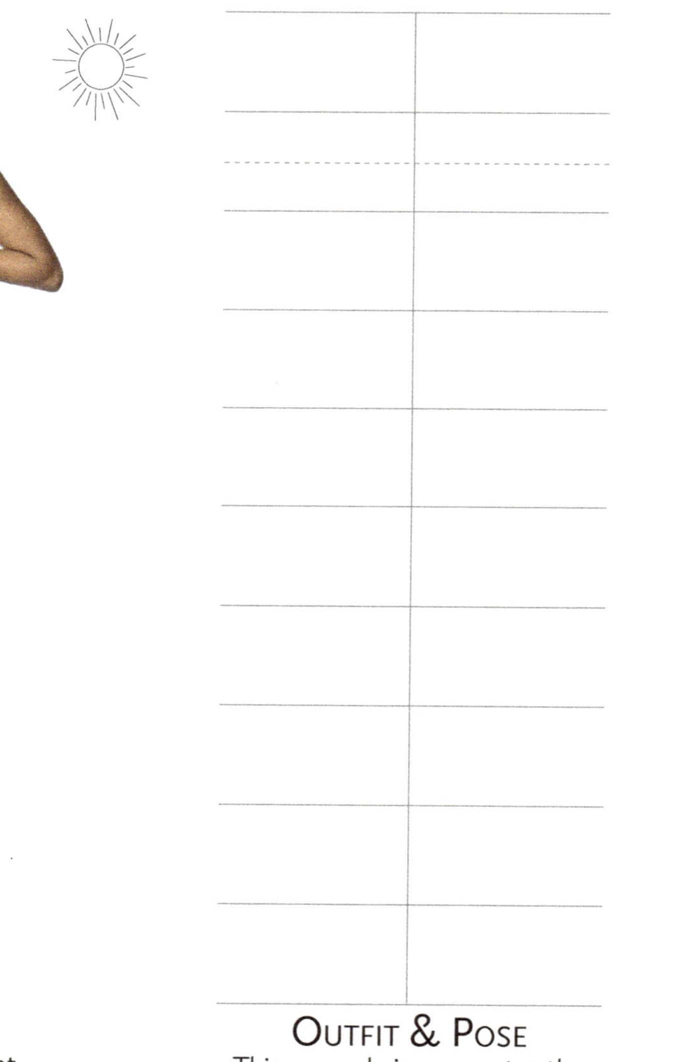

POSE

A simple pose with a light
source.

OUTFIT & POSE

This example incorporates the
outfit, pose and light source.

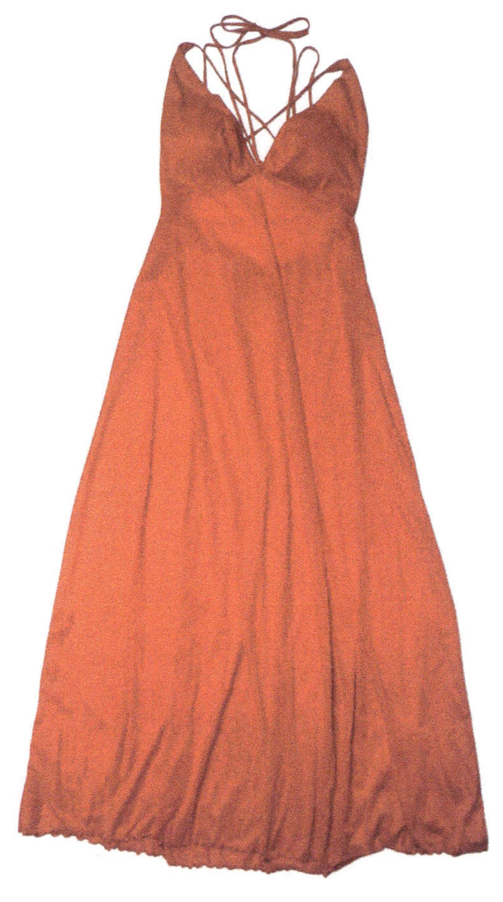

OUTFIT
Strappy evening gown
with full skirt.

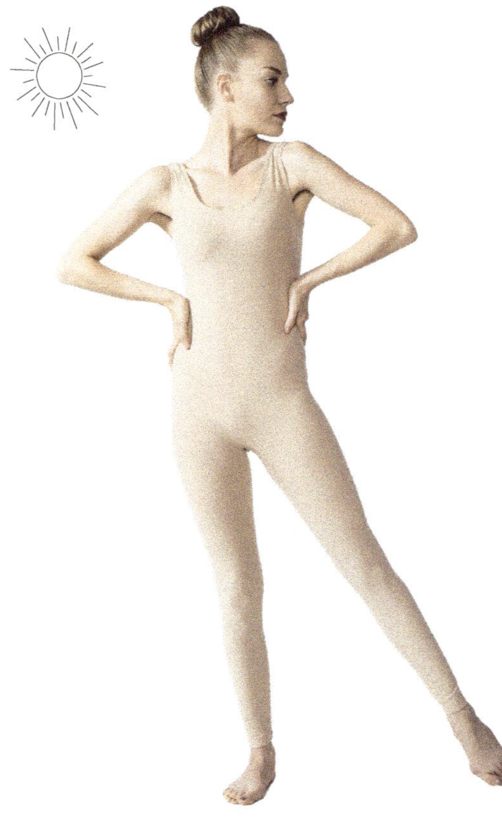

POSE
A simple pose with a light
source.

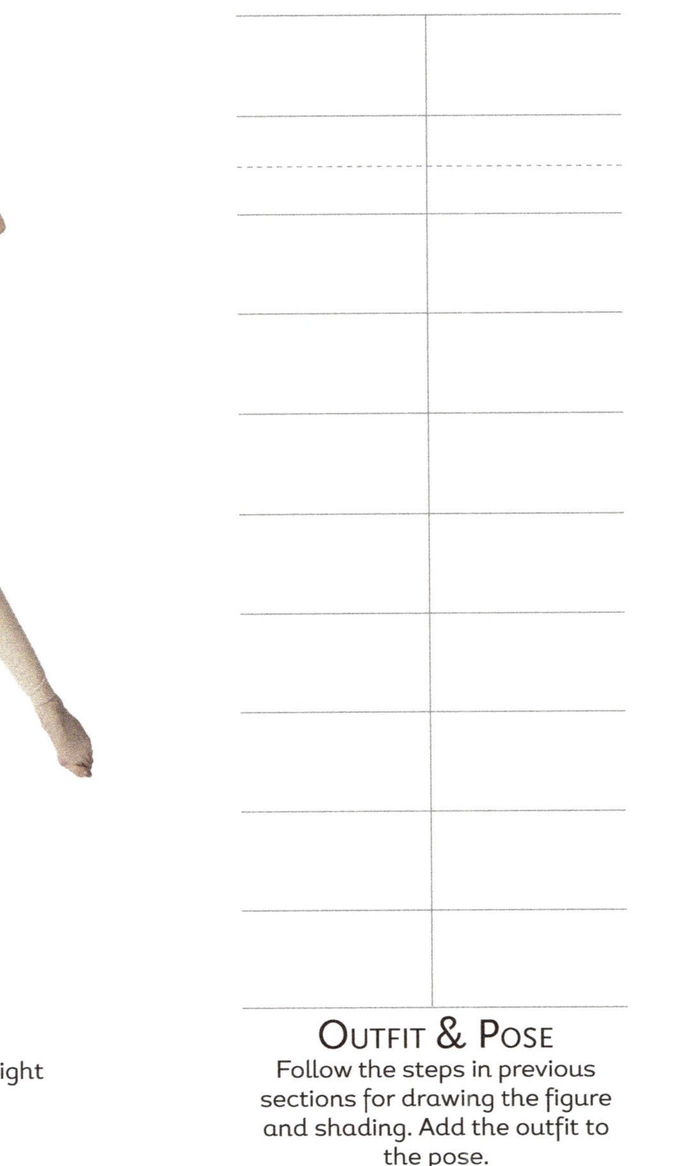

OUTFIT & POSE
Follow the steps in previous
sections for drawing the figure
and shading. Add the outfit to
the pose.

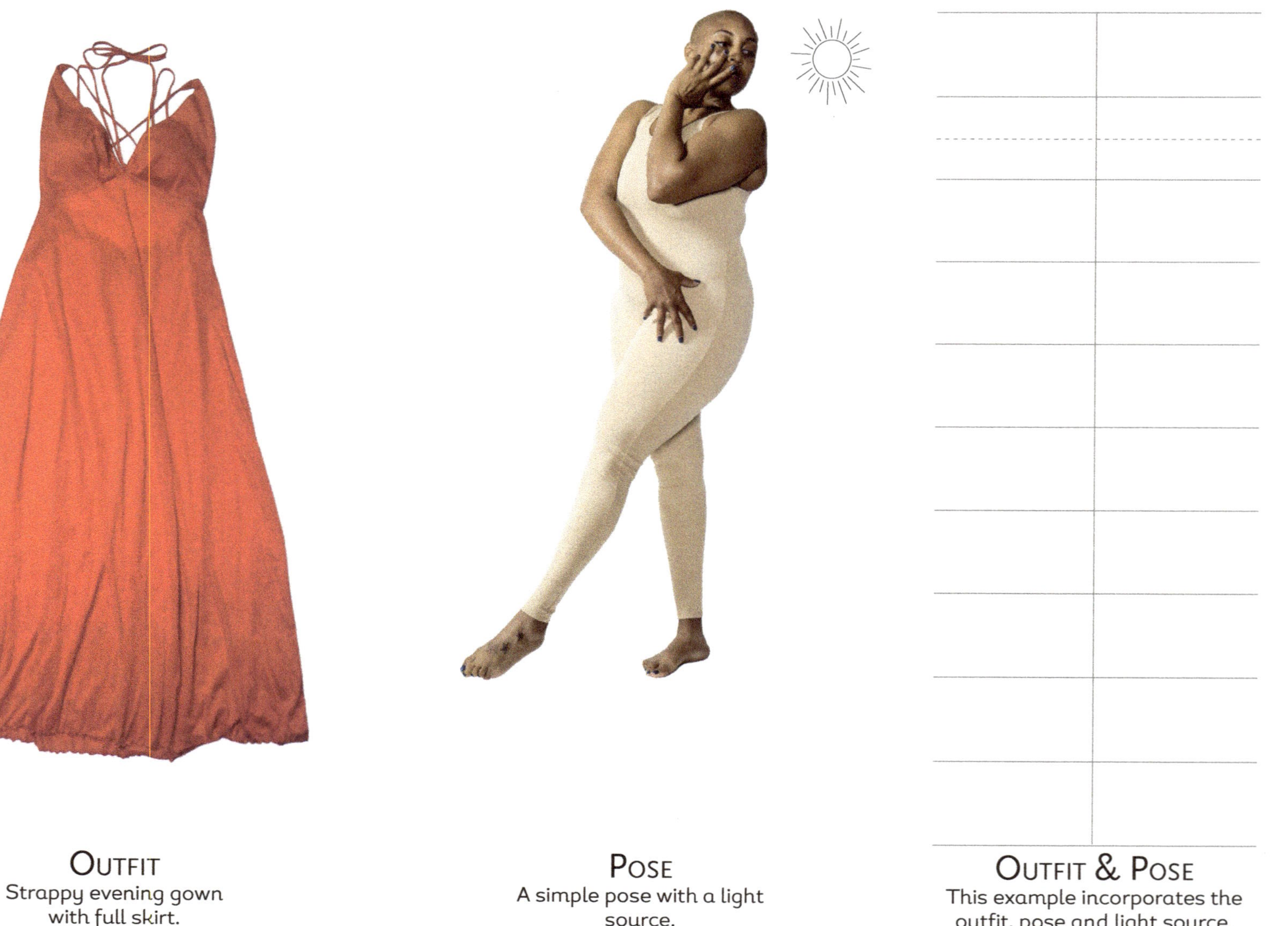

OUTFIT
Strappy evening gown
with full skirt.

POSE
A simple pose with a light
source.

OUTFIT & POSE
This example incorporates the
outfit, pose and light source.

BLOUSE, PENCIL SKIRT & HEALS

The following pages present the same outfit with different models, poses and light sources. Practice skills demonstrated throughout this book.

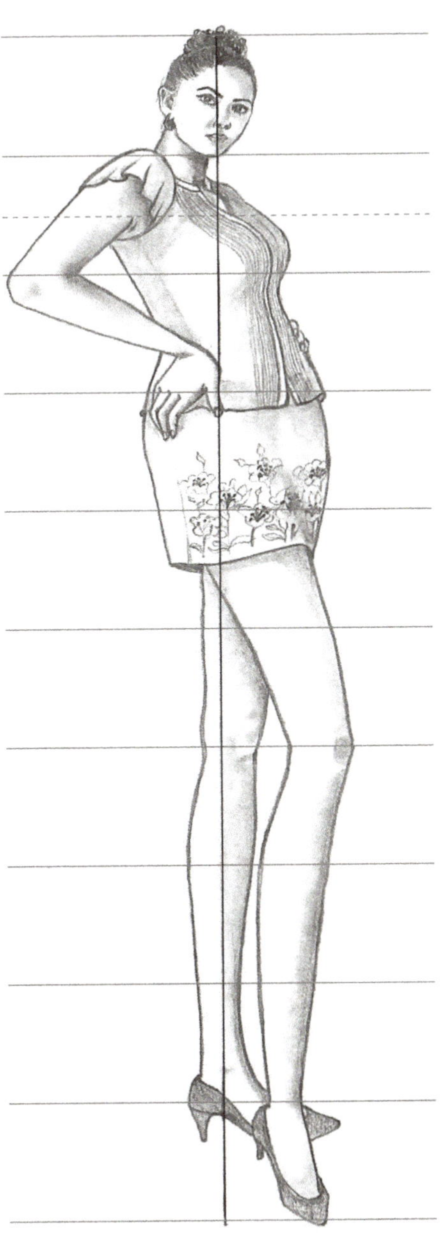

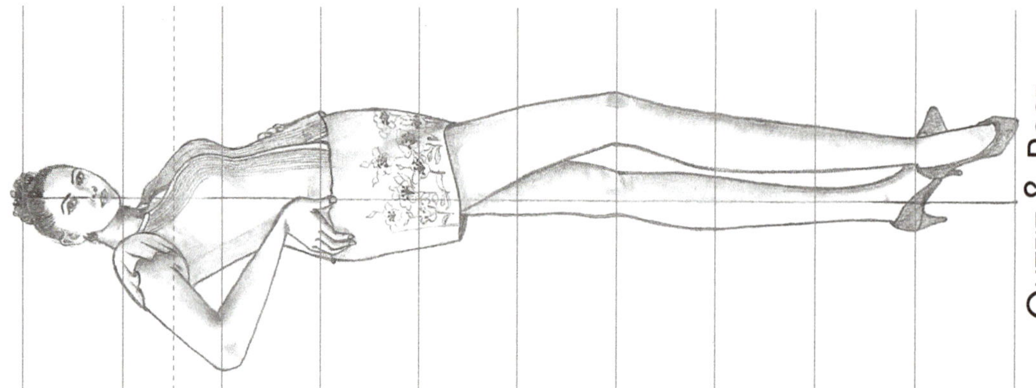

Outfit & Pose

This example incorporates the outfit, pose and light source.

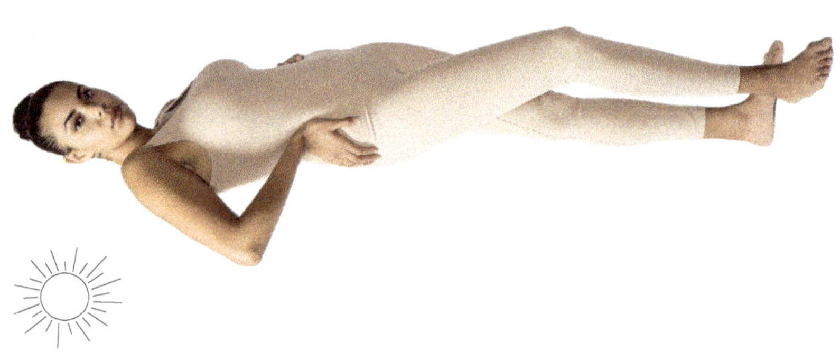

Pose

A simple pose with a light source.

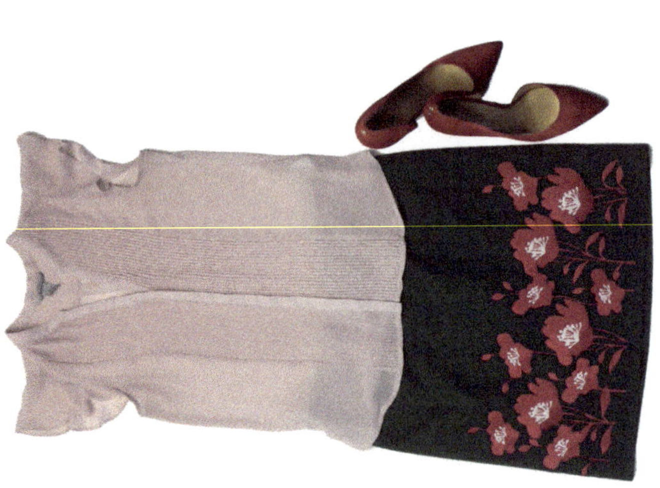

Outfit

Pintucked flutter sleeve blouse, straight skirt and high heeled dress shoes.

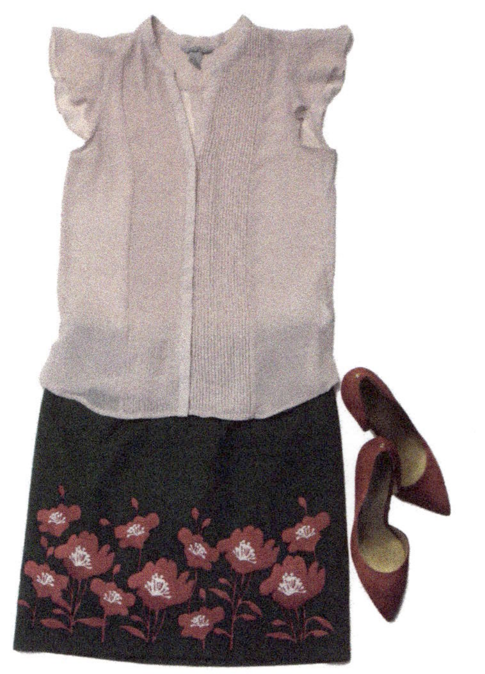

Outfit

Pintucked flutter sleeve blouse, straight skirt and high heeled dress shoes.

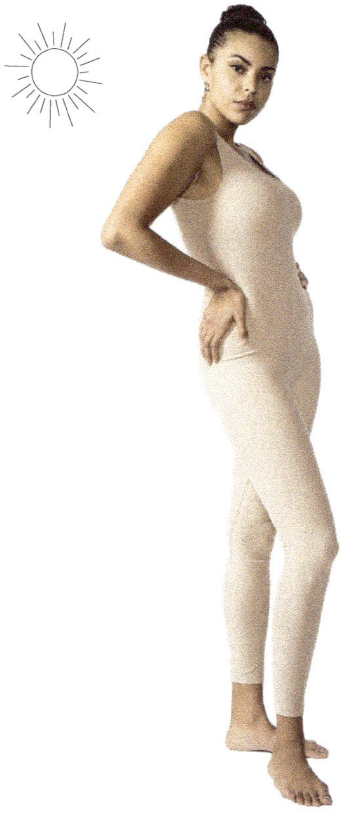

Pose

A simple pose with a light source.

Outfit & Pose

Follow the steps in previous sections for drawing the figure and shading. Add the outfit to the pose.

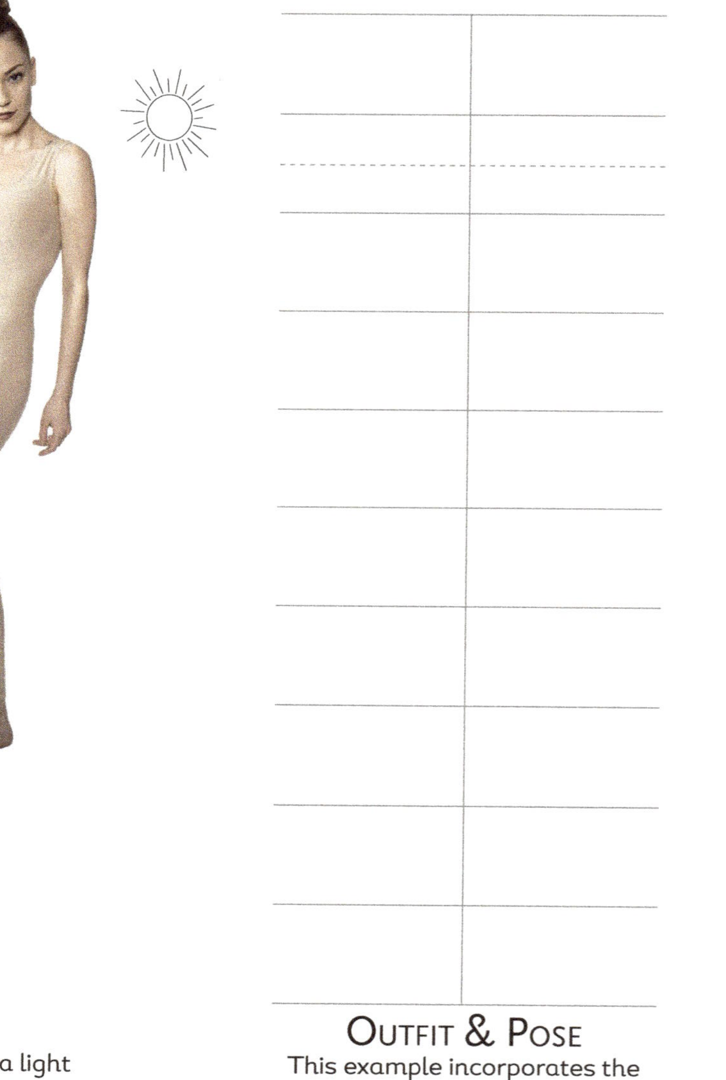

OUTFIT

Pintucked flutter sleeve blouse, straight skirt and high heeled dress shoes.

POSE

A simple pose with a light source.

OUTFIT & POSE

This example incorporates the outfit, pose and light source.

OUTFIT

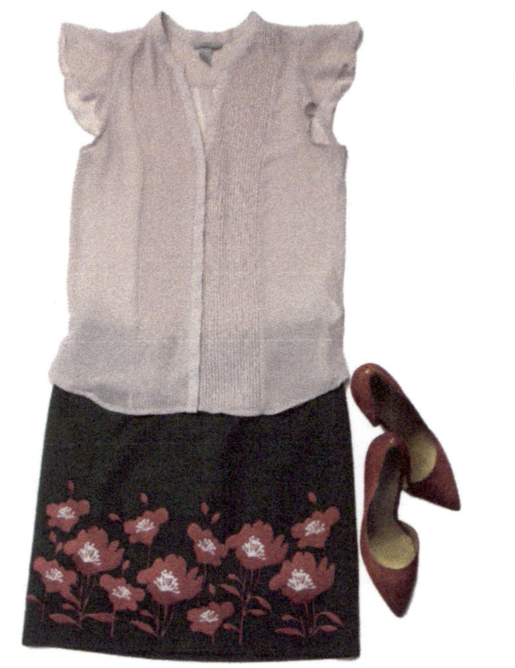

Pintucked flutter sleeve blouse, straight skirt and high heeled dress shoes.

POSE

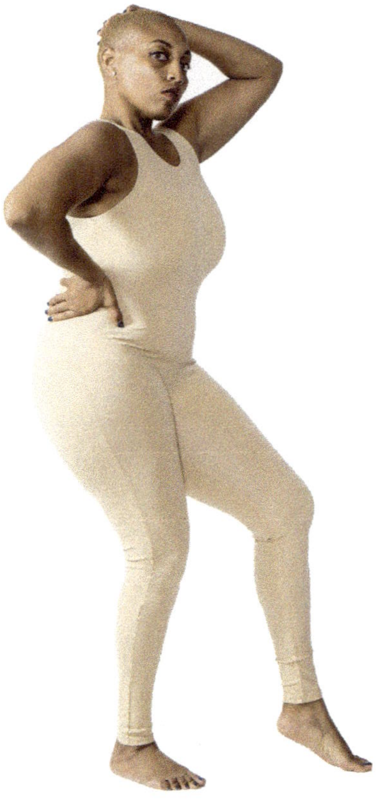

A simple pose with a light source.

OUTFIT & POSE

Follow the steps in previous sections for drawing the figure and shading. Add the outfit to the pose.

Lightning Source UK Ltd.
Milton Keynes UK
UKHW051319200820
368534UK00003B/56

9 781733 274036